DRESSED *to* KILL

DRESSED *to* KILL

CHARLOTTE
MADISON

headline
review

Copyright © 2010 Charlotte Madison

The right of Charlotte Madison to be identified as the Author of
the Work has been asserted by her in accordance with the
Copyright, Designs and Patents Act 1988.

First published in 2010
by HEADLINE REVIEW

An imprint of Headline Publishing Group

1

All photos courtesy of author except p2, top © Getty Images and
p3, top © Cody Images

Cataloguing in Publication Data is available from the British Library

Hardback ISBN 978 0 7553 1960 2
Trade paperback ISBN 978 0 7553 1961 9

Typeset in AGaramond by Palimpsest Book Production Limited,
Grangemouth, Stirlingshire

Printed and bound in Great Britain by
CPI Mackays, Chatham ME5 8TD

Headline's policy is to use papers that are natural, renewable and recyclable
products and made from wood grown in sustainable forests. The logging and
manufacturing processes are expected to conform to the environmental regulations
of the country of origin.

HEADLINE PUBLISHING GROUP
An Hachette UK Company
338 Euston Road
London NW1 3BH

www.headline.co.uk
www.hachette.co.uk

Glossary

AAA: Anti-Aircraft Artillery

AAC: Army Air Corps

AH: Apache helicopter

APU: Auxiliary Power Unit

ATC: Air Traffic Control

BATUS: The British Army Training Unit Suffield

BDA: Battle Damage Assessment

BP: Battle Position

C130: Lockheed C130 Hercules helicopter

CCF: Combined Cadet Force

DC: District Centre

EF: Enemy Forces

EFAB: Extended Forward Avionic Bay (the small side stub wing under the cockpit door)

FLIR: Forward Looking Infrared

FOB: Forward Operating Base

GMLRS: Guided Multiple Launched Rocket System

HALS: Hardened Aircraft Landing Strip

HIDAS: Helicopter Integrated Defensive Aids Suite

HLS: Helicopter Landing Site

HMG: Heavy Machine Gun

IDF: Indirect fire

IDM: Improved Data Modum

IED: Improvised Explosive Device

IntO: Intelligence Officer

ISAF: International Security Assistance Force

ISTAR: Intelligence, Surveillance, Target Acquisition and Reconnaissance

JTAC: Joint Terminal Attack Controller

JHF: Joint Helicopter Force

JMB: Joint Mission Brief

KAF: Kandahar Air Field

LCJ: Load Carrying Jerkin – also known as Life Support Jacket

Loadies: Officially called loadmasters and responsible for passengers and equipment on helicopters

locstat: Location status

LST: Laser Spot Tracker

MERT: Medical Emergency Response Team

MPS: Mission Planning Station

NCO: Non-Commissioned Officer

NVGs: Night Vision Goggles

OC: Officer Commanding

OGp: Orders Group

PID: Positive identification

PNVS: Pilot Night-Vision Sensor

pressel: The switch to allow you to transmit on the radio

PTSD: Post-Traumatic Stress Disorder

RCB: Regimental Commissioning Board

RIP: Relief in Place

RPG: Rocket Propelled Grenade

RTB: Return To Base

SAL: Semi-Active Laser

TADS: Target Acquisition and Designation Sight

TPF: Tactical Planning Facility

TIC: Troops In Contact

TPF: Tactical Planning Facility

UAV: Unmanned Aerial Vehicle

UOTC: University Officer Training Corps

U/S: Unserviceable

VHR: Very High Readiness

This book is dedicated to all the men and women of our Armed Forces past and present, especially to those currently fighting overseas.

Jugroom Fort, Afghanistan, January 2007

'Get some fucking fire down, ma'am!'

My eyes dart from side to side; flashes of red tracer slice through the sky. Scarlet and orange flames blossom across the ground and it is impossible to tell where the friendly troops stop and the enemy begins.

Stay cool, Madison, stay cool. Take a deep breath.

The air smells thick with sweat and fear. I struggle to swallow, and gulp violently; my tongue feels too big for my mouth.

You know you can do this. This is what all that sodding training was for. You can't screw up now.

I blink hard. My eyelids already feel heavy, as if my brain is struggling to keep up with the sensory overload. I'm painfully aware that we're saving our soldiers' lives with our actions.

As we orbit, I see some Taliban fighters attempting to escape. They look like white dots, miniature figures running with what could be weapons strapped to their chests. My eyes strain to see what they're carrying against their billowing Afghan clothing. We have to be sure they aren't innocent civilians fleeing from the heavy fighting.

'Darwin, I can't see . . . maybe that's an RPG, but . . .' I tail off, squinting into my sights.

'I'll fly closer,' my co-pilot, Darwin, says. 'We've got to be sure.'

He's already heading east, reading my thoughts as he watches the telescopic-view videoscreen I control from the front. We work as a team, so while I control the telescopic view from the front, he sits in the back maintaining the all-round perspective.

'Widow Eight Zero, this is Ugly Five Four,' I say into the

radio. 'I've got three leakers heading south along the dirt track. Looks like they've come out of the fort on the eastern side and they're carrying weapons.'

The response from the Joint Terminal Attack Controller (JTAC) is immediate and confident.

'Ugly, there are no civilians or friendly troops anywhere in that area. If they're fighting-age males leaving the area of the fort, I'm happy they're leakers.'

I'm ready. 'Am I cleared to engage?'

Now he's busy with another crew. 'Ugly, stand by . . .' His voice is drowned out by shouting, muffled bursts of machinegun fire and his own heavy breathing. He's on the move.

Jesus. If it's scary up here, I dread to think what sort of hell he's living down there.

I try him again just as we move beyond our cannon's range.

'Widow Eight Zero, this is Ugly Five Four. I have leakers identified.' As we continue our orbit, the leakers slip from view behind a wall.

Come on, come on, we're going to miss them . . .

'Come on, we've got to get round,' I urge Darwin.

He knows, he knows.

'I'm on it, ma'am.'

He's giving a situation report back to our base. He's calm; his voice is low.

The JTAC tells me he's happy for me to fire at the enemy.

'Ugly Five Four, you are cleared to engage on the eastern side. Send BDA.'

Finally.

Widow Eight Zero must have found somewhere to shelter from the hail of bullets. He wants the Battle Damage Assessment – my bird's-eye view of the destruction.

Darwin brings us full circle as quickly as our gunship – fully laden with fuel and missiles – will allow.

Looking down, I panic for a second that I have lost them. I steer the sight around with my thumb, guiding the round grey rocker switch on the GameBoy-style grip. It's stiff, and I use the strength of my whole arm to push it as the aircraft slowly circles. I find the men, crawling on their knees and elbows through the dirt.

'Happy?' Me.

'Happy.' Darwin.

One word that says we trust each other.

My fingers close around the cold trigger. I pause for a split second to think about the gunfire I am about to spray across the battlefield. At that moment, I realize that I have no choice but to be good at my job. There are people relying on me. After today, I'll no longer be the new girl.

'And for the best shot of the year, the award goes to Marksman Madison, who scored forty-four out of a possible fifty.'

I shuffle out of the row where I am sitting. The school assembly hall is musty and smells of teenage boys and body odour. My face reddens as two hundred eyes fix on me. I concentrate on squeezing past the line of combat-clad legs to get to the aisle.

As I walk up to the stage, I hear a whisper: 'That's the American girl.'

I don't look behind me. I hope my arse doesn't look huge in my oversized combats.

What a joke. This result is a complete fluke. I know they'll soon find that out.

I walk up the stairs. My boots don't fit properly and rub against my heels.

'Well done, Cadet Madison.'

I shake the lieutenant-colonel's hand, turn and am forced to sit on stage with a handful of other pupils. I see one of the other girls in my platoon, Mia, and grin at her, feeling awkward on stage. She smiles back, looking equally uncomfortable.

Someone is taking pictures for the fifth-form yearbook. 'Smile,' he says, as the flash goes off.

I attempt a smile, but can't open my mouth. I'm wearing

braces on my teeth and I hate them. They hurt and make me look like some kind of robot. I'm counting the days until they come off. I also feel slightly light-headed. I'm on a special Weetabix diet – two, three times a day – with a few of my friends, in an attempt to shrink our bodies. My stomach growls. Perhaps a Twix wouldn't be too bad . . .

Joining the Combined Cadet Force (CCF) at the local boys' school a year ago, in 1995, had seemed the thing to do at the time. I was fourteen when I started at my all-girls school, and the 'in crowd' went along.

When I moved to England, I'd joined as a boarder. Talk about limiting your options with the opposite sex. My school was very academic and prided itself on its yearly ranking in the league tables. They lost my entrance exam paper, and when I sat it again I knew the answer to every question, because I'd asked my dad the ones I didn't know first time around. I guess I've always been a bit geeky that way. As a result, I was put up a year, having passed with flying colours.

In the boarding house, we spent nearly all our time either trying on each other's clothes or revising for some test or another. I didn't mind too much – the girls were fun and it was quite satisfying to do well at school.

But, of course, there's the usual boy talk. We were all obsessed with the young and handsome history teacher, Mr Laithwaite. He was tall and blond with piercing blue eyes and a tight bum, which we all used to stare at when he turned to the blackboard. He teased us all mercilessly for forgetting our homework, and we were always trying to get into his detention. Just my luck that on the one occasion I managed it, I was lumbered with the massively overweight maths teacher. She was so enormous that when she turned round after writing on the blackboard, she had huge white patches on her boobs.

Kate, one of the coolest and prettiest girls in my class, told me that if I wanted a boyfriend, CCF was the place to be.

'There are loads of fit boys,' she'd said in her sing-song voice as we sat on the grass one lunch break.

'Andrew's in the army, and so are all of his gang.' She gave her shiny blond hair an extra flick.

Andrew was her latest boyfriend. He was in the year above us, at the boys' school, and gorgeous – not unlike a younger and slightly ganglier version of Mr Laithwaite.

'And Jason . . .' Her eyes glinted. She knew I really fancied the floppy-haired older boy.

OK, I was convinced.

So when the time came to decide, my name joined the long list of scribbled Biro signatures on the noticeboard. We also had the option of joining the navy or the RAF, but only the geeks and misfits joined them. We all knew that the army was the best.

Another handful of girls, who smoked behind the lacrosse hut and generally did as little work as possible, went for the other Friday-afternoon option – community service. I think they spent two afternoons serving tea at the local old people's home then bunked off for the rest of the year.

I started to picture Friday-evening dates after CCF – the cinema, followed by a sneaky drink of cider on the way back to the boarding house.

Our housemistress, Mrs Mace, who doubled as the French teacher, was a fierce, rake-thin spinster. We all dreaded having to beg her for permission to spend a night away. When I wanted to go to a club with Kate, her mum had to write a letter – how uncool – asking if I could stay at their house and go to a 'dance', and I had to do a demo in Mrs Mace's office of the kind of 'dancing' I was planning on doing while she sat and watched with a pinched expression, her hair pulled tightly into a bun which perched on the top of her head. I still squirm with embarrassment when I think about that.

The letter to the Mace was a necessary evil – being discovered coming in late prompted her scariest outbursts. But the

5

older girls always seemed to manage to come back from the boys' school after hours, insisting they'd been kept behind to clean the rifles, or to help clear out the stores.

'You can hang around with me,' Kate had said. 'I'll show you how to make the best of the uniform. If you leave two buttons of your shirt undone and tuck your combats into your boots, it can look really good.'

I wanted to be part of a group – and this was it. But no way was I wearing that beret thing . . .

So every Friday afternoon, I joined the coachload of girls piling into the quad, where we were taught to march, given basic rifle and battle drill and spent the odd afternoon wading through tunnels filled with water and scaling twelve-foot walls. There was lots of shouting right from the start, but I loved the feeling of satisfaction when we got through it, and I used to treat myself to a Dairy Milk on the way back to school. I was told that, if I got through two years, I could become an NCO and be the one in charge.

Now, I'm sitting on the stage in full view of everybody and starting to wish that I hadn't concentrated quite so hard earlier that day on the range.

Having completed the compulsory two years, after taking our GCSEs at the age of sixteen most of the girls gladly handed back their musty uniform to the stores and didn't give CCF another thought. But I loved the idea of having a rank and being the one with knowledge to pass on, so I eagerly put myself up for one of the sought-after places on the leadership course to become a junior NCO. The course is a challenge both physically and mentally – and I was game. I was selected along with Mia and a few others to complete the intensive week-long programme, teaching us how to give lectures and educate new recruits. We all pass and are each handed a shiny stripe to attach to our uniform.

I'll always remember the start of the new school year, and a gangly bunch of recruits spilling out into the impressive quad area. The groups the new NCOs were allocated to train were always mixed sex, and we began with basic drill, attempting to teach the fuzzy-faced boys to march properly: right leg forward with left arm; left leg with right.

We rose through the ranks, while, one by one, the other NCOs dropped out, distracted by schoolwork, boyfriends and university applications. But we were still enjoying it, and by our final school year, Mia and I were, respectively, platoon commander and platoon sergeant; the two most senior females in our intake.

Two and a half years after I picked up my shooting award, and just months from finishing school, and we're on the coach to one of the army bases in Kent for the day.

I prise open my eyes. They feel horribly gritty, and the bright spring sun makes me squint. I glance to the side and see Mia's head resting on my shoulder; her dark hair falling over her face.

'Oi, we're here,' I tell her, shaking her slightly. 'Yuck, you've dribbled.'

'What? Oops, sorry,' she says, wiping my combat-clad shoulder. 'God, I'm knackered, and my mouth feels like, just gross, like a little man has stepped into it and pooed.'

'Have some gum, buffalo breath.' I chuck her a packet of Extra from one of the large pockets in my combat trousers.

As we pull into the car park, a crude concrete slab surrounded by a few Portakabins and open fields, we are met by a line of officers and army instructors, who look distinctly unimpressed at the task ahead of them: teaching yet another bunch of cadets about battlecraft.

An hour later, and we're all totally camouflaged up, along with the other cadets – there must be about forty of us. As well as our usual combat gear and boots, we've got grass sticking out of our helmets, long reeds poking from our webbing and green smears across our faces. It's all part of the six 'S's – shape, shine, shadow, silhouette, sound and . . . smovement – the measures you take to blend in with the countryside and not be detected by the enemy.

We congregate at the meeting point and are met by three instructors; they are all young, beefy and extremely good-looking, and they clearly know it.

The middle one comes forward. He reminds me of a fitter version of Jim Carrey, with all the arrogance but none of the humour.

'So, which one of you lot is the platoon commander?' he asks, and there is a definite sneer in his voice.

Mia takes a stride forward. 'Me,' she says, as confidently as she can manage. He looks appalled as he clocks her stripes, then he raises his eyebrows, looks at his colleagues and sniggers.

'And your platoon sergeant?' he continues, thinking it has to be one of the boys; they're definitely in the majority here.

'Yep, that's me,' I say, stepping next to Mia.

Now he's totally amused. 'What, two girls?' he laughs. 'You're kidding me, right?'

'Ha, let's see what you're made of. Give a battle command from over there by that tree. You can do it in front of the whole platoon so they can see what you're made of, too.' He snivels, 'Blondie, you can go first.'

Mia gives me an encouraging 'Sod them' look. I take a deep breath.

I know this is a test. I look around me, and rows of eyes are staring back at me. My heart starts hammering.

I muster up every bit of energy I possibly can and let rip – I'm mindful of the fact that I need to keep my voice low. Squeaky shrieking would get me laughed right out of there.

Everything goes in slow motion, and as I start hollering it feels like the ground underneath my feet is shaking. I yell as if my life depends on it.

'Enemy, 150 metres in treeline. Watch and shoot, watch and *shoooot!*'

I look round, and the instructor is standing open-mouthed; and his eyes are so wide I can barely see his irises. I don't dare look behind me at the cadets, but I catch Mia's eye. She's grinning from ear to ear.

'Well, well,' he says, quickly regaining his composure. 'Not bad.' But it's pretty obvious he's determined to make fools of us.

'Platoon Commander, call yourself a commander, let's see it then,' he says to Mia. As she moves towards centre stage, I can tell she's terrified, but she starts bellowing the same instruction as I did.

It's impressive. It's so impressive, in fact, that when we turn round, it's as if there is a whole new bunch of instructors facing us. The slightly patronizing looks on their faces have been replaced by genuine smiles, and wide mouths and teeth have replaced the pinched cheeks and squinty eyes. From that moment on, they are totally respectful. They don't think to question our sex, our rank, our knowledge, they just let us get on with it.

We spend the morning barrelling through muddy fields, our platoon around us in various formations, looking for enemy and mocking up battles. In the afternoon we make a platoon camp and practise an ambush scenario.

As Mia and I pack up, pulling off our sweaty helmets and webbing, the main instructor comes over. He's changed into a tight T-shirt and his chest and arm muscles bob as he walks.

'Oi, girls.'

We look over, slightly apprehensive. 'You've surprised us today, good work. You can tell all the cadets respect you too. I'm impressed.'

Three months later, and I'm sitting in a military waiting room before my medical for a Short Service Limited Commission.

I've just finished my A-levels and will still only be seventeen if I go straight to uni. Freshers' Week and still below the legal drinking age – not an ideal way to begin my post-school life of freedom.

The idea of a gap year in the army came up during a chat with one of my CCF officers. It would involve four weeks' training at Sandhurst, rather than the year a 'proper' officer spends, and ten months working in a regular army unit as a junior officer.

I can feel my tummy churning. My paper gown is open at the back, and the plastic chair feels cold on my bum. Why does the army doctor need to see my bum anyway?

So far, the worst part about joining the army has been never knowing what's going to happen to me next. Everything comes as a complete surprise, and no one ever reacts to me the way normal civilians would.

My CCF officer sent me some brochures. The cover featured a girl who was about to jump out of a plane. Underneath the picture were the words: 'Amazing opportunities to see the world – adventure training.' The girl looked confident and sun-tanned, and she was smiling. I've always loved flying; everything about it, from the way time almost stops when you take off, to floating high in the sky, one minute in clouds, then high above them. One glance at that brochure and I was sold.

Two days later, I picked up the phone.

The conversation didn't go at all how I'd imagined.

'Army Careers,' the gruff Northern voice barked.

I was sitting on the floor of my bedroom, surrounded by army leaflets and bits of paper.

'Um, hi . . . I'm thinking about joining the army . . . and I . . . er . . . have some questions.'

I scanned my list of questions.

'Go ahead.'

I could hear the tapping of a keyboard in the background and the faint whir of office machinery.

'Well . . . is it hard?' I squeaked.

There was a hostile silence; I could feel the man on the other end of the line wondering if I was serious.

'What?'

This was going badly. 'Umm, you know. Joining.'

'Depends what you consider to be difficult. Listen, miss, I suggest you go and have a think about whether you're serious or not, then come in and see us.'

After the phone call, I was more determined than ever.

I'd been so nervous about this assessment that, apart from a Nutri-Grain bar, I'd been unable to eat all morning. I just had no idea what was going to be required of me. The train journey to Warminster was pure torture; I alternated between biting my nails down to the quicks and wondering what the hell I was doing.

The Nutri-Grain bar on the walk here had been the final straw for my stomach; it started churning so much I had to pop into a hotel to use the loo.

I walked in looking relatively smart in the M&S suit my mum had bought me the month before for these army interviews. I enquired where the toilets were and was directed downstairs by the pretty receptionist.

'Stairs are off limits though; they're painting. Use the lifts.' She smiled and gestured towards the corner of the foyer.

By now my stomach was complaining loudly and I was working hard to keep everything under control. My pelvic-floor muscles went into overdrive as I pressed the button for the basement. The lift stopped downstairs and I stood perfectly still, poised to dart through the doors at the first available opportunity. My bowels were gurgling like a food processor.

But the doors remained resolutely shut.

I started to think that maybe a teeny-weeny fart would bring me some relief while I waited. I decided to go for it. I tilted my bum slightly towards the back of the lift. There was an explosion like a car crash, followed by a huge wave of relief.

11

I heard a small cough from behind me.

I turned in slow motion to see the doors open behind me . . . and a waiter with a little silver food trolley and three hotel guests with surprised looks on their faces.

Good start to the day, Madison.

'Miss Madison?'

I followed the nurse into a large, cold, uncarpeted examining room with peeling paint and a few dog-eared anatomy posters on the walls. An old man who looked like a corpse sat behind the desk, a stethoscope around his neck. His skin was transparent and I could see the blue veins pulsing softly around his temples.

The doctor asked me a few questions, noted my responses in some papers on his desk, then directed me to the scales.

As I turned my back to him, I was mortified to realize that I was wearing a barely-there G-string. I felt my face flush and did my best to hold the back of my gown closed.

'Over to the measuring rule now, please.' His voice crackled like parchment.

The nurse took the reading then resumed her place against the wall. I was standing uncertainly in the middle of the room, one hand shielding my bare arse.

The doctor indicated the examining couch. He wasn't hostile, exactly, but he unsettled me.

He came over and listened to my chest, front and back. The stethoscope was like an icicle. 'We're just going to have a quick feel of things . . . Hope you don't mind . . .' He folded back the side of my gown.

I grabbed a peek at myself as he reached over and got the shock of my life.

My nipple! It was poking out of my nice lacy bra! There was a hole in my bloody bra. I felt myself start to sweat and went an even brighter red.

Maybe he won't notice.

He worked his way up my abdomen, checking for God

knows what. He was heading for my boobs, appearing not to notice my ridiculous choice of underwear.

I glanced at the nurse, who looked faintly amused.

The doc replaced my gown. 'Hop down please, Miss Madison. We need to see how you move.'

They both stared at me, waiting.

I climbed hesitantly off the couch and stood in the middle of the room again. *What's happening now? 'See how I move'?*

'Walk towards me please . . . and away . . .'

My knuckles whitened as my fist clenched over the opening of the gown.

'Just swing your arms naturally, Miss Madison.'

Pervert! He wants to see my arse! And the nurse is in on it . . . No wonder she looks so amused.

'OK . . . Now face me and bend side to side.'

I did so, right then left.

'And forwards.'

Ohmygod, he's having another look at my boobs. I leaned tentatively forward, keeping my head over the neckline of my gown.

'Mmm . . . hmm . . .' Apparently satisfied, he jotted down something else in his notes.

'Face the wall, please, and run your left hand down the outside of your left thigh.'

I swivelled slowly on one foot until I was facing the wall and stood with my bum on show and my heart pounding. *I can't believe this. I was expecting a check-up, not an audition for Spearmint Rhino.*

I took a deep breath and lifted my left arm slowly into the air. I cocked my left leg to the side and then slowly, almost sensually, ran the tips of my fingers from the line of my G-string down the outside of my thigh, all the way to my knee. It seemed to take for ever.

As I turned to face them, the nurse made a noise like a bark and started laughing uncontrollably. Realization dawned on me. The doctor just wanted to check my spine.

The doc can't bring himself to look me in the eye. He's even more embarrassed than I am.

I can't believe I just did that! Does he think I'm trying to sleep my way in? Ohmygod, get me out of here nownownow.

The last five minutes in the examining room are a blur.

A letter arrived a week later, with ticks in all the right boxes. My little performance hadn't damaged my chances. And no one needed to know anything about it.

I was invited to spend two and a half days at Warminster with the Regimental Commissioning Board the following month. There, we were put through a number of tests – a short run, an individual assault course – then given some lectures and participated in some discussions. Finally, we went through a series of interviews, each one harder than the first.

It felt as if everyone was much older than me, but none of it seemed to faze me as much as it did some of the other candidates, even when they told me my military knowledge was crap. I just told myself I was still not totally sure I wanted to do this, and that if I failed it would be a sign.

At the end of it, the RCB held a dinner to show us some of the good things we could expect if we passed – silver-service four-course meals polished off with a small vat of wine is the norm at these regimental meals, apparently. I wasn't even able to have a drink, though, and had to sip my water as demurely as possible. Turning eighteen wouldn't come a moment too soon.

The water is cascading down my body; my hair is soapy and smells sweet. My legs and armpits are freshly shaven and smooth to the touch. I'm bronzed, exfoliated and buffed. There isn't a hint of orange peel; I've been using a special, ultra-expensive cream to shift it. Chicane's 'Offshore' plays softly in the background. An enticingly fluffy white towel sits by the shower, a crisp waffle dressing gown and big slippers beside it. A huge carrot cake topped with butter cream and eighteen candles waits invitingly, as does a chilled bottle of rosé . . .

'Second Lieutenant Madison!' A gruff voice breaks into my daydream. 'We'll be moving in five.'

Despite the fact that it's my long-awaited eighteenth birthday, the possibility of my first legal drink is still months away.

We're on the last day of a six-week exercise. The British Army Training Unit Suffield (BATUS) is 1,200 square miles of open prairie in Canada where we have free rein to fire our rifles and drive our tanks at breakneck speed. It's one of the army's biggest and best training areas, and every unit comes here to be put through its paces at least once a year.

I was the youngest cadet and one of only a few girls to have made it through the short Sandhurst course for gap-year students. I'd accepted an offer to read civil engineering at Nottingham but deferred it for a year and instead had been posted to Osnabrück, Germany, with the 21 Royal Engineer Regiment for ten months.

Coming to BATUS is our biggest exercise of the year. I'd been on a handful of adventure training courses, learning to ski, sail and climb, but it was always a relief to escape from Osnabrück. The only things there are the military base and Europe's largest sex shop. I've been sentenced to six weeks in a tank at BATUS. It's inhabited by four men – and me. One of the men is the officer commanding my squadron in Osnabrück, but far from being an honour to share his, bigger, tank, it's turned out to be a death trap.

We crashed about two weeks into the exercise. As the tank nose-dived into a trench, I was slammed against the metal grille separating the driver's compartment from the radios and bombarded with the OC's camp bed, solar shower, several plastic buckets, and his flip-flops and bright red shorts. Unforgettable. The door slowly opened in what had now become the roof

and through it I saw a puffy cloud go by, followed by a helicopter.

The stench in the tank is something special – a mixture of
BO, feet and general decay. I've only managed one shower in
the last six weeks, and my hair is plastered to my head in greasy
clumps despite my regular use of the dandruff-inducing dry
shampoo spray (which, misleadingly, has a picture of a shiny-
haired lady on the tin).

We've been in this position for four days, and the boredom
is indescribable. Amazingly, the boys all seem to think this is
great – real-life playing soldiers.

I go back to my shower fantasy . . .

I'm too scared to drop off; I got an almighty bollocking for
resting my eyes for a few minutes too long one day, so I fill
the time in the half-darkness by counting down the hours until
I can step into the wall of steam and lather up . . .

And planning my next shopping trip.

I make mental notes of what I need for my next holiday
with Paul, the man of the moment, whom I met when I was
at home. Maxi dress, tick. Wedges, tick. New bikini, tick.
Hawaiian Tropic factors 8, 15 and 30, tick, tick, tick. I won't
burn my boobs this time round.

Despite my junior-officer tag, I know I'm next to useless
after my paltry four weeks' officer training at Sandhurst, especially as I am now working alongside a bunch of guys who
have done this job for years. I've been manning the radios,
transcribing the code as the different platoons communicate
with each other across the vast plains, so I haven't been able
to get out of the tank.

It doesn't matter too much – there are some things against
getting out. I've developed an irrational fear of going to the
toilet in the open. Out on the prairie, there's one tree, the 'shitting tree', which everyone avoids unless the situation is really,
really urgent. If the smell in the tank is anything to go by, it's
not going to be pleasant. Inside, there is nowhere private where

I can go to the loo, so I wait until dark – but of course the guards wear night-vision goggles and I just have to accept their ribbing the next day.

We do everything with the tank: sleep by it, service it, dress it up in camouflage nets . . . it's like a very demanding boyfriend who never even takes you to dinner or to see a film.

Our final day is an endless stream of radio messages punctuated by periods of driving at three miles an hour to lay imaginary minefields to foil the imaginary enemy's imaginary plans. I fear my heart might stop through lack of stimulation – I'm so relieved the end is in sight.

At long last, I decode a radio message with the words I've been dreaming about for six weeks. It's not quite 'Your bath is ready, Miss Madison,' but it is second best: 'ENDEX'.

It's over.

I press the 'open' button next to the tank hatch.

As I stumble through the door to freedom, a helicopter is landing 100 metres away, on its way to the debrief. The blades slow and whoop, whoop, whoop, throwing up a cloud of dust. The air smells suddenly exotic: aviation fuel.

The pilots climb out of the cockpit. They're blond and their uniforms are clean and freshly starched; I bet they smell of washing powder and home. I long to run up and sniff them, but I manage to restrain myself.

'Would you like a ride?' one of them asks.

Is that a joke?

'Yes, please!'

The next thirty minutes are blissful – I can see the whole prairie from up here! And all the stupid tanks and cardboard minefields. And that God-awful tree.

As I watch the pilot's hands making tiny movements on the controls, I'm fascinated. I think about how amazing it would be to do his job, and realize that, maybe one day, I *could* do it. I land and tell anyone who will listen that I want to be a pilot. As I say it, I know it sounds a bit lame – as if all it took was one helicopter ride to make anyone want to be a pilot, rather than it being a life-long, burning need of mine.

They snort with laughter. I'll show them I'm more serious than that.

University passed in a blur of drunken nights out, the odd lecture and Wednesday afternoons at the University Officer Training Corps (UOTC), where I instructed new cadets on all the basics: drill, rifle training, fieldcraft. I kept my commission and earned £50 a week – big money to poor students living on baked potatoes, pasta and vodka. I also surprised myself by being a good instructor. I liked all the cadets in my platoon and hoped the feeling was mutual; they certainly didn't dive out of the way when I saw them on campus. The only tricky thing was the fact that I was a fresher teaching fellow freshers, but as long as we all made it to Club ISIS together every Wednesday night, we all got along fine.

During my first long summer holiday, I was asked to go back to school to help out on the regular army camp, and when I was there I was called 'ma'am' by all the NCOs and cadets. I felt totally in my comfort zone for once, and even the teachers seemed slightly in awe of me, which was a bit weird, considering how recently they were shouting: 'Stop laughing at the back of my class, Madison!'

By my second year of uni, I'd decided I wanted to make a career of the army, but I hadn't enjoyed my time with the Royal Engineers enough to want to join them. Each time I thought back I could only muster images of the shitting tree, the stinky tank . . . and then the amazing helicopter and Persil-fresh pilots. I put aside any memories I had of the engineers' faces when I told them I wanted to be a pilot and decided to take a leap into the unknown: to try for selection for the Army Air Corps (AAC).

I wrote off and, a month later, I heard back. I would have to have yet another sodding medical. The list of requirements was so long, anyone would've thought they were looking for an Olympic athlete: perfect hearing, flawless vision, no joint problems, limbs of certain lengths so you could fit snugly into the ejection seat. One guy failed because his arms were too short. Thankfully, I was deemed a well-formed, healthy specimen.

Having passed, along with the other AAC candidates who had made it through the medical, I was sent on a two-day selection course at RAF Cranwell during the Easter break from uni. We had to sit endless tests. Some of them were just like those computer games where you control the action using a joystick, and were designed to assess our speed of learning, coordination and general aptitude for flying. It was good fun, but the stakes were high: usually, only between two and five people in every twenty pass, and our group was no different – only three of us made it to the next stage. The whole thing reminded me of *The X Factor*, but without Simon Cowell.

A few weeks later, a brown envelope fell through my letter box. Luckily, I'd been looking out for it, and I plucked it from amidst the takeaway-pizza leaflets and unpaid bills and ripped it open. I'd been invited to the three-week selection course at Middle Wallop (the AAC headquarters) in the summer for some intensive flying training.

Alongside eleven other AAC candidates, we learned to fly fixed-wing aircraft called Fireflys. There's no way to describe the feeling of floating above England in those small yellow planes – I felt freedom like I'd never felt it before; it was as if flying was what I was born to do.

The instructors loaded us up with new information every day to see how fast we could learn; they plotted each candidate's learning curve to ensure it didn't start 'flattening out' – a sign of being overloaded. They told us that anyone could train to be a pilot but that only a few could master the skills quickly enough to make becoming a pilot feasible. Of the twelve people on my grading, four failed. I'm lucky to have an almost photographic memory, so I found it easy to retain the checklists that many would-be pilots fell down on. So far, so good.

There was still no guarantee that I would make it on to the notoriously tough Army Pilots' Course. It's like A-levels: you may get the right grades, but it doesn't necessarily mean you'll get that coveted place at your university of choice. The medicals, aptitude tests and flying grading were just my ticket for a place in the race.

I returned to my final year of uni with a clear idea of what I wanted to do. I sat smugly in the back of my lectures daydreaming about flying high in the clouds and imagining the lives of hard-hatted site visits awaiting my fellow engineering students.

I'm at Sandhurst on my commissioning course, which I started straight after uni. We're on the Yorkshire Moors – although it could be anywhere for all we can see across the bleak countryside. I can only make out rows of fields, stone walls and barbed wire, with the odd cow dotted on the horizon.

The light's closing in and I'm absolutely freezing. I've been on sentry duty with another girl, Michelle, guarding our all-female platoon camp for what seems like a week although, according to my Casio watch, it's only been two hours.

'Fucking hell, those ration packs play havoc with my guts,' Michelle groans, pulling a face.

'But imagine a double hamburger and fries,' I say dreamily.

I'm wearing a ridiculous gas mask and helmet combo, and when I whisper I sound like Darth Vader before he went through puberty.

'Ohh, or a hot chocolate with marshmallows, that would be amazing.' Her eyes roll upwards in her steamed-up mask.

Michelle's stomach gives a loud and ominous gurgle, and we giggle, then shush ourselves loudly, remembering that we are meant to be being 'covert'. I count my blessings that I've been paired with her; she's the funniest girl in the platoon. She's a complete gem, making what could be just the most depressing of experiences bizarrely enjoyable with her brilliant sense of humour and hilarious face-pulling.

Another five minutes go by. I'm lying on my front, supposedly looking out for 'threats', and it's so cold my toes and fingers are starting to ache. My rifle is jammed into my shoulder, and I peer across the sights to look at my arcs. My whole body is numb and sopping wet and my elbows are slowly sinking into the icy mud.

I'm four months into Sandhurst 'Take Two'. It's the scariest experience of my life, and the most challenging, but it's better that I had imagined. In all my worst nightmares before I came, I pictured myself on my own – on my own trying to clean my room with a toothbrush, on my own trying to climb a six-foot wall, on my own being told to iron everything I have by morning. What I didn't account for are the twenty-odd like-minded girls that are also here so, no matter how bad things get, there's always someone beside me, going through the same thing with a smile – or a grimace and some blood, sweat or tears – on her face. Most of the time, as we run along the corridors of Sandhurst's halls, we laugh so hard I once thought I'd wee myself.

When I did that gap-year month at Sandhurst, I remember thinking it was pretty hard, but this year-long course is, predictably, much more gruelling. It's divided into three terms, and I've just completed the first, which everyone says is the hardest. It's physically tough and, some mornings, when I try to get out of bed it takes a good five seconds for my legs to work; it's as if my brain has lost the power to communicate with my body. I ache all over, my heels bleed constantly from the stiff leather boots and I haven't worn mascara in weeks. In fact, I can't remember ever even owning a make-up bag.

We're all severely sleep-deprived, working on an average of just a few hours a night. It's a common sight to see one of the girls falling asleep on the march and veering off into the bushes, or for someone to nod off in a 'holding area' at night and just get left behind. Both of those things have happened to me over the past three months, and every morning it feels as if my eyelids have barely closed the night before. But, on the plus side, all the exertion and lack of sleep seem to be good for my figure – I've just bought some size-eight skinny jeans from Top Shop, and they actually go over my thighs.

Our schedule is packed, but no two days are the same. We're trained in basic military skills such a fieldcraft, operating the basic army rifle, the SA80, drill and fitness, as well as military knowledge and history, instructional techniques and leadership skills. I have a bit of a head start because of my seven years of CCF and UOTC, but there are definitely areas where it would seem I hadn't been paying enough attention first time around.

I know that, if I want to be a pilot, I need to be at the top, or at least near it, to fulfil my dreams. The AAC only take the top cadets, and I'm desperate to be given the chance. From the start of our time at Sandhurst, we are graded on virtually every aspect of our training: from our fitness, officer qualities, intelligence and confidence to how well we perform in the classroom, at giving lectures and writing essays. Out of the thirty people in my platoon, I come in the top five for everything. I'd always hated being near the bottom; it feels as if the climb upwards is impossible.

We're told that the commissioning course, where we are trained to become officers, will teach us all sorts of wonderful personal skills that will help us 'be the best', such as decision-making, negotiation, self-confidence and discipline. I think they need to add having a good sense of humour to that lot.

We need it.

An average day might go like this: we're forced out of our hospital-style beds by the shouting of our scary, automaton-like colour sergeant after what feels like two seconds' shut-eye.

We flail around trying to find the right kit while trying not to make a mess in case there's an on-the-spot check later, then run outside to be inspected for smartness, shininess and correctness. We're often then instructed to change at speed into any number of outfits, and each change is timed.

In the first term we had a cleaning period between 4 and 5 a.m. I remember squatting in my doorway cleaning the door jamb with a cotton bud and listening to *Farming Today* on Radio 4, the only radio station we were allowed. Someone's cow had broken free; I listened closely for any tips the broadcast might offer to aid my escape.

During our PT sessions we have to run for miles in full combat gear, which roughly equates to the weight of a small person attached to your chest. And that's on top of what my Aunt Margery calls the 'legendary Madison boobs', which are becoming a right pain in the arse. Actually, if they were on my arse it would be a bonus; I could use a padded chair at times.

Most of my friends are starting their careers as medical students, lawyers and journalists. We write letters to each other, or send each other funny cards and have the odd telephone chat during my rare weekends off, but it's really hard to describe what I'm up to, so I stick to asking them questions, or swapping gossip about other friends.

I once tried to get some sympathy from Rachel, a fourth-year medical student I lived with at uni. She'd rung me and said she'd had a shit day.

'Tell me about it,' I said. 'We were up at 0400 for a room inspection, then we had a log race; I fell off a wall and bruised my face. Then we went straight in for three hours of lectures, and I fell asleep and got shouted at and was made to stand at the front of the room for the rest of the period. After lunch we practised digging holes before going to the gas chamber and being gassed.' I gave a hacking cough as evidence of my recent gassing.

There was a short silence.

'I know! My day was hideous!' Rachel started. 'I sat in the library for five hours waiting for Rich, who was too hung over to make it for our study period, and then on the way home I broke my heel and my bus was delayed . . . talk about shitty days. What are we doing with our lives?'

Hmm, not exactly the response I was hoping for.

I pull myself back from these thoughts and look over at Michelle. She's nodded off. I give her a prod to avoid her getting a bollocking from the colour sergeant.

'Thanks, you cow. I was dreaming I was on holiday with my boyfriend!'

With an hour to go, I'm practically counting down the seconds until I can get back to my bivouac, my best attempt so far at hoisting my poncho between two trees to provide some shelter. My eyes are now primed to spot the perfect bivouac site: big tree, trunk not too fat, right distance from its neighbour, nice soft leaves on the ground, not too wet, no ants' nests. My musty-smelling sleeping bag is heavenly in comparison to this muddy ditch.

Michelle and I have a running joke about what we'd do to get medevac-ed off every exercise. It's like a scale of how bad things are. I might run past her during a platoon attack and she'll shout, 'Would you shoot yourself in the foot?', and I'll respond, 'Not yet', or, 'Maybe the face!' depending on how dire things are at the time.

We're both struggling to stay awake as we look across the slowly darkening horizon through our rifle sights. I consider sucking on the mouldy chocolate I've got in my jacket pocket and wonder whether that would make me just the right amount of ill to get to go to hospital but not kill me.

I shuffle along the ground a bit in an attempt to get my circulation going. It feels as if my blood's stopped flowing and that everything might just turn blue and drop off.

Despair is seeping in when my eyes sweep over a big cowpat

nearby. It's the size of a large wok, a strange greeny-brown and crusted over in large bubbles, like a green curry from a bad takeaway. There are some rancid flies buzzing around it. It's only about two feet away from my face, and it's testament to my state of mind that I don't even feel the need to move away from it. I nudge Michelle and gesture towards it.

'If I ate that, do you think I'd be airlifted out of here?' Michelle whispers, her eyes scrunched up behind her mask. 'It would make me really ill, like a-week-in-the-sick-bay, ill. And think of the weight loss! Look at the colour of it!'

'Go on, I dare you,' I say.

'Seriously, though, how much money would actually make you eat that?' Michelle looks serious.

I consider the taste, texture and possible hospital stay.

'A grand?'

'Hmmm, I reckon if someone waved ready cash at me I'd take five hundred.'

'Fuck it, three hundred!'

We amuse ourselves with more childish poo-chat until two of the others come over and tap us to let us know our shift's up, and then we crawl back to our bivouacs. I struggle out of my combat jacket and helmet and climb into my sleeping bag with my rifle stuffed down the end. I take huge pleasure from listening to the noise the zip makes going up – to a trained ear, so totally different from the noise of a zip going down prior to going on sentry duty. I drop off, cold but happy, wearing my gas mask, muddy clothing and boots.

The Army Air Corps is the most selective unit in the army, and the only combat arm which women are allowed to join. There are lots of things I could choose to do, but this is the biggest challenge – to be on the front line.

The next hurdle is the interviews with senior AAC officers, which take place a few weeks before we finish the commissioning course. Our performance in these interviews, together with our conduct during the past forty weeks, will be the deciding factors as to whether the AAC wants us.

'Apparently they can ask us anything about the whole Army Air Corps – when it was formed and who is in charge – as well as current affairs and general knowledge stuff,' I say in a panic on the phone to Mia the night before my interview.

'What kind of general knowledge? Like "Which football team won the World Cup in 1970?" kind of thing?' she laughs, clattering around in her kitchen in London.

'No, dumb arse,' I giggle. 'But I've heard of them asking people to name all the countries in South America.'

'Go on then, have a go.' I hear toast popping up in the background.

'Ummm, Brazil, Mexico – no, wait. Oh, *shit!*'

The day of the interview comes, and I wait in an echoing Sandhurst corridor in my unfamiliar-feeling and now much-too-big suit. I'm the fifth cadet to go in, and during my hour-long wait I go to the loo six times.

'Cadet Madison.'

I jump as a female voice calls my name, smooth down my skirt and follow a dumpy-looking secretary down the corridor. The clicking of her heels hurts my ears as the sound ricochets around us. She ushers me into a cream-carpeted room where a long table stands before me. Three uniformed men sit on the far side like judges in a court, and a single wooden chair sits in the middle of the room. It feels as if I stand for ever in the doorway watching the unseasonal summer rain spattering against the grimy window behind the judges.

'Will you have some coffee, Miss Madison?' the judge sitting in the middle asks in a surprisingly low voice. The room feels suffocatingly quiet when he stops speaking. This judge is the tallest by a whole head, and his face is politely blank.

My hands are cold and shaking slightly with nerves – I reason that a cup of coffee will warm and steady them.

'Yes, please,' I say.

There is a slight pause before the tall judge nudges the man on his left. Short and slight, he reminds me of a small, nervous feline, and he is clearly at the bottom of the judges' pecking order. He scurries off to a table in the corner which I hadn't spotted before. I notice with anxiety that there are four utterly untouched stacks of cups and saucers on it. The feline judge is battling with the plunger on the cafetière, and then I see him ripping the seal off the milk.

No one has had any coffee yet – maybe I wasn't supposed to? Why do I always get these things wrong?

At a signal from the tall judge I sit on the wooden chair, cupping my coffee and trying not to spill any on my lap. Five minutes of questions about myself, my education and interests and my time at Sandhurst put me at ease. Then the third judge, who looks incredibly serious, speaks for the first time. His voice is thin and threatening.

'Now, Cadet Madison, just some general questions to check that you have a good working knowledge of current affairs.'

I gulp.

'Do you know who is currently the vice-president of the United States?'

Ha! They don't know that I'm half American.

'George Bush. George "W." Bush,' I correct smartly.

'No, Miss Madison, the vice-president.'

'Oh, yes, of course.' Then I have a mind-blank. 'It's ummm . . .'

The serious judge looks down and starts jotting something in his notepad.

'Oh, it's Dick, errr, Dick, ummm, Dick . . .' I scrabble around in my panicked brain for a surname, but nothing comes. I realize there are three men staring at my increasingly pink face as I just say 'Dick', over and over again.

'Sorry,' I say. Silence replies.

'And who is the UK defence secretary?'

I have no idea. Why would I ever need to know that, I wonder – in case I need to phone him up? *Hello, Bob, it's Charlie. You know, Charlotte Madison from Sandhurst. Just wanted some money for my personal defence budget.* Hardly.

I suppress an urge to say, 'He's the one who's always refusing to give us more cash to make sexy uniforms,' before realizing that too much time has gone by and the judges have taken my daydream for a wrong answer. They are all shuffling to their feet.

'Thank you for your time, Cadet Madison,' the tall judge says, extending his hand. I shake it and then back away, unsure whether to salute or not. I remember that I'm not in uniform, so I'm not supposed to, but isn't there something about not turning your back on senior officers? *Or is that just the Queen?*

The three men are looking at me, waiting for me to leave, and in my frenzied attempt to make a final good impression, I find myself doing a horrifying, slow-motion bow in the style of a maid from *Upstairs, Downstairs.*

As I stare at the carpet on my way up from the low bow, I feel my chances of getting into my dreamt-of Army Air Corps slipping away.

'Thanks,' I mumble, not meeting the judges' eyes as I dive out of the room at top speed.

Bollocks.

Just days later, with two weeks left to go until the end of my course at Sandhurst, it's crunch time: the remaining AAC candidates will find out if they have made the grade. Of the original seventy applicants, there are now only twelve of us, and we are sent to a small, plush room at the back of the headquarters. I'm so exhausted by this point that I have to concentrate hard even to put one foot in front of the other as I walk across the polished wooden floorboards, but the closer I come to the room, the more adrenaline pumps through me. I feel my heart beating faster as I see a sign on the door: AAC CANDIDATES 1030–1100.

As we walk in, sunshine pours through sash windows on to several plump armchairs and sofas. I squint.

'Come in, welcome,' a colonel from the AAC greets us. I recognize him from the interview phase. He looks immaculate in an expensive civilian suit, but his face is unreadable.

'Help yourself to tea,' he tells us.

On the far side of the room is a table laid out with china teacups and saucers, posh-looking biscuits and gleaming silver cutlery. We edge over, too anxious to eat but politely pouring ourselves tea nonetheless.

I recognize a red-haired cadet from the all-boys company and make my way over to him.

'Hi, I'm Charlie.'

He breaks into a big friendly grin. 'I'm Steve.'

'I'm so nervous. Are you?'

'I guess. I know I don't want either of my other choices of regiment, but I'm pretty confident the Air Corps will have me.'

'Why?' I ask, envious of his confidence.

'My interviews went well. They asked me lots of political questions, and I like to keep up to date with politics.'

'Oh,' I say, remembering the awkward moments in my interview.

'And my grading was awesome – I loved it. How was yours?' I smile just at the memory of flying high above Wiltshire in a Firefly.

'Amazing. I loved it too. That makes this worse, though, don't you think? To know you want something so much and to know that you enjoy it, and then have the selection completely out of your hands?'

'At least we've both done ours . . . some people here haven't even done theirs yet. The Air Corps has to take a gamble on them – they know what they're getting with us.' I like Steve already; he's so friendly and positive.

After a few painfully nerve-racking minutes, all twelve candidates are assembled, and the colonel addresses us.

'I am now going to read out two lists of names, separate you into two groups and announce who will be accepted into the Corps.'

'Oh, God,' I whisper to Steve. 'I don't think I can take the suspense.' What if I end up back in that awful tank with the Royal Engineers, I think to myself.

The colonel reads down his list, calling off six names and motioning for those called to be seated on six armchairs at one end of the room. I am not among them, but Steve is, and so are two other cadets I know by reputation – they performed well at Sandhurst and are bound to be accepted into the Air Corps.

He calls out another six names, ending with 'Officer Cadet Madison. Now if you six could sit over here.' He gestures towards a ridiculous red sofa.

I sit down, numb with shock and anticipation of the crushing blow about to be dealt to me. I think about the year of sheer effort and exertion I have just been through, about how I have striven continuously to be in the top few in the platoon.

'Now for the results. The cadets who have made it into the prestigious Army Air Corps, who will be starting their flying training within weeks, are . . .'

My stomach lurches with yearning to be allowed to start the pilots' course.

'All of you! Ha, ha, ha, ha! Tense, wasn't it?'

It takes a few moments before any of the bone-weary cadets stir, and then realization spreads through the room like an electric shock. I'm too happy to be angry about our *Pop Idol*-style acceptance.

'We're in!' I shout. Everyone is grinning wildly and there are handshakes and back-slapping.

I rush over to Steve. 'Well done, Charlie,' he greets me. I grin back, speechless with relief.

My official 'passing out' ceremony from Sandhurst falls on a drizzly day in September, a month later. As I stand to attention for perhaps the last time in front of the grand white stone building, I reflect on my time there. Through the pain of cracked heels and bruised shins which glow like a map of the assault course through my tights, the overriding emotion is a huge sense of achievement. Looking over to the sea of faces watching the ceremony, I can make out Mum, Dad and Mia smiling in the front row. I don't dare smile back but raise my eyebrows in recognition.

Afterwards, we gather for a meal in the vast dining room and I pick mine out among all the proud parents and friends and hurry over.

'God, you look a bit rough,' Mia tells me while my parents chat to my platoon commander. 'Are you all right?! I mean . . .'

'Just fucking knackered,' I tell her honestly, then wince at my language as I realize my parents are standing right beside us. 'But thanks. I thought I could pass it off as looking *wiser* or something.'

'And the flying stuff?' she asks. 'How are you feeling about it?'

'I can't wait!' I tell her. 'It feels like my whole life is about to start.'

Now I am officially qualified, I am sent to spend five months flying Fireflys at Barkston Heath, near RAF Cranwell in Lincolnshire. There are twelve of us at the starting blocks. Every flight we make is assessed; it's three strikes and you're out. I bond with the group really quickly.

They're a mix of navy, army and RAF; I already know Steve and immediately click with one of the other girls, Sue. She has long flowing dark hair and hasn't compromised an ounce of her femininity for the RAF.

Making my way through the various rounds of training and tests, it becomes clear I have found a place where everyone is like me. After a lifetime of Mum telling me off for running around with a glass of water or a plate of food

31

in my hand, now I'm in a place where everyone runs up-and downstairs with cups of tea in one hand and a phone in the other. I'm with other coordinated people. I'm in my element. Christmas that year comes and goes in a whirl-wind of fun and learning, and in the spring we switch to learning to fly Squirrel helicopters at RAF Shawbury, near Shrewsbury, and are taught the basics of rotary-wing aircraft. I've known for ages that I want to fly for the AAC, so I've always known it would be helicopters for me. Who wants to just go fast when you can go fast, then stop, hover and check out your surroundings?

I'm nervous and excited before my first helicopter flight, not knowing what it will be like and having such high expecta-tions, but as soon as it begins, I'm hooked. My instructor is a short, slightly plump man who's recently left the army, and he tells me he's doing the job he loves most in the world. His enthusiasm is infectious.

As we take off, I feel like I'm in the middle of one of my thousands of dreams about flying, lifting off the ground lighter than air, on a smooth magic carpet. The blood rushes to my head, and I feel weightless.

'What was it like, what was it like?' My course mates crowd around me when I land; I was the first one to go up and they are dying to know the details.

'Like flying . . .' I say dreamily, oblivious to the sniggering from behind me at my stupid remark. I'm the happiest I've ever been. Most evenings I go out with my course mates and we sit chatting in the pubs by the river, watching the hazy oranges and pinks of the sunset over Shrewsbury and swap-ping stories of our mishaps during that day's flying. I'm convinced I've pulled out the trump card with this job, and it seems I'm quite good at it too.

In early autumn we move down to Middle Wallop, where we continue to fly Squirrel helicopters, but now solely with army instructors, and begin to learn army tactics. Sue stays at

Shawbury to continue her training with the RAF, and I'm gutted to be leaving behind a girl I'd grown so close to. The next phase turns out to be even more exciting, as we embark on the very serious job of preparing to go to war. By now people are being dropped from the course thick and fast; there's no time for stragglers. Our set of four, which includes Steve and me, is too small, so we join another group, to make the numbers up to eight. For the most part, I find it OK, and I'm overjoyed when I pass the course, with the highest possible grade in my final test. Two more people fail. Each time someone leaves it's like a punch in the stomach, but I know I can't take my eye off the end goal and have to stay motivated. I start to learn that people come and go in the military; like Sue, one week you spend twenty-four hours a day with someone – waking them up in the morning, studying over tea, having the, now odd glass of wine in the evening, comparing notes – and then you never see them again. I decide to have fun with my course mates but never let them get too close.

Now we've completed our final test, we'll be recommended to fly either Lynx, Gazelle or Apache craft, but we are also asked to state our preference. I know deep down that flying an Apache would be the most challenging, but I don't want to tempt fate or end up disappointed so I put off thinking about it too hard.

It's party time. Five friends from uni have come to stay for the weekend. The six of us spend hours in my bedroom in the mess perfecting our outfits: angel wings, tutus, wands and roller blades – the theme is 'children's party', complete with kiddie food and games.

I first laid eyes on Jake when he was throwing a broken toaster out of the window of the officers' mess, but we haven't spoken. I've been telling my friends at home about 'The Fitty' for ages, and can't wait for them finally to lay eyes on him. He arrives downstairs in the bar dressed only in a long fawn trench coat and a leopard-skin thong, and carrying a stuffed animal. He's come as a paedophile. Charming.

Tonight, at last, Jake crosses the room to chat to me, and we sit in the pool of brightly coloured balls we've put together for the party and spend hours discovering how much we have in common and making each other laugh. I'm hooked. He moves to his next posting – in Somerset – two days later, but most weekends we will be inseparable.

Two months on, and Jake is posted to Bosnia on a peace-keeping role for five months. Before he goes we have a serious conversation. He asks me to wait for him.

I don't hesitate for a second before giving him my answer, and he promises to keep in touch as much as he can.

True to his word, he rings me every single day. The phone call always follows a similar pattern.

'Hi, it's me,' he says. I feel a rush of butterflies in my stomach and try not to squeak with excitement. 'How are you?' He always asks after me first – this is a refreshing change from other men in the military who tend to push themselves forward in the hopes of impressing you with a roll call of their rank, sporting prowess and a list of tours.

'Yeah, good thanks,' I say casually, as if my life hasn't been made instantly better by this one phone call. 'You?'

He tells me about his day in Bosnia, where he is flying his Lynx helicopter almost every day, but he can't tell me any of the details of with whom, why or exactly where, so we soon run out of that line of chitchat. Then comes the good stuff – the stuff I lie in bed thinking about for hours. As he can't talk about what he's doing every day, he asks me about my family, school, work, aspirations – everything. He listens like no one else and I am filled with proud and secret delight when, during my long days at work, I suddenly find myself remembering one of his cousins' names, or recalling one of his old family stories. But the best thing about Jake is that I don't feel like I have to play a part or act in a certain way.

I feel comfortable just being me. I know that this relationship is different.

I'm at home one weekend lounging in a minging shorts and
T-shirt combo on one of the ancient blue sofas I've inherited
from a distant family member. As I hang up the receiver after
one of my long conversations with Jake, I walk towards the
kitchen to pour myself a glass of wine, but something doesn't
feel right; it hasn't for days. It's a horrible, nagging dread deep
inside that I just can't shift. I carry on my everyday life as
normal, but that feeling sits heavily, rooted in the pit of my
stomach.

And then I realize I'm terrified that he is away. We've grown
so close that I can't imagine how I would feel if something
happened to him. It's warm in the house, but I'm suddenly
covered in goose bumps and want to shiver. My breathing
quickens.

I inhale deeply and count slowly to five. Taking my wine
with me, I sit back down on the tired sofa and tuck my legs
under me.

I could never change Jake, or make him leave the armed
forces. He went straight into the Marines from school; he knew
it was his vocation. And I can tell he is a brilliant officer.

My mind drifts towards the future: engagement, weddings,
children. I know it's years away, but it dawns on me that I
could never be a mother while I'm in the army. Losing a partner
would be terrible, but a baby or child losing its mother must
be so much, so much worse.

I make the decision there and then. I'll leave, I think. I'll
just get out. When the time is right.

I feel instant relief. My breathing slows, my head clears and
that lead weight starts to subside. It's the first time I have ever
thought about leaving.

I hear that I've been posted to Apaches when one of the guys
in the mess comes over and congratulates me.

'Well done, Charlie,' he says. 'Apache, eh?'

I'm confused. My posting preference proforma, the form that I needed to fill in to say which aircraft I wanted to fly, lies untouched on my desk still, as I wasn't sure what I wanted to do next. All I know is that I don't want to be a million miles away from Jake. But this guy is now telling me that he's seen the course nominal roll and I'm definitely on it.

I know the Apache course is sought after, and I'm thrilled to have been selected, but I'm apprehensive about the infamously challenging Apache conversion course. At the moment, the AAC chooses only the top three per cent of its pilots for it. We all know how many decent pilots have failed the course; that it requires your eyes to work independently of each other and that it costs almost £10 million, just in flying time, to put someone through it from start to finish. I also know that the AAC has been looking to select a girl for a while, and wonder whether my card had been marked earlier on in my pilots' course.

It's going to take me six months to learn to fly the Apache, six more to learn how to do battle in it, and another six before I'm combat-ready. With a few other courses tagged on the end. And when I complete my training, I know I'll be posted to North Yorkshire, hours away from Jake . . .

The good news is that there is a special 'Apache wing' in the officers' mess at Middle Wallop so I get to move immediately into a big, shiny new room with a shared en suite bathroom. This is pure luxury compared to my grotty old room, where the bathroom was shared by the entire corridor; not long after I joined the forces I realized that my dressing gown was more important than any other piece of kit I would be issued. Another bonus is that, because Apache pilots are also required to work night shifts, the cleaners don't come until the early afternoon, allowing us the odd lie-in. At this stage of the game, this is the best bit.

*   *   *

When the new course starts a month later at Middle Wallop, I'm surrounded by new and unfamiliar male faces brandishing little Yorkie-bar-style stickers saying 'APACHE – IT'S NOT FOR GIRLS'.

I have something to prove, big style. Lots of people may fail this course, but I am determined not only to be the first girl ever picked but the first to pass, too.

The night before the course begins I go to the bar to meet the other guys – again, there are twelve of us. All I can see is a row of backs – five or six men huddled together, deep in conversation. I squeeze myself into the ring of steel. It's never easy meeting new people in these situations, but I try to overcome my apprehension. In the military, you are expected to just get on with it. I know there is no time for girly worry about what to say.

'Hi, I'm Charlotte.' I force a grin. My voice sounds like a whisper alongside the booming, beery outpourings of the boys.

They don't even look up.

One of them, who apparently goes by the name of Jon, is recalling how he brought some friends to a recent party at the mess.

'. . . and they said, "God, you pilots, you're all so *arrogant*!", and I said, "Yah, I know!"'

He's part caricature British gent, part Ice Man from *Top Gun*.

Everyone in the circle snorts and whoops. 'Oh yah, ha ha ha, we *are*.'

At first I think they're joking but, I soon realize, they're not.

I christen the group of offenders – there are six of them – the Dicks. Jon is tall yet weedy with a prominent nose and small eyes that are half an inch too close together. His skin is pitted as if he suffered from serious acne as a teenager. I look anxiously around me for anyone else who looks like they are on the course, but it's only me and them. So I tell myself to at least try.

I make an attempt to join their circle, but no one makes a move to create a gap; they stand shoulder to shoulder and I feel too awkward to push in. I linger waiting for an opportunity to join the conversation and physically scoot myself into the circle.

'And do you remember that time at Sandhurst when we came first in the inter-platoon competition?'

Four of them snort away together, amused. They start describing the competition in detail, so I walk off to the bar to buy myself a drink. I turn towards the group while my red wine is being poured, looking to see if anyone else needs a drink. As this bar is inside the mess and most people know each other, it's unusual for someone not to catch your eye and raise an empty glass with a smile. I've had more than my fair share of drinks bought this way, but clearly the Dicks don't know the score and not one of them glances around.

'Just the one?' the barman asks me, hinting that this is a surprising breach of etiquette.

'Just this, thanks – no takers. Will you have one?'

'Go on then.'

I take my wine and head back to the fringe of the frightening clique. I've never felt ill at ease in this bar before – it's part of my home while I'm stationed here – but tonight the air tastes hostile and foreign.

'Anyway, so I was trying to explain to him that you have to remember to talk down to the other pilots, keep things simple,' another of the Dicks is explaining in his patronising voice. He seems even more offensive than the others and I christen him Dick Number One. The others nod blankly like those tacky plastic dogs you sometimes see in car rear windows. I do notice a raised eyebrow from one of them but he doesn't disagree.

'You have to remember that we have been specially selected for this. We are the *crème de la crème*; the best pilots in the corps, and you have to bear in mind that other pilots' brains don't work the same way. Dumb it down.'

There are more mutters of agreement. I stand in my group

38

of one, astonished. I certainly won't be joining in this particular conversation.

We start ground school, the first part of our training, with Tech (the technical side of the Apache, all the engine workings and the hydraulic system – the boy stuff). I'm bad at this. I've been dreading it for weeks. I'm sure this is the bit I'll screw up, and I'll never even get to fly the helicopter. The boys will be right after all, and I'll be a disgrace to women everywhere.

I enter the classroom and sit down without looking around. After my terrible start in the bar, I'm not sure entirely how to behave or what to say. With the Dicks at the centre of every conversation, I feel like I have nothing in common with most of the group, and their whispering and smirks are unnerving me. They're worse than the nasty, cool gang at school, the girls who smoked behind the lacrosse hut, wore loads of make-up, scraped back their hair and passed notes around about everyone else being frigid.

I get my pad and pen out and wait. The tech teacher enters. He is famously knowledgeable and infamously fat. I can see pink flesh straining against his shirt buttons. I try to avert my eyes.

The teacher introduces himself, then starts the first presentation with a question.

'Now then,' he says in his broad Yorkshire accent, 'who can tell me how many engines the Apache has?'

Relief washes over me. *I know! It's so easy. The Apache is a twin-engine helicopter; it says so in the pile of handouts we were told to study.*

I sit up extra tall and beam at the teacher, willing him to let me tell him the answer is two. Get it over early, then he won't ask me any difficult ones later . . .

'You . . .' he says, pointing to the opposite side of the classroom.

My enthusiasm instantly deflates like a left-over party balloon.

'How many?'

'Three,' comes the reply.

I smile knowingly and shake my head, showing the teacher that I know better. I imagine we're sharing the joke about the silly man who thinks 'twin-engine' means three.

'Correct,' the teacher says matter-of-factly.

'Now then, why are there three?' he asks, looking around the classroom for another victim.

I avert my eyes, panic-stricken. *Three? What? Where? But . . . twin . . .*

I hear the teacher explain about the small third engine, the auxiliary power unit. I'm not really listening now. Shit, am I in trouble.

A few days in, I see my first Apache for real. There are loads flying around the base, but I've never set eyes on one up close. It takes my breath away. It's awesome. Forty-nine feet and one inch from nose to tail, its rotor blades stretch out another eight feet. It's seventeen and a half feet high and sixteen feet four inches wide, and weighs a hefty 23,000lbs when fully laden.

A monster.

It's angular, black and angry-looking. It's like I shouldn't be anywhere near it. No wonder the US pilots call flying it 'riding the dragon'.

Our instructor shows us around, pointing out various parts of the airframe and armament. This is one highly intelligent bit of kit.

The high-tech rotor blades slice quietly through the air; the Rolls-Royce engines give the helicopter extra power and speed. While the fuel burns at 800°C, the advanced cooling system makes it more difficult to track with a heat-seeking missile than any other helicopter. The state-of-the-art integrated defensive aids suite (HIDAS) recognizes the heat signatures of rocket-propelled grenades, activates counter-measures to defeat them and sends a verbal warning to the crew.

The Target Acquisition and Designation Sight System (TADS) is composed of a number of cameras housed in the cone-like nose on the front of the Apache, providing the pilots with 127 times magnification in daytime – enough to see the face of the man on the ground. At night, with the Pilot Night-vision system (PNVS), it can detect a person from over two and a half miles away.

Then there are three weapons systems. There's a 30mm cannon on the underside, with 1,160 rounds in the magazine for starters. Then there are the rockets – HEISAPs (High Explosive Incendiary Semi Armour Piercing); point detonating; MPSM (Multi-Purpose Sub-Munition); and flechettes – a maximum of seventy-six rockets are loaded into four rocket pods located on the side wings of the aircraft. Both the cannon and the rockets are fired with the traditional crosshair aim. Finally, there is the *pièce de résistance* – the Hellfire missile. Each Apache can carry up to sixteen of them. They're laser-guided from the cockpit, and are accurate enough to be posted through a letter box and powerful enough to destroy any known armour.

And at the flick of a small switch all the weapons can be automatically slaved to the pilots' line of sight.

This type of Apache has been around since 1998. It's more deadly than its predecessors, the most significant update being the addition of the Longbow radar, which can detect over a thousand potential targets from up to five miles away, classify them and identify the sixteen most threatening.

'The UK bought sixty-seven of these for a whopping £46 million each,' the instructor informs us. Wow, that's one hell of a lot of shoes.

With a £30,000 an hour price tag to fly one of these, I wonder if I could do forty-five minutes and go shopping with the rest . . .

'It's the most expensive attack helicopter in aviation history

41

and the most technologically advanced helicopter in the world.'

The enormous instructor climbs the ladder and stands on the Extended Forward Avionic Bay (EFAB), the small side stub wing under the cockpit door, his buttons bulging.

'This can take the weight of two pilots, plus kit. It's surprisingly hardy.'

He moves swiftly on to talk about the ballistic tolerance of the Apache to enemy fire.

'What can it take?' Rich, the guy next to me, pipes up, referring to the calibre of the incoming round. He's older than us, in his early forties, and I never see him joining in with the Dicks; at the end of every day he goes back home to his wife and teenage kids. He's as bald as a coot with teenage braces across his bottom row of teeth, but he's strangely attractive with it because of his super-fit body and expressive face. He is a qualified helicopter instructor but has decided to up his game and convert to Apache.

'Oh, it'll take me easily.' The instructor smiles, thinking the question was about the weight of a pilot on the EFAB.

'Fired from *what*?' someone asks. I picture the instructor wedged into a cartoon plane's rocket launcher, like a circus cannon.

He looks around, alarmed.

'No, he means the side wing. It can take his weight.'

'Thank God for that.' Rich and I try and stifle our giggles, disguising them as coughs.

At least I'm not the only one laughing.

'Do you know, they call you the Robot?'

I'm at the bar one evening with Steve. It's the only place to socialize within the building – and serves dirt-cheap alcohol. Most of my course mates congregate there after mealtimes in the evening to try and unwind from the day's studying.

By then, Steve has become a firm friend. He is extremely

kind and sociable – I've never known him to turn down a trip to the bar, the cinema or out for supper. I've lost count of the number of times he's bailed me out of trouble by letting me borrow his car or bike, or picked me up or dropped me at the train station after weekends away.

Tonight, the Dicks are all out at a party for one of their girl-friends at a pub in a nearby village. Neither Steve nor I was invited or even told about it.

'Doesn't surprise me,' I tell Steve as he waits for me to sit down. 'In fact, if that's the worst of it – which I'm sure it's not – I'm relieved.'

I drink a big swig of my Pinot grigio, enjoying the rare occasion of being able to use the bar without Jon and Co. being there.

'Why "the Robot"?'

'Dunno, really. And as if they'd tell me! I only overheard it, but I know they all joke about you having no personality . . .'

I think about it – it could be worse. Imagine being known for being stupid, or for having a huge arse or a face like a horse. The Dicks clearly think that this job should be the preserve of men and that I'm intruding in their cosy men's club. I know they think I might not be able to hack it; that I'm the token female given a chance in some weird bid for equality.

Steve and I spend a pleasant hour or so before The Dicks come barrelling in from their party, drunk. Dick Number One is in the lead and heads straight for the bar.

'Can't believe we've got another "Bag" sortie tomorrow, I'm not in the mood,' he says.

'You said you were pretty good in your last one – no debrief points, according to the instructor. That's what you said,' another Dick points out. I've christened him Panicky, as he is always in a flap about something or other.

I see the two of them nudge each other and look in my direction.

'Hi, guys!' Steve says happily, and waves over at them. They're already heading our way.

Panicky, Number One and a sidekick slide into the booth next to Steve. I feel torn between being ridiculously rude and leaving, or sitting here trying to think of things to say for another twenty minutes. I decide to give it five minutes.

Panicky Dick is mumbling something about tomorrow's 'Bag' trip, and I'm sure some insider info I have could make him feel a bit better. I take a deep breath.

'I spoke to the Met forecaster before I left work today and he reckons there'll be thunderstorms all day tomorrow. I don't think any of our sorties will go ahead.'

Panicky Dick looks up at me, a bit surprised that I'm speaking.

'How many hours have you flown so far?' he asks.

'Umm, about three hundred and fifty.'

'Exactly. Less than half what I've done. Anyone else need another beer?' He stands up and leaves the table.

I take the opportunity to excuse myself to go to the loo but instead head straight for my room and phone Jake.

It's fairly miserable. Steve and Rich are my allies, but I never feel comfortable. The Dicks are only six of a twenty-man course, but I still feel quite isolated. They're loud and consider themselves the leaders of the pack, so no one ever questions their behaviour. It's pretty obvious they don't think they should be sharing the same space with me and, to my discredit, I go past the point of even making an effort with most of the other men and, as a result, I imagine that the wider group dislikes me just as much. I skip going to supper and eat carrots and sandwiches in my room to avoid mixing with them. I simply can't stomach any more bouts of macho bragging – willy-waving competitions as I call them. About half of the students on my course are married and have houses outside the camp with their wives. I jealously imagine being able to leave this world behind at the end of every day and going home to a warm house where everything is my own. I try to construct my own equivalent right here in the mess, making my room as homely as possible, buying cushions and rugs and making sure that nice music is always playing. I come back and change into civilian clothes as soon as my day is over, then go running or to the supermarket. Anything to have a little bit of normality.

Apart from when we're working, the only other contact I have with my course mates is when I rush to and from the shared en-suite in a very large, fluffy blue dressing gown, like some sort of live-in hooker.

I am horribly lonely on days when the pace is slow and live my life for weekends away from the base and life after training. I join a local orchestra, where I play my double bass. At our weekly rehearsals, I'm so relieved to be somewhere where people don't know the finer details of what I do, just that I'm in the army. It's a brilliant release and, as I drift off into a haze of classical music, I don't give work a second thought. Some days I scare myself with the thought that my entire career could continue in the same way, with Dicks at every turn. The idea makes me feel sick but, as much as I'd love to give up my course, I'm not a quitter.

On my original pilots' course there were Sue and myself and plenty of women who had gone before us, but training on the Apache is a whole different ball game. I always knew there would be men who would take the piss or might not accept me along the way, but I never bargained for people to be willing me to fail. I'm rewriting their rulebook – but I never anticipated feeling quite so alone, vulnerable and exposed.

Every weekend I make plans to see Jake, my friends and family. I think nothing of climbing in my car, switching on the radio and driving a few hundred miles on a Friday night to get away. I don't really share the true depth of my feelings of isolation with anyone but Jake and, to an extent, Mia. She knows I hate it, but it's hard to explain, especially because she isn't in the military. One weekend when I'm visiting her in London for a shopping and wine blow-out, she starts to talk about the overweight and ineffectual men she manages at work. She's coined the term 'beardos' to describe them.

'God they're useless,' she says. 'Did I tell you about the one – the Goth – who spends half his life on World of Warcraft or whatever the hell it's called, when he thinks I'm not looking? And one of them – the one who looks like a weasel – is so snotty; if he sniffs one more time, I think I might lose it. I even bought him a new box of Kleenex as a not-so-subtle hint. He didn't take it.'

'They sound awful. But imagine going home with them, eating dinner with them, showering next to them and then saying goodnight, only to sleep a few yards from their rooms. It's like a mix of *The Apprentice*, where you fear everyone will stab you in the back as soon as you turn round, and *Big Brother*, where you are literally trapped. Then in the morning, you get into the shower after one of the beardos, only to discover a weird pool of gunk by the plughole which definitely isn't shampoo, and wee under the toilet.'

She spits out her wine. 'I don't know how you manage. Thank the Lord my working day only lasts ten hours.'

The days drag by. It takes four weeks of long days in the classroom for us to have a sufficient understanding of all the technical stuff, from how the engines work to how a four-bladed helicopter stays in the sky. To my great relief, the teachers treat me exactly the same as the boys; if anything, in the classroom, I feel I'm doing better than many of them. I've always been a quick learner, so I thrive on the fast pace of the course. It's frustrating that the Dicks can't accept me for what I bring to the group; they never ask me for help.

After the classroom phase, we move on to the simulator,

a stage that lasts almost a month, and we fly all times of the day and night. We know it's a great training tool, but sometimes your brain becomes so overloaded at the beginning that you may as well not have bothered. It's as important to pass this stage as the final flying stage; again, it works on the three-strikes-and-you-fail principle. There are new challenges at every turn, and we're all dreading the 'Bag' phase, the infamous killer section of the course. It's where we'll be trained to use the night-vision system, when the whole cockpit is blacked out and we have to rely totally on the picture in the monocle which you clamp over your right eye. It has a dozen different instrument readings projected on to it, and I can call up a number of images behind the faint green glow of the numbers: the night-vision system; camera images from the TADS; or the Longbow radar's targets.

When we finally start flying the 'Bag', I find that the picture is a bit of a joke, like one in a bad video game: green and black and fuzzy around the edges. But the trickiest thing about it is that the PNVS is located three feet below the pilot and eight feet in front, so the picture displayed is not what your brain expects: imagine sitting in the pilot's seat and looking over your left shoulder. On the PNVS picture there is a tree right across from you, but in reality the tree is eight feet in front of you. Now imagine the cockpit is not bagged up and you can see out clearly across the moonlit sky. You look over your left shoulder, and the monocle over your right eye shows that there is a tree level with you. Your left eye is also looking out but sees the tree at the front of the aircraft. Your eyes are basically crossed over, just trying to look at the tree. Now picture doing this while you're flying at 50mph at fifty feet above ground, in the dark, trying to find a safe path for the aircraft. It's not that your eyes need to work independently but that your brain has to interpret the information from each eye separately.

I sit in the crew room drinking ridiculously milky tea, just the way I like it, and waiting for Sean to come and get me. He's my instructor for my first Bag trip, but he's still debriefing the last student. A long debrief is a bad debrief, so I feel a pang of worry for whoever it is. Sean is short and portly, like a Hobbit, and he behaves as if he's been teaching Apache for at least a thousand years and as if going for another flight is about as exciting as going for a trip to the urinals.

Eventually, half an hour after we were meant to take off, he breezes in, grabs a Coke and sits down next to me.

'Ready?' he asks.

'Yep,' I say, trying to act like it's just another trip.

'Read the aircrew manual on this?' Sean asks nonchalantly, sipping his drink.

I nod.

We quickly brief, but it's nothing I haven't heard from the other students or read in the aircrew manual. This is just a 'get-to-know' trip, so I can feel how it is to use the Bag. We walk to the aircraft, and Sean chatters happily about his plans for the weekend. I tell him that Jake and I are off to a friend's house for a barbecue. It reminds me that I haven't decided what to pack and gets me thinking about what to wear. In my happy reverie, I almost forget what I'm doing out here on dispersal, but when I finish checking my side of the aircraft, ending back up at the cockpit door, I remember. Oh shitty bollocks.

Kit stowed and harness strapped on, I grab my helmet from the EFAB and pull it on. It's taken three months, but I finally have the right combination of padding and strapping to make it comfy. I clip the monocle on to the side of it and swing it around so that it's directly in my eyeline.

After starting the engines normally, at the last minute I close my canopy door. Everything goes completely black. God, this is what it's like to be a blind person. My eyes gradually become aware of the faint green glow of the PNVS, but it seems my brain would rather concentrate on the dingy clues available to

48

me inside the cockpit – I can just make out the outlines of the controls and can't force my brain to 'see' what my right eye is seeing. This is a problem we've been warned about, but apparently we'll 'get used to it'.

The first hurdle is taxiing, and I make a predictable hash of it, despite vague hopes that perhaps I would turn out to be a natural at night-flying. I find it impossible to tell where the taxi lines are, because when I think they're going underneath me, they're in fact only going underneath the PNVS. I turn early on every corner.

The next hurdle is getting over the fence to dispersal. Rather unfairly, I think, the fence has stuck shut and now presents a 25-foot dice with death between me and the runway. We lift slowly into a shaky hover, me struggling to detect when we start drifting one way or the other. I've watched other students taking off in the Bag, and it's laughable – they do everything so slowly, and badly. And now that's me.

I taxi forward from my 25-foot hover and try to gauge when enough space has passed behind me to make it safe to descend. I pick my point and lower the collective, the lever control used to adjust height, only to feel Sean grabbing it and pulling back up.

'Not yet, you'll chop us in half,' he laughs, unconcerned.

My stomach knots in frustration, the way it always does whenever I'm not good at something the first time, and I redouble my concentration.

We don't leave the airfield for the whole ninety-minute sortie; instead we spend it doing ridiculous tricks with the PNVS, which are designed to build confidence. I'm told to look directly at the ceiling, then taxi smartly sideways, keeping the helicopter on a line. All the symbols I need are right there in my eye: I have a velocity vector telling me which way I'm moving; I have an acceleration cue which tells me which way the cyclic – the joystick, which controls direction – is telling the helicopter to go; I have speed and height information as well as engine information; I have boxes telling me whether the attitude hold is in, to give me information to help me hover and whether the height hold is in (it will beep if I start descending). So there is no excuse, but still I find it hard and have to have two gos. It's like trying to ride a bike along a straight line by looking up at a mirrored ceiling – there's no reason you can't do it, but it feels very weird.

Then Sean coaches me through 360 degrees and backwards flying. All the while he is peering out of the window into the clear blue afternoon checking that we're not going to fly into anything.

By the time we taxi back over the broken fence, I'm feeling much more confident. I taxi in, missing fewer of the taxi lines, and park. Sean chuckles, but won't be drawn on why until I've fully shut down the engines.

'What are you laughing at?' I demand, giggling despite myself.

'Open your canopy,' he says.

I do so, and see that not only have I missed the taxi line by yards, but I've also barely made it into the parking space; we're hanging out of it by miles. Sean is still laughing.

'Women and parking, hey?' he says to the civvie engineer who has come to monitor our shutdown.

'Shouldn't be allowed to drive, in my opinion,' he answers, smiling at me.

I grin. 'I've heard to all before, boys.'

There's a huge amount to learn both in the air and in the classroom. I don't find any of it particularly difficult; there's just lots of it. The course is divided into phases, and for each one we have lessons in the classroom, then time in the simulator, then in the air. The Dicks spend hours in their rooms testing each other, I spend hours in my room flicking through magazines and chatting on the phone and doing the right amount of work to keep me here. Some evenings I go to the cinema with Steve or break up the tedium with gym sessions with

Rich, during which we run on adjacent cross trainers and quizz each other on the latest Apache systems. As an instructor, even though we're learning together, I feel he's taken me under his wing; him as the eldest and with the benefit of fifteen years' flying experience and me as the youngest, eager to learn. He encourages my questions, and we spend free hours in one of the classrooms or one of the dimly lit hangars practising our checks together.

We then start to be trained to go 'combat-ready' – to learn how to fight with the aircraft. On the ranges for the first time, we fire 30mm but, disappointingly, it's just like the simulator, except that you can't even see the impact of the rounds here because they bury themselves into the dirt. The Dicks love it and crow about it for days, giving each other high fives and saying, 'Welcome to the gun club.'

The other thing that starts to grate is that the squadron only has two small girls' loos. One of these is also used as a stationery cupboard, with the toilet shoehorned in between cabinets, and the other is a general junk room. I go to the loo with my knees up against a broken overhead projector, while people rattle on the door mid-flow, in search of a fresh box of staples.

It's gone midnight and I'm laden with kit. My stomach is churning with nerves. My Final Handling Test (FHT) marks the end of my Apache training at Middle Wallop and will make me a fully fledged Apache pilot, but even though it'll all be over in three hours, it feels like I have to climb Everest before I'm done.

The trip is the culmination of all our training so far: a low-level, night pairs mission. I'm going to go flying in the dark for two hours only ten feet away from another Apache while the instructor loads me up with as much information and tasking as he thinks I can handle . . . and then a bit more.

Rich has been my 'stick buddy', my regular partner, throughout this phase of training, and we have planned everything together: our exact routing, the manoeuvres we plan on practising and what we'll do if it all goes tits up.

My stomach gives a lurch and I think how nice it will be when this is over. Jake is waiting for me in my room in the mess with a bottle of champagne – he's always had the utmost confidence in me and is sure I'll do well enough to warrant a celebration. I'm not quite so certain.

I reach the aircraft alone; Sean is at least thirty minutes behind me. I do the walk-round by myself and start the Auxiliary Power Unit (APU) to get various systems spooling up before he joins me.

I dump my Load Carrying Jerkin (LCJ), otherwise known as Life Support Jacket, helmet bag and nav bag underneath the right EFAB and pull my gloves on to start my checks.

As I reach the top of the aircraft, I see Rich starting the long walk towards the aircraft from the REME hut (where the men who look after the aircraft are based). I wave and he waves back, pointing his torch at his crossed fingers to signal me good luck. I grin at him and make a show of crossing all my fingers; probably all he sees is my head torch bobbing around madly.

A civilian engineer arrives to monitor my start and plugs his headset into the wing. This will enable him to talk to me and to Sean, when he arrives.

'You OK, Charlie?' he asks kindly.

'Pretty nervous, actually,' I admit, and start gathering my things up from the floor.

I pile my gear on to the EFAB, zip on my LCJ and climb into the back seat, dragging my stuff in after me. The cockpit smells like dust and nervousness; almost every flight I've had in an Apache has been a test of some sort and the musty smell of the cockpit reminds me of exam halls and sweaty panic. I put my soft-leather-gloved hands over the hard metal of the flying controls and briefly close my eyes; at least these are starting to feel familiar.

I press a button to power up the APU, then start turning on all the systems we'll need for flight: the Longbow radar, the TADS and PNVS, and the Back-Up Control System (BUCS), which will take over if the main controls fail. Each system runs through its own power-up checks as it turns on, and these checks, plus the ones I need to do once the systems are up, can take up to forty-five minutes to complete.

As the PNVS picture slowly comes into focus, I squint through my one-inch monocle.

Gradually, all the systems come online and Sean walks out to join me. I need to be in the front seat for this trip, so I climb out and let him get into the back, then crawl along the EFAB and squeeze myself into the front seat, realizing for the millionth time how bloody cramped it is in here.

Sean says nothing as I strap in, which is fairly unusual – he's so relaxed normally that his silence unnerves me. I busy myself trying to make sure my maps, nav information cards and other notes are in order before we go. I pray that nothing will go wrong with the checks we still have to do, or I'll be late – the very worst crime for an Apache pilot. I would be massively marked down before I'd even taken off, and there are enough hurdles to jump without starting on minus points. Sometimes the PNVS doesn't 'follow' your head properly, the BUCS can fail at the last minute or something can go wrong with an engine just before taxi. These things are out of my control, but they would still put a big, thick black cloud over the test.

With Sean strapped in, we run through some of the checks that need both pilots to complete, including the weapon operational checks.

'Actioning gun,' I start.

'Roger, C-GUN,' Sean answers, reading out the display that shows in his eye.

'Up. Down. Left. Right,' I continue. The engineer on the wing acknowledges that the gun is moving.

We repeat the process throughout the weapons systems and,

eventually, all checks are, thankfully, completed successfully and on time. The clock shows 0125, the time allotted for engine start.

'Shall we?' I ask Sean.

'Roger,' he answers. His replies are more formal than usual and, for once, he doesn't seem quite so horizontally relaxed about the whole affair.

From the light cast by the landing lamp, I see the engineer on the wing nod that he is ready and Sean pushes the first engine power lever forwards; this has to be done from the back, otherwise I'm sure I would be made to do it. The rotors start turning almost immediately, and I look over at Rich's cab and see with satisfaction that his rotors are also just spinning up. Perfect timing; a good start.

When both the engines have fired up, I lift. The black-topped dispersal gets smaller below me and I feel a tiny shiver of elation. It isn't over yet, but after this trip I'll be allowed to fly without an instructor and I know how it'll feel: free – exactly how I felt the first time I drove alone after passing my driving test.

Normally the back-seater does the flying so the front-seater can concentrate on running the mission, but today I am being tested to capacity, so the controls are all mine. I start to feel overloaded. My head begins to ache as I squint into the monocle. Beads of sweat prickle at the back of my neck. I taxi slowly at fifteen feet until I reach the Hardened Aircraft Landing Strip (HALS), with Rich right behind me. Sean gets permission for departure and I concentrate on not screwing up the take-off; I don't want to leave him with anything to debrief me about. I am setting myself the highest bar to reach and I know I'll be angry with myself if there is a list of points where I haven't quite reached it.

Moments later, I am positioned on one end of the HALS, and Rich is behind me. I pull the collective smoothly up to about 60 per cent torque and we slowly start moving across the tarmac. As the speed builds, I push forward on the cyclic and watch as the altitude indicator changes, showing that the tail wheel has lifted off the ground. As we reach the end of the HALS, I pull the torque up to 80 per cent and we lift smoothly off the ground, climbing high above Middle Wallop with the lights on the runway disappearing below me.

Our route takes us west, above a small local village, and from there north, on to the Salisbury Plain training area. I feel I know this route like the back of my hand after almost nine months, and as I follow the nearby railway line, I run through the outbound checks: Fuel – sufficient, start an automatic fuel-consumption check; radios – say goodbye to Wallop Tower and dial up the next frequency, Salisbury Plain Ops; engines – I look on my Multi-Purpose Display (MPD) and see that all engine-oil temperatures and pressures look fine; data-management systems – no faults showing; direction – I check that the standby compass is showing the same as the digital one in my eye; altitude – I check that the other standby instruments correspond with the digital outputs; if we have an electrical failure I'll be relying on these standby instruments to get me home.

'Check harness, please,' I instruct Sean.

'Tight and locked.' He's still answering with only the minimum of words. It's unnerving.

Outbound checks complete. Rich follows me through the first twenty minutes of our planned route in his own bubble of nervousness, the trees and hills rushing past the PNVS in a green blur. I feel as if we're going too fast, but I don't want to be late to the target. After what seems like an age, we reach the northern end of Salisbury Plain and take up our Battle Positions (BPs). Rich and I spent hours poring over the maps on the Mission Planning System (MPS) choosing these; we have to have a good view of the target area but be hidden from view ourselves. The BPs have to be safe for us if something goes wrong with the aircraft as well as allowing us to fire any weapon we choose without firing through trees or earth.

Hovering at thirty feet, I can see that we chose well – I can see everything I wanted. The target we've selected is a windmill about two miles in front of my aircraft. The time is now 0215, and 'H hour', the time we are going to engage, is 0218.

Timed to perfection. Concentrate, Madison.

I bring up a 'weapons' page on my MPD and select a Semi-Active Laser (SAL) missile. Of course, we don't have any on board, but we are using a system that makes the aircraft think it has a full weapon load – kind of like inserting a video-game cartridge. I press the 'Wpn Arm' button on my control panel, which is level with my left eye, and press the small cocked-hat-shaped button on my left 'Gameboy grip' with my thumb; the missile icon on the weapons page starts flashing.

I select the pre-stored target file for the windmill and slave the TADS to it with my right thumb. 'T-10' shows in my monocle, letting me know which target file I've slaved to. The thermal imaging picture in my eye now displays a green and black image of the windmill.

Perfect.

I zoom in with my left hand and start to make out the details; how many windows it has, whether there are trees in between the windmill and my aircraft that could 'block' the laser signal.

All OK. Come on, you can do this.

I pull the laser trigger with my right index finger to find out the exact range to target – 2,750 metres. It's not a real laser, as that would be a dangerous weapon to deploy in the UK; it's a training one we use to practise, but it still gives me a pretty accurate range. The missile needs to impact at exactly 02:18:00, so I quickly calculate that it has to leave my aircraft at 02:17:49. The time is now 0217.

'Happy?' I say to Sean.

'Sure, if you are,' he answers, and I immediately feel as if

I've missed something. I mentally go through my checks, but can't think of anything. I can feel stress starting to cloud my thought processes.

'Umm, OK . . .' I trail off. *Fuck, fuck, fuck . . . what is it?*

I set up the tracking gates over the windmill with my left thumb; this will make the TADS 'grab' the target so that the laser spot is steady for the missile.

I pull the training laser again and watch the missile icon change to a solid line; it's letting me know it can see and track the laser energy from my trigger. I'm all ready. The time ticks past: 02:17:41, 02:17:42 . . .

'Forgotten anything?' Sean asks. It's the first tip he's given me since take-off.

I panic. *Bollocks. What? You don't have long.*

'Ummm, I guess so. What?' I'm stumped, but I've got to get it right, even if it means asking for help. My heart is starting to thump loudly.

'Video recorder,' he says.

Damn.

I stab at the record button on my left grip and watch as 'RECORDING' appears in my monocle. It's vital to get into the habit of recording every engagement so we can discuss it afterwards in the debrief. I know that, when I get out to a war zone, they'll need everything taped for legal reasons.

It's 02:17:49. I keep the laser pulled and squeeze the left-hand trigger as well. An electronic whoosh fills my ears as the 'video game' fires off a missile. As I silently count the seconds until impact, sneaking thoughts about how I missed the video recorder crowd into my brain.

You've failed, you've failed . . . I ignore my traitorous brain and concentrate on counting.

'Impact,' I announce when the time is up.

The windmill stands there defiantly, surviving the blast of my imaginary missile. In my head it's a smoking wreck with flames licking it angrily, like in the simulator. The lack of smoke and rubble is quite an anticlimax, really, I think, but I'm glad the timing of the shot is spot-on.

The next hour of our sortie takes place at 2,000 feet above ground level, and is to practise tactical formation. Ten minutes in and I'm sweating with the stress. I just hope it's going to get easier. My back feels wet as I lean into my seat, and my head is throbbing as the muscles in my neck and through my shoulders tense.

This has always been the most difficult part for me. The FLIR picture is terrible even on a good night – the world looks grainy and surreal, and the boundaries between earth and sky are blurred. Rich's aircraft looks like a giant murder weapon in my tiny PNVS picture; it fills my vision with all its whirling, knife-sharp rotor blades. I'm supposed to be able to anticipate his every move so that I can move in tandem, but it takes me a split second too long each time to assess what he's doing. The helicopter is only ten feet from me, and one wrong move by either of us would end in disaster. The cockpit is filled with the sound of our roaring engines; neither Sean nor I utter a word – we're both concentrating on not flying into Rich. I make hundreds of tiny movements on the controls, and I can sense Sean's hands covering the collective and the cyclic, preventing me from doing anything dangerous. Far from being offended by his lack of trust, I'm maniacally delighted by this extra safety measure – this is terrifying. Over the scream of the rotors I can hear my heart thudding in my ears.

'Tac left . . . GO.' I hear Rich's voice over the radio. It sounds like it's coming from far away.

While I try and remember what to do, Rich's aircraft wobbles slightly and my heart almost stops. Tac(tical) left means a turn to the left where the outside aircraft turns first. In this case, that's Rich, and my foggy brain finally analyzes the PNVS picture enough to see that his cab is now turning dangerously close in front of mine. I resist the temptation to squeeze my eyes shut and wait until he is in my 12 o'clock before snatching the cyclic hurriedly to the left, staying on the left-hand side of Rich's aircraft.

'Battle,' orders Rich's cab, and with my sweat-sodden, gloved hands I pull the collective to 95 per cent. I need as much power as possible so that I can pull level with Rich's aircraft and achieve 'battle' formation.

Once we're in position, 'Rotate . . .GO,' says Sean's voice over the intercom and the radio. This is where both aircraft turn towards each other and do a 180-degree turn, passing each other right-hand side to right-hand side. I think . . . Or is it left to left? I decide to go left to left, but the indecision, coupled with the fact that to ask Sean would be an instant fail, makes my hands shake. I feel like I'm outside of myself, barely in control of my weakening limbs.

I'm on the outside of the turn, so at least I don't have to change direction as sharply as Rich, but this is still one of the most uncomfortable manoeuvres. I breathe rapidly and imagine Sean staring boreholes into the back of my head, willing me to do this correctly and not kill us both.

The worst that can happen is that Rich feels the same indecision as me and his aircraft tries to pass mine on its right-hand side in the heat of the moment, creating a dangerous head to head. I concentrate on staring at the right side of Rich's cab as I lean the cyclic over.

I stare into my monocle, but my turn doesn't seem tight enough: all I can see is the front of Rich's aircraft – I should be seeing the sides. It isn't right; his aircraft isn't leaning away at all, and I turn even more tightly. The cyclic presses into my thigh and I feel like we're on our sides, falling out of the sky. I peer at Rich's cab, trying to be objective: it still looks like it's getting closer.

'Knock it off, knock it off,' Sean says suddenly and loudly into the radios. 'Knock it off' is the emergency code for when it's all going wrong. I roll the wings level just as Rich's cab does the same, and we pass each other with only feet to spare.

It happens too quickly for my overloaded brain to take it in, and all I feel is joy that I'm alive.

Ohmygod, what the HELL just happened?

Sean had seen what I was too unsure to notice – I got it wrong. Rich was correctly going for a right to right and, with me trying to do the opposite, we could have crashed. I curse myself for not noticing. When we finally arrive back at Middle Wallop, my helmet liner is soaked with sweat. The shutdown checks seem to take ages, and I am acutely aware of Sean's silence in the back. I listen for any hint, any nuance, that will tell me whether I've passed or not. Either I'm a free woman, or I have another few weeks of retraining and another final handling test awaiting me. It's agony not knowing, and I can't gauge myself how the trip has gone. I feel bedraggled and wrung-out after concentrating so hard for so long.

We dump our kit in the crew room inside and grab cups of tea before sitting down in the debrief room. I'm convinced I've failed and feel furious with myself.

You always think you've failed, Charlie. Calm down.

'How do you think that went?' asks Sean. I hate this question, and look at Rich for help.

'Well, the timings all worked out well,' Rich says. 'The BP work was good and the tac formation was fine apart from one wrong manoeuvre, so I'd say it went OK. You, Charlie?'

I nod and say something about there always being things you can improve on. I'm always really hard on myself, and can never stop thinking about the thousands of tiny things that could have gone better. Most tests seem like they were a disaster to me when I debrief, but in reality they have generally gone well. I tend to be a glass-half-empty kind of girl when I'm assessing myself.

There is a silence, and the two instructors glance at each other, before Sean clears his throat.

He begins, 'I agree that there were several areas which could have been much tidier. The tac form was pretty bad, and the transit to the BPs was sloppy . . .'

He keeps talking, but I'm not listening any more.

We've failed. How will I tell Jake?

I'm not even interested in all the things Sean thinks were crap; I bet I can think of all of them and another three hundred things.

Dammit.

Sean is standing up, beaming and shaking Rich's hand. He reaches for mine, and I stand uncertainly.

'Congratulations, Charlie,' he says, shaking my hand. 'You are a fully fledged attack pilot, and the first British woman to achieve that. You could try looking a little more pleased.'

We've passed? I should have listened – I look around at three Cheshire cat grins and break into a wide smile myself. *YES!*

As soon as we have left the room, Rich and I embrace in a giant bear-hug.

'Wow! We've done it, Charlie,' he grins. 'Can't wait to tell the missus. She's gonna be chuffed to have me back at home more – no more fifteen-hour days for us.'

'Ha! Don't speak too soon – you know what this place is like! I'm off to see Jake. Have a brilliant evening.'

I cycle back to the mess on cloud nine, and Jake is waiting in my room. He's come to visit specially on his evening off and jumps up, sees my huge grin and gives me an enormous, too-tight cuddle. We pop the champagne.

'Well done, gorgeous,' he says, and I feel exhaustion and happiness finally washing over me.

He pulls my arm until we're sitting side by side on my bed – the room is too small for an armchair. 'So how was it?'

'Disastrous,' I tell him.

'I'm sure it wasn't, Super-pilot. Otherwise you wouldn't have passed,' he reasons. He pulls me closer and I feel ridiculously comforted. 'Well, I did a rotate the wrong way round and my instructor had to call "Knock it off".' I'm glad that Jake flies too, and understands all the terms. I don't have the energy to explain anything tonight.

'Is that the only manoeuvre you messed up?'

'Yes.'

'So in an hour of tac flying you screwed up a single two-minute manoeuvre?'

'Well, yes, but . . .'

'What else?'

I tell him about the video recorder.

'Mmm hmm. But you arrived in the BP on time, got the missile into the target on time and destroyed it?'

'Ye-es.'

'Isn't that your whole job description?'

'Yes, but . . .'

'Come here, you silly worrier. I'm proud of you, Charlie. You're so hard on yourself. You've passed – the first female Apache pilot in the country!'

I nod and raise a smile. I feel so comforted by the fact that I can completely unload on to him. I long for his reassurance and, when I get it, I instantly feel lifted; it's like he's protecting me from the world.

Next comes the phase of the Apache course that teaches us the final skills we'll need to go to war. We spend more hours in the simulator, where they test us to the limit. It's fast and furious, and my brain literally aches from the pressure. It takes almost eight months, and when we all finally pass, there is a very puffed-up ceremony. We shake important people's hands, are welcomed to the 'Attack Pilots' Club' and given the coveted Apache badge. No reference is made to my sex or to me being the first girl to pass through the course, but that's fine with me. I don't want anyone – namely the Dicks – to think I have had to do any less than the boys to earn my position or that I have had, or will have, any sort of special treatment. At home, of course, there is a little part of me that enjoys the fact that my job is so different. People are always surprised and interested, although the military world is so far removed from most people's lives that it's hard to explain.

I am posted to 656 Squadron in Dishforth. I know for a while beforehand that I'll be joining them, and I'm pleased; all the pilots there have excellent reputations, but beyond the normal day-to-day niceties, they are all virtual strangers. My new home in North Yorkshire turns out to be much like any other RAF or army base, but I immediately feel more welcomed by my colleagues here. I briefly meet my new flight – the three other men I will be working in a team with – but I have no awareness of the dirty undercurrent that has plagued me since I started: that there is no way the girls can be as good as the men. I'm sure I've caused a stir among them, but they're careful not to show it.

On my first day of work, I'm straight in the simulator with my new boss. I've heard a lot about the squadron's new officer commanding, Major Christopher James. He's new to the job, but I already know he's a whizz at the Apache and was one of the first British pilots to fly the new American model, the AH64D, on the US Army's first Longbow conversion course. In Arizona, he blew all the Yanks out of the water, and was awarded the Top Gun prize and then an MBE by the Queen.

I'm so nervous I've got butterflies and go to the toilet at least three times in the half hour before our flight, but as soon as he comes to greet me, I'm at ease.

'Captain Madison,' he says, proffering a hand. 'Pleased to meet you. I've heard lots of things about you. All good, of course.'

I extend my arm and literally cannot believe the size of his hands. His fingers are like Swiss rolls or giant udders. God knows how he gets those around the controls.

'Great to meet you too.' I tear my eyes away from his omni-hands and look up. I'd expected him to look far older, but I'm guessing he is less than ten years my senior. He has thick dark hair, a round smiley face and a chiselled jaw.

'After you,' he says as we make our way to the simulator.

We climb in. The sortie takes us over the town of Now Zad in Afghanistan, escorting a Chinook to pick up an injured soldier. The console flashes menacingly as we are shot at, and I struggle to keep up with the constant lists of demands from the cockpit: sorting weapons, the radar, numerous radio calls, as well as dodging bullets. The boss never instructs me and just lets me get on with it, as if I'd been in the squadron for ever.

As I step out feeling dazed and blinking into the light, he's full of praise.

'Great work, Charlie,' he says, and I start to feel more confident about my new colleagues. We walk to the mess room, and the six pilots stand up respectfully when they see Major James. And, for once, the smiles feel totally genuine.

The men are professional and straightforward and actually seem to enjoy having a girl around the place. I think they get a kick out of showing off their chivalrous side and open doors in a gentlemanly fashion. They are clearly prepared to give me a chance in the way that the Dicks never did. I'm keen to try and be part of that team before I face the biggest challenge of my life so far: three months in Afghanistan.

The journey to Kandahar in November 2006 is no fun at all. No comfy chair, no complimentary mini-bottle of wine and certainly no in-flight movie to keep me entertained.

I sit next to my new flight commander, Nick, who chirps away throughout the entire eight-hour journey like an over-excited child on the way to Disneyland. He's one of life's optimists and a brilliant guy to be around. After he won the Sword of Honour at Sandhurst, he became the first pilot to start training directly on the Apache. He really is the golden boy; good-looking, über-talented and modest as well. It's impossible not to like him.

'I can't wait. Are you excited, Charlie? My first tour was great.'

'I'm not sure what to expect, to be honest,' I tell him. I feel very apprehensive but am keen for it not to show. I ask him a host of questions: How do I do my laundry? What's the accommodation like? Are there girls' toilets? Surprisingly, he can only accurately answer questions about work and missions, so I secretly fantasize I will be arriving at a luxury safari lodge and provided with a maid who does all my washing.

It is 656 Squadron's second tour of duty and my first. I try not to feel nervous about the prospect of three months away from home in a hostile war zone; after all, it is what I signed up for. I desperately hope I'll walk away from this tour as well regarded as they are. But I feel I'm going to work twice as hard to prove myself as any of the men that are out here for the first time. My squadron all seem to be welcoming, but I'm still aware that, as I am the first girl, all eyes will be on me and some of the men will have their doubts.

We arrive at Kandahar in the middle of the night. It's safer touching down in the dark – this huge base is located in the middle of the city, so anything beyond the barbed-wire fence is dangerous territory. The first thing I notice is the smell of rotting shit. I have heard tales of the 'shit-pit', a giant hole in the ground smack bang in the middle of camp where the waste from all 25,000 men is filtered. I resist the urge to heave and tell myself I'll get used to it.

'God, I'd forgotten how much that stinks,' FOG says as we trudge down the steps. Affectionately known as the granddad of the squadron, FOG has two obsessions that dominate his time, food and Google, which have earned him his nickname. He is never more than a few steps away from the computers, rota in hand, pointing out that it's his turn next. He also carries his laptop around with him as religiously as I carry my lip balm. And, as for food, I have enviously observed that, despite being in perfect shape, he eats enough for three and invariably gets grumpy if we ever miss a meal.

'I thought that was your arse,' Darwin shoots back.

I am already looking to Darwin and FOG for my cues and follow them as they head off to collect their bags. Darwin has a playful face with prominent ears, dark cropped hair and a small forehead, just like a chimp – hence his nickname as Charles Darwin's missing link. There's always a practical joke brewing in his sparkling brown eyes. As a dad of two young children, he's matter-of-fact and funny and I'm enjoying his company.

Nick and Major James appear oblivious to the assault on our nostrils and go bounding off across the burnt earth to find some transport. We have affectionately nicknamed him 'the Boss', and he has already won our hearts and minds. He's fought across the world, but this is his first time in Afghanistan. He keeps telling me we're both new, that we're learning at the same time, and I don't need to worry. He fills me with confidence.

'OK, Charlie?' he says when he and Nick get back, having established that we need to dump our stuff in some sort of temporary accommodation until the final leg of our journey towards Camp Bastion, the main British army base in Afghanistan, tonight.

'This is all a bit crazy, isn't it?' he says, gesturing around. The camp is huge – many of the American soldiers are out here for up to eighteen months, so they have to make it comfortable.

We have a choice between sitting on the wall-to-wall camp cots in the temporary accommodation tent, or getting out and seeing Kandahar Camp, so we dump our stuff and my flight decides to go and get coffee.

I follow the guys towards the boardwalk. It's a huge, raised wooden walkway, square and about 160 yards along each side. The inner quad has a small enclosed hockey pitch and some areas of wooden picnic chairs and tables nestling in the dirt. All around the outside of the square there are trucks and iso-containers backed up against the walkway selling various things: trinkets and local gifts, Afghan rugs and hats, knock-off sports gear of every description, baseball caps and pistol holsters. There are mobile-phone stores in wooden shacks against the walkway, a tailor and an embroidery shop. And there are food outlets of every description – from a Pizza Hut truck and Subway van, to a noodle stall, and a Burger King.

'Tim Hortons?' Nick asks, pointing in front of us. 'It's the Canadian version of Starbucks.'

A dozen people – some military and others who look like contractors – sit outside eating doughnuts and sipping lattes in the weak November sunshine. The Canadian radio station The Bear plays through speakers.

We sit down on the wooden steps and FOG and Nick go inside and come back with a variety of goodies.

'Oh, I've missed these iced coffees,' Darwin says.

'It's not exactly the Bahamas here – I don't know how you can drink a cold drink,' I point out, zipping my combat jacket up to my neck. I take a tentative sip from my boiling-hot, milky tea.

Nick's voice is muffled by his cinnamon Danish. 'We'll go for a run later and burn this off,' he says, patting his finely honed torso.

FOG nods his agreement vaguely, distracted, his biscuit sitting ignored in its bag. His laptop is open on the table in front of him.

'I won't.' Darwin's eyebrows shoot up meaningfully. 'You all right, FOG? You haven't said a word since we sat down.'

'Mmmm. Just wondering why my laptop isn't connecting to the Wi-Fi here . . .'

'There's *Wi-Fi* here?' I'm astonished. 'In Afghanistan?'

'Sure. None in Bastion though – have to make the most of it while I'm here.'

'Surfing porn again, old man?' Darwin reaches for his Marlboros.

FOG ignores him, so Darwin looks for fresh bait.

'I hear they're running a half-marathon competition here this afternoon,' he says casually. FOG smiles almost imperceptibly and glances at Darwin out of the corner of his eye. This seems like a well-practised routine.

Nick springs to attention as soon as Darwin mentions 'competition'.

'Are they? Where? Who's running it?'

Darwin just laughs. 'Oh, no, wait. There's no competition.'

FOG draws himself away from his laptop for long enough to chuckle lightly at Nick. I again get the feeling that this is a long-running joke.

Nick doesn't seem the slightest bit fazed and eagerly announces, 'There is a ten-kilometre race on at Bastion not long after we arrive. I saw a poster in the air terminal when we got here last night.'

FOG slams his laptop shut. 'Curses. It just won't connect.'

'Curses?' Darwin teases.

'I don't think swearing is always necessary,' FOG answers.

'I agree. Anyway, who's up for the 10k?' Nick hasn't been distracted.

'Me, definitely,' I say.

'I'm in too,' FOG agrees, taking the first bite of his biscuit.

No one bothers to ask Darwin. I realize I'm going to have to keep my eyes peeled to avoid becoming the butt of one of his practical jokes, but congratulate myself on my extreme good fortune – my flight are a great bunch.

That night, as we fly west over the Red Desert, I peer through the window. It's hard to imagine that anything lives down there – it looks like the surface of Mars; rusty red, arid and barren; like the most unforgiving place on earth.

Running vertically through the middle of Helmand is a strip

of land known as the Green Zone. But here, green definitely doesn't mean 'go'. No more than ten kilometres wide at the broadest point and well irrigated by the Helmand river, whose muddy waters snake their way towards Iran, this is where the Taliban fight their battles. The whole area is laced with underground bunkers, rat runs and tunnels, so our men seem to spend much of their time playing a macabre game of bat-a-rat.

The vast majority of Afghans live in small towns, scratching a meagre living from their poppy crops, which more often than not end up as heroin, which itself ends up putting the fringes of British society on a slow road to an early death.

The Hindu Kush stretches far into the north, on the border with Pakistan, as if it has been punched out of the earth in a fit of rage by the ancient gods. Snow-capped and weathered through time, the vast mountain range only has one path through it. It reminds me eerily of Mordor in *Lord of the Rings*. Camp Bastion is located on the west side of the river, in the Dasht-e Margo, the 'Desert of Death', home only to a handful of nomads who raise small herds of animals and forage in the dusty land.

As we descend, the broken rock and gravel shimmers like waves on a silver sea.

I'm keen to settle myself in. We do everything as a squadron, so I'm sharing a tent with my three colleagues – Nick, Darwin and FOG – and the opposite flight, who we'll be working closely with. We are paired up and put together according to our levels of experience. This is the first time Nick, Darwin and FOG will be teamed up together too, but they've all been in the squadron for at least a year and they've all flown with each other before. The squadron as a whole is divided into four flights – HQ, 2, 3, and 4 – with four pilots manning two aircraft in each. We are treated and treat each other as equals; officers call each other by their first names, and other ranks are often called by their nicknames.

'This one's mine.' I rush over to the corner spot and fling down my Bergen rucksack, desperate for a shower. I start to unload my kit. Our small sleeping spaces only have room for a bed and some portable canvas hanging shelves, but I'm desperate to make it as homely as possible and give my fake flowers pride of place.

FOG and Darwin offer to show me around, and I jump at the chance.

We walk out of our tent into damp, sandy-smelling air. The ground looks dry and dusty, but when I step outside my boots sink ankle-deep into the sludge.

Bastion is home to just over two thousand soldiers. At 1,500 square metres, it's the largest British military overseas camp to have been built since the Second World War. It's hard to imagine that every last piece of kit had to be airlifted in or transported by road from Karachi Port in Pakistan, over 1,000 miles away. However, there's a good tactical reason for being here: surrounded by hundreds of miles of sandy no-man's-land, we're relatively safe from enemy attack, because you can see for miles from the watchtowers dotted around the fenced perimeter.

We head out into a grey-skied day. A mist of sand seems to hang in the air, and the powdered-dirt ground matches the scum of dust on everyone's faces. It's cold but thankfully wind-less; I stick my hands deep into my pockets. The air smells exactly like the shitty-smelling air at Kandahar and I wrinkle my nose as I catch a fresh waft.

'Oh yeah, there's a shit-pit here too,' Darwin says. 'No escape.' He lights a cigarette and I jealously breathe in the fumes to disguise those from the poo.

There's a tent for everything at Camp Bastion: tents to sleep in; a plastic cookhouse tent the size of a warehouse; tents with metal showers and toilets; office tents with haphazard bundles of maps and computers; recreation tents with board games with bits missing and well-thumbed magazines, and a variety of gym tents.

Fifty yards outside our line of tents is a large tent standing on its own.

'Crab and Archer?' I ask, reading the sign hanging wonkily from the door.

'Squadron rec tent,' FOG explains. 'The soldiers can go and hang out in there, play Scrabble or Ludo or read their books. I think there's a TV in there that the last guys bought with the welfare budget. Be careful about going in there on your own, though, probably better not to.'

He's being really protective for some reason, but it's comforting rather than stifling, and I'm relieved they're taking the trouble to guide me through the unknown.

I put my head into the Crab and Archer for a quick look – mostly it is just a big, empty tent; it has a really high ceiling and is pretty chilly. There are two wooden benches in the corner set around a big TV. There's some sort of sports match on and my eyes skim over it.

'Ooh, cards,' I say, spotting a home-made wooden table and some canvas chairs. On the table is a half-finished game of poker. 'I love cards.'

'There'll be plenty of time for that,' Darwin chuckles mysteriously.

Halfway across camp, past a high-walled, barbed-wire-topped area, we reach our office.

'This is the main drag?' I ask, looking at yet another mud road snaking past lines of tents. The only thing to mark it out is a gravel-lined path leading off the road with three tall flag-poles towering above it. Today, the tops of the flags are licked by the low cloud.

'The shop's over there . . .' FOG points into the distance.

'There's a shop?'

'Oh, don't get excited, unless you like jars of clams and weight-gain powder.' Darwin laughs.

'What?'

'Yep, that's pretty much all you can buy there. Oh, and last month's *FHM*.'

As we walk down the gravel path leading to the flagpoles, I

notice a group of four or five soldiers looking at us. They're in a huddle and immediately stop talking when I notice them. When we walk past, they don't try and hide the fact that they're ogling us.

Darwin and FOG are silent.

'What are they looking at?' I ask, smiling but nervously pushing a few stray stands of hair behind my ears.

FOG answers: 'God knows – might be the first time they've seen a woman in a while. Ignore it.'

We head to the shop which, true to the boys' word, sells nothing of interest to me whatsoever. I make a mental note to ask Mia to send some extra mags.

We walk back to the main drag and turn up the gravel path.

'And this,' Darwin says with a flourish, pulling aside the flimsy wooden door that's embedded in a massive tent, 'is the JHF.'

'Joint Helicopter Force?' I check.

'Er, yes.' FOG looks slightly doubtful, as if this should be unspokenly obvious. It's the control centre for all our missions.

I stick my head in and am practically knocked out by the rancid stench of BO and stagnant water. I survey the room: desks line all four walls, and wires and lights are strung in every direction across the low ceiling sending a bright, neon glow over every surface. Along one wall, radios stand and hang from every desk, and groups stand round them listening in.

In the centre of the room are two big bird tables, planning tables, crowded with papers and diagrams. The place is crammed with people, and there is a low-level buzz of conversation, with the occasional loud shout.

'Out the back is the brew area,' FOG adds, pointing through a plastic flap at the end. 'There's a slightly collapsed trestle table and a kettle, but it's a relief being out there sometimes.'

As we walk through the JHF, the Boss immediately greets us.

'Two flight!' He looks around. 'Where is your illustrious flight commander?'

'Not sure,' Darwin answers. 'He went off to the flightline ages ago.'

'No matter.' The Boss is already herding us into the heart of the operations room.

He talks us through what happens at each of the desk areas around the room, reeling off the names of all the important personalities. I try to take them in, but mostly I just stare around the room marvelling at how it looks exactly like the tented HQs in Second World War films.

As the Boss finishes off, I realize I can hear a female voice coming from somewhere. It's almost like it's on a different frequency to all the men's low grumbles. I turn to see a pretty, petite girl with neat brown hair briefing a group of pilots.

'Who's that?'

'Ah, good. There she is – I thought you'd like this, Charlie. Louise here' – he points in the direction of the briefing – 'is one of the intelligence officers. She'll be briefing you every day before you go flying.'

I'm gobsmacked. Another girl? I feel a bubble of excitement rise through my chest. Hopefully Louise can show me the ropes; where we can shower, the best way to wash clothes and where the cleanest Portaloos are.

As soon as she finishes talking, I go over and introduce myself.

'Hi, I'm Louise,' she says. Up close she is even prettier; beautiful clear skin and bright blue eyes in a tiny frame. 'I saw you walking in – your boss said he had someone to introduce me to this morning.'

'I had no idea there would be another girl here – I'm so relieved.'

'Me too,' she tells me. 'I only got here a few weeks ago, and I'm totally starved of good conversation already! If I have to talk about cars, computers or engines one more time, I might cry!'

She checks her watch. 'Want to go to lunch?'

'Sure.'

As we make our way towards the cookhouse, I notice heads turning at the sight of two girls together and chuckle. Louise and I chat all the way to the dining tent and through the twenty-minute queue to get in. She tells me that she is engaged to Tom, who is in the army and due to deploy to Afghanistan soon; they are getting married next year when they both get home.

'I'm engaged, too! We can compare ideas and share wedding magazines.'

We swap notes on what we have planned and, as we chatter, move along the queue, pick up a tray each and make our way along the human conveyor belt. Angry-looking chefs shovel piles of food on to our plastic plates, and by the time we pause to draw breath we're sitting at a shiny trestle table in the middle of a hot, sweaty tent filled with hundreds of impossibly young-looking soldiers, many of whom are looking in our direction or nudging friends to do the same. I smile self-consciously and look back at Louise.

'Oh, just ignore them – they're girl-starved and have been here so long they've forgotten how to behave.'

I pick up my knife and fork, which appear slightly crusty, and look properly at the food on my plate for the first time. To one side is what is supposedly curry, which is a funny orange colour. Blobs of grease are swimming on the surface of the sauce. Next to it is a giant portion of egg-fried rice. The bits of egg look seriously congealed. Pudding is some sort of frozen cake.

'This looks absolutely rancid.'

'Yep,' Louise says. 'It's pretty greasy, but considering what the food goes through to get here, it's not too bad.'

'I'm going to have to go to the gym twenty times a day to burn this off – I have to fit into that wedding dress!' I scoop some of the curry up with my fork and post it into my mouth. It tastes good. Like Friday school dinners.

'Tell me about it. Mine's a size four,' Louise says matter-of-factly, without a hint of bragging.

I look up at her; she is tiny. 'OK. Gym thirty times a day, then.'

I'm so glad she's here. I feel the gnawing anxiety that has been with me for the last few weeks starting to melt away.

British forces first deployed around the Afghan capital, Kabul, in the months following 9/11, as part of a coalition whose primary mission was to root out al-Qaeda. In February 2006, Defence Secretary John Reid ordered several thousand troops to Afghanistan as part of the expanding NATO stabilization mission. He said that he hoped troops would return home having 'not fired a single bullet'.

One of the main tasks of Operation Herrick is to combat the resurgence of the Taliban. The underlying long-term aim is to help the people of Afghanistan build a democratic state with strong security forces and an economy that will support a civil society.

The British have taken on Helmand in the south; the biggest province in the country, which is largely run by lawless drug lords. The Soviets tried to control it in the 1980s with a force of twelve thousand and failed. Opium production was increasing at the time and impoverished farmers were selling their crops to the local Taliban leaders. It's anarchy, with President Hamid Karzai's government existing here in Helmand in name only.

Resistance to the aims of the British deployment is vicious and relentless. The Taliban and drug barons club together and form a more aggressive and desperate opposition than anyone had at first imagined; the District Centres (DC) around Helmand in Now Zad, Sangin, Kajaki and Gereshk are constantly pummelled with small-arms fire, RPGs and rockets. In September, troops were forced to retreat from the DC in Musa Qaleh because it was becoming increasingly hard to deliver much-needed supplies of food, water and ammunition.

The death toll has spiralled, and the Apaches' role in supporting troops under attack is crucial. As far as neighbourhood-watch systems go, they don't come any better than us. The message to the enemy is clear – we're not here to dish out sweets, and if they take us or our troops on, the consequences are fatal. The Apaches also reassure the men on the ground; they've quickly become the support aircraft of choice. The Taliban are desperate to take out an Apache; they call us 'mosquitoes' and hate us with a passion. We pack a punch, and they know it. As their war becomes more asymmetric – with the increased use of suicide bombers and Improvised Explosive Devices (IEDs) – ours has too: our destructive power is greater than an entire platoon's on the ground.

But it's also a war of hearts and minds; we must win over the Afghan people and convince them we have come to deliver them a better future. Our troops spend hours holding 'shuras', or meetings, and talking to local leaders. Many have grown beards and learned Pashtun to try and blend in. A whole host of locals work inside the wire, as cleaners and labourers, even though their integrity is questionable. The Taliban are quick to play catch-up and adapt their plans as they go. It's impossible to know when the region will be stable enough for the Afghans to run it themselves; at the moment, I can't imagine it ever happening. Yet I know we have to stay positive and remember the good we are doing for the ordinary people on the ground. Otherwise, what are we fighting for?

We negotiate the handover with 664 Squadron. Although every one of them seems to be an identikit tall, handsome, impressive model, they also look dog-tired and relieved to see us; our arrival is their signal that they'll soon be on their journey home.

We, on the other hand, are gnashing at the bit. Nick and I will be in the front seats of our Apaches for the duration of the tour, in charge of all the awesome weaponry. FOG and Darwin will be in the back seats taking care of the tricky business of flying in a desert – dusty conditions, thin air and tiny, treacherous landing sites. It's all a bit alien, and I decide the only thing to do is to take each day as it comes.

I soon find myself settling into an easy rhythm; we live our lives in twelve-day cycles. We have three duty operations days in the ops room to plan future missions, track the progress of ongoing missions over the radios and do paperwork. It's a bit like being in an office, but a very strange one: there's a lot of shouting, the constant buzz of radios in the background, and all the statistics and briefings are to do with missiles and enemy forces.

The following three days, we fly deliberate, pre-planned missions. Each is normally preceded by an Orders Group (OGp), which ensures that everyone knows what's up, and the tasks themselves can happen as far away as the Pakistani and Iranian borders. Some are planned days in advance, while for some, we are only given a few hours to prepare. In the first few weeks, most missions are to escort Chinooks as they drop off supplies at the various DCs or pick up casualties. We're often scheduled to appear overhead when the Marines push out of their bases on exploratory patrols. If they're alone, they're often met by vicious opposition, but the low growl of the Apaches issues a warning to any enemy hoping to infiltrate.

The three days after that we're on Very High Readiness (VHR), during which we can be called out at any time of the day or night on a 'shout' to help out when there are troops in contact (TIC) from Taliban fire on the ground. Sometimes there are four or five call-outs a day, sometimes nothing for the entire duty. We have thirty minutes to be off the ground once the call comes in on our hand-held Motorola radios, or sixty at night to wake up and adjust to the night-vision systems. Initially, I find it terrifying springing out of bed at three in the morning never knowing where we're going. We have to sprint to the aircraft as fast as we can, and before long I learn that VHR really means Very Hard Running. Every second counts, so the

VHR tents are close to the flightline and the aircraft, alongside mini-hell: a tiny, three-metre-square Portakabin containing three loos, three showers, four sinks, eight people, sixteen unflushed man poos and a big fart cloud. Everything is metal and grimy – and the floor has an array of soggy toilet roll, mud, dust and God-knows-what else slicked across it. There are some mirrors but, like the ones in garage service stations, they're dingy and it's like looking at yourself in tinfoil. To add to the excitement, the shower curtains are wafer-thin, harbour a generous amount of green fungus and are made of that gossamer-type material that crawls right up your bum crack the second the water goes on. After every shower I feel I need another one to wash the dirt off from the first one. There seem to be naked man-bottoms everywhere I look in the Portakabin – and they're not exactly the tanned, buffed ones of my teenage imagination – so I've decided that staring at the floor is the easiest option.

Because VHR can be very tiring, the three days after it are spent doing 'Testing and Maintenance' at Kandahar Air Field. When one of the helicopters breaks, it's flown back to KAF. We only have eight aircraft out here, and four need to be fully serviceable at Bastion at any one time. Once fixed, the cabs always need flight-testing around the airfield and the makeshift shooting range next to it – in between cups of coffee and cookies at Tim Hortons.

The only pitfall is the giant cesspit in the middle of camp – wherever you are, there's always the stink of other people's shit. And the American Marines' ultra-smooth chat-up technique is pretty amusing too.

On my first break at Kandahar, I have an afternoon off and decide to go to one of the three huge gyms to work off yet another man-size meal (this time, steak and kidney pie and chips, followed by a wedge of cake and a gratefully received and well-travelled apple). I am walking along the road, when an open-top Hummer comes past and slows down beside me. Inside are four men, all muscly and tanned.

'Hey, pretty lady, can we give you a lift?' the one in the passenger seat calls. His voice has an unmistakable American twang.

'Er, no thanks.'

'But you're too pretty to be walking on your own.'

'Er, I'm fine, honest.'

'Well, we'll be in the disco tonight if you want to see us again.'

'Disco?!'

'Yeah, the Dutch run it. It's near the Boardwalk. See you there.'

'Not if I see you first,' I say under my breath. There's no alcohol here, and I'd have to consume at least three bottles of wine before I even considered hitting the dancefloor with my body armour on.

They speed off at an embarrassing 15mph – the fastest speed we're allowed to drive. I chuckle to myself as the dust is kicked up in their wake.

One morning in the second rotation back in Bastion, I lie on my cot, freezing and trying not to need a wee. My watch says it's four in the morning, and after tossing and turning for a while in my sleeping bag, I realize I'm not going to be able to drift off unless I go to the loo. Considering the time, I reckon there won't be anyone around, so I manoeuvre myself as quietly as I can from my camp cot, stick my flying boots on over my shorts-and-vest-top PJs and unzip the tent flap. The cold hits me as I emerge into the early morning, and I put my hands over my boobs, hoping not to bump into anyone and wishing I'd stopped to put a bra on – the Madison boobs hardly go anywhere without a bra for fear of knocking someone out. I creep down the dark alley between the tents, glad for the hint of pale dawn light to show me the way. I round the corner towards the toilet block and, just as I think I've made it safely, I practically run smack bang into a huge, poker-faced sergeant.

He's one of the firemen who live in the same compound we do. I've had a few unpleasant chats with him before, and he looks at me with his usual disapproving scowl. Thick-set and tall, and with a puckered and weather-beaten face, he looks about sixty years old, but I'm guessing he's probably in his mid-forties. He might be missing the odd finger or toe, I'm guessing, and is so at home in his uniform; he's the type that wears bad Next trousers and high-ankle trainers when he's on leave because, without his combats, he's lost. All he knows is the army.

He's also the kind of person I struggle most to gain respect from. He's been in the army for ever and climbed the ranks straight from coming in as a private at the age of sixteen – as young as you can. He's the sort that thinks officers are mostly too young and unnecessary – and that the fast-track year at Sandhurst can't even begin to equate to twenty years' experience on the ground. And because we pilots are in the air (obviously) rather than down on the dusty ground doing hard labour, he acts like he thinks we're weak and arrogant. What he thinks of a female officer pilot standing in the cold in a vest and flying boots holding her hands over her nipples at four in the morning – I daren't even go there.

'Morning, sergeant,' I say, as if running into him is just totally fine and I'm not dying inside. I can feel my cheeks glowing, despite the cold.

'Morning . . . ma'am,' he replies, with just the right withering pause between 'morning' and 'ma'am' and a lingering glance at my boobs which is a fine blend of distasteful (all women should be at the sink) and lecherous (he can't have seen any female quite so exposed for months).

I practically sprint away, heart hammering, towards the loo, thank heaven when I find that the unisex toilets are vacant, go for the longest wee ever, like some sort of camel that has been storing it up for a few days, and then hotfoot it back to my cot as quickly as possible, my head firmly down.

At half six, I'm awake again, having got over my humili-
ating encounter and been able finally to fall back to sleep at
about five. We're on duty ops and not on the programme to
fly until this afternoon, and I lie on my cot listening to snoring
and a light rain falling. Since my flight had agreed to go for
breakfast at eight, I decide to go to the gym. I swing my legs
down, avoiding the cold metal frame of my cot, and hurriedly
shove on my gym kit.

When I pull the poncho-wall around my cot aside, I see
FOG and Nick also hopping into their gym shorts.

'Gym?' I whisper.

'Going running,' Nick whispers back, beaming at me as if
he'd said he was off on a luxury holiday to Bali. 'Coming?'

I'd been wanting to see the running route but hadn't wanted
to explore on my own; I'd only managed to find the gyms so
far. I'm keen to maintain my fitness – no way am I going to
develop a paunch like some of those RAF types. I call my
regime the Afghan Plan, my version of a diet and exercise
combo. I'm determined to lose that extra half a stone, even
out here. And with all those fatty meals, I know I'm going to
have to work doubly hard at it.

I've started to work my way around the different gyms so I
don't get bored, but my favourite is the smallest and most ragged,
between the main ops room and the VHR showers. It's through
a random wooden door; you'd never go in unless you knew it
was there. It contains a few sand-clogged machines and an
opening at the far end so the breeze can bring some kind of
relief from the heat you generate. It's normally almost empty –
a handful of people working out as the likes of Mika and the
Scissor Sisters blare out from the dust-choked speakers, day and
night, on MTV.

I'm always happy when I'm working out, and I do my best
thinking as I move rhythmically on the cross trainers and tread-
mills, my feet pounding the dusty rubber surfaces. But I'm also
keen to get outside. The barbed-wire perimeter isn't clearly

marked, and it looks as if it's fairly easy to end up on the wrong side of it. I don't fancy my chances against the Taliban just wearing my Asics and cycling shorts. I give Nick a thumbs-up and go to wait outside.

'Let's go,' says Nick when he bounds out of the tent a few minutes later.

'Morning.' FOG nods in my direction, hopping from one foot to the other to warm up. They're both wearing those ridiculously short running shorts that some men seem to favour, the ones with the unnecessary slit up the side of the thigh. They both look like well-muscled gazelles bouncing around, and I feel like a lead weight.

We set off towards the perimeter track, slide through a gap in the twenty-foot-high HESCO wall and turn left. These huge constructs are made with wire mesh and heavy duty fabric liner to act as a barrier against small arms fire, and seem to be every-where I look. We're running in a fifty-metre-wide channel between the HESCO and the barbed-wire fence that surrounds Bastion. We could be anywhere – and it's so foreign and deso-late, I imagine this is what the moon must look like. The powder-fine dust has been churned into deep mush and then frozen into an ankle-twisting ocean of icy mud. The fine rain makes the sky look almost the same colour as the dirty ground. I concentrate on my feet, as the view isn't much to look at. All I can see is diarrhoea-brown-with-a-hint-of-blue sky and vomit-coloured mud. At least the wind is blowing the shit-smell the other way.

I find myself out of breath just keeping pace with them, so I give up any hope of joining in FOG and Nick's conversa-tion and content myself with listening. There's no way I'm letting myself fall behind.

We round the first corner of camp, and I look up from my trainers, ready to take in the new sights. I'm greeted with a mirror image of the last leg of camp: brownish-blue sky, brown death-trap floor, high walls either side. They pick up speed again and, although my whole body is burning, I feel a familiar rush of endorphins surge through me. I've always loved running, and I've missed not doing it in the open since being here.

'Great training for the fitness test, this,' FOG announces.

'What time do you normally get for the mile and a half? I get eight minutes forty-five,' Nick says proudly.

'Oh, around eight minutes thirty,' FOG answers, smugly speeding up once more. 'I'm allowed extra time now that I'm in my forties – twelve minutes – but I don't ever intend to use it.'

I stumble in surprise. 'Forties!' I wheeze. 'You're never . . . in your forties.' I heave a huge breath in. 'I thought . . . more like . . . thirty-five.' I stop talking before I expire.

'Yeah, yeah, FOG is for "fucking old guy", I know what you lot think of me,' he chuckles. But we know he's kidding – he looks much younger than forty. He's tanned, healthy and toned. In fact, looking ahead at them, neither of them has an ounce of fat on their bodies. How annoying.

'I like to stay healthy for my boys. I do a lot of orienteering – I really enjoy that.' FOG sounds happy mentioning his kids.

'How old are they?' Nick asks.

'Oh, both teenagers now. Scary, really.'

'I like to keep fit so I can do all my kite-surfing, skiing and climbing and stuff,' Nick says.

'So you can come first in all of it, you mean,' FOG retorts.

Camp still looks the same when we turn the corner of the perimeter fence, except that, on this leg, the rain is blowing into my face and the wind is carrying the sweet smells from the shit-pit straight into my nostrils. I breathe through my mouth to minimize odour-trauma, then realize that I'm breathing in tiny particles of everyone else's shit. I close my mouth, gagging, and concentrate on my feet again. The wind has picked up, and I can no longer hear much of what FOG and Nick are saying. I let my thoughts drift to home. I calculate the time – we're four and a half hours ahead, so it will be the early hours of the morning at home. I think about Jake sprawled across the bed with all the covers over him, and Mum at her house in Oxford beneath her favourite quilt, sleeping peacefully. I wonder what their days hold. Shooting with his mates, a session in the gym and a drink at the pub for Jake; and collecting a million rogue apples from the over-ambitious apple tree for Mum probably. I desperately miss everyone, but I want to be here and to get on with it so that I have some exciting stories to tell when I get back. Jake sends me daily eblueys (emails which are printed off like letters and given to us). He writes about what he's been up to – perhaps even more than he'd tell me if I was at home – and constantly tells me he misses me. And Mia has promised to write as much as she can, so I feel that maybe I won't be missing out on all the gossip too much. They're all there, always in my head, but I know that I just have to get on with it, homesick or not.

Turning into the final stretch, I'm relieved when the wind dies immediately and the stench clears.

'. . . back seat? I think it's more interesting in the front,' Nick is saying. I guess they're discussing the merits of the front seat versus the back in the Apache. Nick is often in the front, like me, whereas FOG spends most of his time in the back.

'No way,' FOG says, gesturing with his hands. 'You can see more from the back, and you get to do all the flying.'

'But you don't get to pull the triggers,' Nick says, as if he's closing his case.

'I've fired the gun plenty from the back. Plus, we do every rocket shot from the back, and they're the most fun,' FOG points out.

When we reach the opening in the HESCO that leads to our tent, I start veering left towards it, checking my watch. We've done thirty minutes of sprint-speed running on the frozen mud-ocean.

'Not coming round again?' I hear Nick's voice, and turn to

see FOG and Nick sailing past the gap in the HESCO, neither sweating nor even breathing hard.

I'm a bit annoyed at myself for not keeping up but I'm knackered, so I make a face that I hope will explain my decision and, as soon as I'm through the gap in the HESCO, I walk. Back inside, it's like I'm emerging into a different world. In here, there are muddy-brown tents in little brown rows, dirt roads in nice straight lines and hundreds of matching soldiers making their way to breakfast. They look ever so slightly robotic. Their faces are unreadable, but they don't even try to hide their staring. I know it's because I'm a pilot and a girl and blonde, nothing else. It's like I'm on the front of a giant Wonderbra billboard ad. It makes me feel slightly uncomfortable, but I still try to laugh it off. It isn't as if I ever expected to be serving behind the Waitrose cheese counter with lots of women, after all.

At times, the boy-heavy environment does verge on the gross, though. In some of the unisex blocks, there are signs up saying, 'PLEASE DON'T LEAVE SEMEN ON THE SEATS.' It's vomit-inducing, to say the least. I'm sure the other girls on camp get the same sort of attention. But I'm the only female Apache pilot and I guess that marks me out as different. When I'm with them, my flight always seem to draw me into conversation, as if they're helping me to ignore the eyes looking me over.

I try not to catch anyone's eye and drag myself back to the tent. It feels like a warm cocoon. As I walk in, Darwin is strolling cheerfully back to his cot, a towel around his waist. His semi-nakedness doesn't bother either of us one bit, although I am meticulously careful about getting changed behind my makeshift poncho wall so I don't embarrass anyone. Even my strappy tops make them a bit red-faced. But they're all trying to include me. When one of the groundies – the guys who work with the aircraft when they are on the ground – suggested calling the aircraft after famous porn stars, that got everyone's vote. So we fly Lolo Ferrari, Tabatha Cash, Jenna Jameson, Tera Patrick, Taylor Rain and Silvia Saint. Cue hours of crude jokes about their 'hours inside Lola', 'riding Jenna' and 'Isn't Taylor a goer?' Boys . . .! But, so I didn't feel left out, the final aircraft was christened Ron Jeremy. I must remember to Google Ron Jeremy in my next internet session. Apparently he has the biggest cock in Hollywood.

'Morning! Been running?' Darwin asks, screwing up his nose, as if he's asking whether I've been rolling in broken glass for fun.

'You really missed out,' I say, but feel the exhaustion in my voice will give me away.

By now, I've begun to realize that, most of the time I spend here, I'll have sand in my hair, in my boots, even in my knickers. After the run, I'm as finely coated as a chicken nugget. I head to the showers and spend the whole three minutes visualizing a shower where the water is hot, it doesn't start by you pushing a button, there's a tiled floor and fluffy white towels and slippers. Afterwards, gingerly patting myself with my dusty towel, I still don't feel clean. It feels like there's a film of grime clinging to my skin, which I long to scrub off.

I reach for my uncomfortable flying shirt. I always strip down to a T-shirt when I can; the scratchy, hot shirt is my least favourite item of clothing. The army needs to get Trinny and Susannah on the case, if you ask me. The whole outfit is ridiculously unflattering. There's the desert shirt and matching trousers, and I can only imagine the trousers were styled on someone totally square with a really wide waist and very short legs. I look like some kind of rapper, with the drawstring pulled really tight around my middle, the crotch down by my knees and the legs barely skimming my boots.

When we go flying, everything we wear is fire retardant and it all looks like the uniform regular infantry soldiers wear, with no markings that would label us as Apache pilots. If we were shot down and they realized that's what we were, well

. . . it doesn't bear thinking about. Over our shirts we wear the LCJ that contains all the kit we'd need if we ever went down, such as spare ammo and a vial of morphine for pain relief. It's just loose enough for us to be able to breathe, and more than tight enough to hold in our innards if we ever get shot. Clipped to the LCJ is a rock-hard, bullet-proof Kevlar breastplate. The whole get-up makes me look like a barrel-chested butch lesbian, especially when the outfit is finished off with a crotch strap.

Now fully dressed, I head for some food with FOG.

The whole camp is split up with HESCO barriers. The only way to cross them is to climb the ladders placed sporadically along their lengths. The only snag, as I found out on day one, is that it is unbearably 'uncool' to climb down the other side facing in – you have to walk down forwards, like stairs. This is easier said than done, and it's not like I haven't been putting in the practice. The other, favoured way to cross is to reach the top and then launch yourself off from there.

As we approach one of the barriers, I see a platoon of Marines standing in a neat line on the far side, like a crocodile of children waiting at a zebra crossing.

I feel the familiar rush of panic as I clamber up the rickety ladder. It's ridiculous, I know, but it suddenly seems to stretch ahead of me like a giant banana skin. I make it to the top without mishap and my confidence returns. I decide that, in light of my audience, I'll play safe and jump down instead of using the ladder, and I rest a hand on the wall and launch myself off it, thinking how suave this nonchalant manoeuvre must look to the thirty young soldiers staring up at me. Just this once, I'm enjoying being watched.

Suddenly, I'm aware that my booted foot has remained at the top of the HESCO, while my head and body travel down. There's no way out of this. A second later I'm spread-eagled across the hot gravel, flatter than I've been in my entire life. I haven't even broken my fall with a knee or an elbow. Every part of my body is in contact with the ground apart from my forehead, and my eyes, which are fixed on the Marines.

I long for the gravel to swallow me up. My cheeks burn as I blink, wishing that, when I open my eyes, the Marines will no longer be there. But they stare at me impassively and don't move a muscle.

FOG is still climbing over the HESCO, studiously pretending everything is going as normal. I make a point of never asking for help, so he knows I'd probably bite his head off if he scrambled down and attempted to pick me up. I climb to my feet and dust myself down. As I walk away, I feel a warm trickle of blood running down my leg and the stares of the young soldiers on my back. Boy, will they have fun with this one . . .

FOG's eyebrows are raised in concern, but I can see he's stifling a grin.

'There better be something good on the menu,' I croak.

Two weeks into my tour, and the sun is shining in through the Perspex of the cockpit windows as we head towards Now Zad. FOG flies at maximum speed and the cab shakes as if it's going to fall apart. We don't speak much, as this is a VHR shout and we're both working hard. I can see FOG's eyes moving rapidly between the huge blue expanse of the sky and the confines of the cockpit as he checks the instruments. After more than five thousand hours' flying time, so much of this is second nature to him, and I imagine his fingers using muscle memory while his brain considers the next three tasks.

I'm listening in to Nick's conversation with Widow Seven Zero, the JTAC, and try to keep up with all the grids he's sending. For every one, there are more than thirty button pushes to be made before I can send Nick the target file by email, and it all has to be done at the speed of the radio conversation. To make matters worse, I'm desperate for the loo. I feel like I spend 50 per cent of my time worrying about when I can wee next and dehydrating myself on purpose and the other 50 per cent hopping from one bum cheek to the other in my seat, the in-flight equivalent of crossing my legs. It's become my obsession, and sometimes my bladder physically hurts from holding on so much. During flights when I think I'm going to burst, I try to think about anything other than the moment when I can finally relieve myself, but my thoughts keep turning back to it. Could I wee into my water bottle? Would my nav bag be big enough? Why did I drink that tea five hours ago? This is the only thing that truly takes my mind off what I am doing.

In the breaks between calls, alongside plaiting my legs I'm making sure my cockpit is ready for the fight: TADS ready to slave to the enemy; weapon systems set up with correct trajectories and ranges; and no errors in the weapon processor, the brains behind the whole thing. Widow is taking incoming fire and has sustained two T2s, who need immediate assistance. Casualties are given a grading by the medics on the ground: a T1 is in grave danger and needs to be in the operating theatre within an hour; a T2 needs to be there swiftly enough not to become a T1; a T3 is more often than not walking wounded. There's nothing you can do for a T4 except carry his body home.

I can see the Chinook icon on my radar screen. It's slightly ahead of us and off to the left, aiming for the Helicopter Landing Site to collect the injured soldiers. Through the TADS I can see tiny figures surround the HLS, making sure it's safe for the Chinook to come in and pick up the casualties.

We reach the overhead of Now Zad as the mighty Chinook lands in a huge cloud of dust. Sometimes they remain enveloped for up to a minute. It takes balls to do that when you can't see and under enemy fire; I don't envy the pilots one bit.

Nick decides to look after the Chinook while we take the

wider area, scanning for any of the blighters who may be responsible.

'Ugly Five One, this is Widow Seven Zero, this last incident originated from the area of RPG alley, but I think that was more shoot-and-scoot than anything. Could you look for any rocket firing points in the eastern woods?'

'Roger, Widow,' I reply. 'We'll let you know what we see.'

RPG alley is one of the Taliban's favourite firing points, a mere street away from the platoon house but protected by thick walls and the darkness of the tight urban surroundings. They set up their RPGs to land inside the British area then melt away into the nearby markets and join the stream of other men in cream dishdashas (the long tunics worn by the men in Afghanistan) as if nothing has happened. There is little or no chance of catching them unless we're actually overhead when they attack – but the Taliban are too wily for that. So we're off to look at the woods instead.

FOG is already a step ahead, flying towards the zone Widow is talking about. I flick between Day TV and FLIR to try and make out any telltale signs. The Day TV is better for picking up movement, but the FLIR can see through the foliage and pick up the heat signatures of people, warm metal and recently disturbed ground. I scan the whole woods methodically, like a fingertip search from the air.

'There – what are those?' FOG says five minutes later, jerking the cab into a tighter arc so that the TADS can look down at a steeper angle. He's been watching my screen, and his experienced eye has picked up some hot spots I've missed. 'They look like people. What do you think?'

I follow the icon in my eye that tells me where he's looking. I slave to it, then scan back along the tree line with my TADS until I see a point where a small pathway broadens into dusty, scorched dirt track. Along the side of the track is a ditch and along it is a line of hot, evenly spaced blobs. I struggle to see more detail and switch to Day TV. No bodies; they've obviously moved on, probably only moments ago, leaving the ground warm beneath them.

'Dammit,' I sigh, moving the TADS immediately back into a wider field of view and taking up my scan. FOG sees what I see without us having to speak; we each know where the other is looking, where the TADS and the aircraft are pointing, what radio the other is working on. He sees my TADS picture and I see what he's looking at with the radar or the PNVS. It saves all the chatting and pointing.

The radio crackles into life.

'Ugly Five One, this is Five Zero, we've got movers!' Nick says. 'Stand by for laser spot.'

I make sure my Laser Spot Tracker (LST) is set up to look for Ugly Five Zero's laser code.

'Ready for spot.'

My TADS swings wildly around, then homes in on Nick's laser spot, which is moving slowly across the woods.

I can see four figures on the Day TV, darting in and out of the trees. They obviously think they're relatively safe under the thick vegetation, because they're only jogging, not really going for it.

Widow confirms there are no friendlies or civilians in the area; these men are definitely Taliban, and probably the very ones who were firing rockets at our soldiers thirty minutes ago.

Nick has a plan.

'We're going to set up south-east to north-west for a flechette run; you follow up with another salvo and watch for BDA. '

'OK,' I say. 'Turning east now.'

We'll be doing a co-operative shoot, where I aim the TADS and squeeze the laser but FOG flies the aircraft towards the target and pulls the trigger – it's the most accurate way. Each time FOG pulls the trigger, four rockets will fly towards the target that I'm tracking, each spraying eighty six-inch tungsten darts which punch holes in everything they touch.

'Nick's tipping in,' FOG says. We're flying at 90 degrees to them, ready to turn north-east, towards the target, when Nick pulls away.

I slave the TADS to where Nick is firing, and the screen shows Nick's rockets splattering through the trees. Neither of us can see any of the targets now though; they've gone to ground, seeing us changing our wheel into something more threatening.

'Resetting.' Eight rockets have been fired from his aircraft, and Darwin's voice is calm. We see the darts rip through the canopy of trees below and disappear.

FOG pulls us around to face the enemy. I slave the TADS to the last known target location.

'Go co-op,' I say, the drills feeling natural after hundreds of missions in the simulator.

'Co-op,' FOG answers, actioning his rockets as I action mine.

I have a last check that the crosshairs are on target as we fly towards it at over 100mph.

'Match and shoot,' I say: FOG's cue to line up his steering cursor with my crosshairs and pull the trigger.

'Five One firing,' I tell Nick over the radio. It'll help Darwin position his aircraft where they can see our BDA and tip straight in to fire again if needed.

'Firing.' FOG pulls the trigger. 'Good set.'

I watch the trees for movement but see none. That doesn't mean they aren't down there, though, and we have the time to fire another set.

'Repeat,' I tell FOG. He does, and I watch with satisfaction as the rockets hammer down into the woods.

He pulls the aircraft away once we've seen the rockets land, and we both reset into a wheel over the area and all eyes search for movement.

We see none.

Nick updates Widow, and I hear the Boss's voice telling us that, unless Widow has taken incoming fire in the last five minutes, we have to return to base. Widow hasn't, but sounds like he wishes he had when Nick tells him we're leaving.

We start back towards Bastion, and I fold away the Now Zad maps. I hadn't needed them; we are all so familiar with Now Zad that I hardly ever have to look up a building location.

'So?' FOG asks.

'Fuel's fine, aircraft's fine.'

'That was your first real engagement, wasn't it?' FOG asks. 'How do you feel?'

I hadn't given it a moment's thought until now – it all seemed so natural after almost two years of training. The Taliban we've just taken out had been firing rockets at British soldiers only a short time before; I'm glad we did what we did. On a professional level, I'm happy; I know I've passed the test. I didn't crumble under the pressure of the real thing, didn't decide I couldn't pull the trigger, didn't whoop unprofessionally as our rockets went off. I was . . . just as good as one of the boys. And I know that a large part of my calmness has to do with FOG.

'Felt fine,' I say. I don't need to add anything more.

As we shut the engines down and walk away from the flight-line, a creeping sense of uncertainty starts to bubble through me. I feel slightly nauseous as I look around me and see the guys on the ground working: two men are loading a giant missile into the rails on the side of the wings of one Apache; another aircraft is being refuelled. Everything is just going on as normal, but I have this creeping sense of unease about what we're really here for.

Now I am a killer.

I walk fast; pumping my legs to try and push out the uncomfortable feelings. With each stride, another grim thought sneaks its way into my brain. Who were they? Did they have families? Children? While I know I have done the right thing professionally, I feel horribly agitated.

I stop and lean up against one of the HESCOs. My heart is hammering and my breathing is ragged.

This is my job. I push the feelings away but it's hard; like a wardrobe overstuffed with coats, to get the door shut you have to push down twenty things at once. I suddenly realize that thinking too hard on a human level about what we do would make it impossible for me to do my job. I create a heavy trapdoor deep in my consciousness where I will hold everything from now on; anything that disturbs me I will push inside and lock it down. I have to cut away and feel nothing.

I start walking again and deliberately will the unhappy thoughts away by thinking of other things: Jake in our house with his feet up and a cup of tea in one hand watching some action drama; Mia sitting at her computer in her office surrounded by beardos, who are now a bunch of hilarious caricatures in my head.

I step into the JHF, and the Boss comes over.

'Good work, Charlie.' His smile is honest. He's heard everything on the radio.

Genuinely interested in people, he talks to everyone regardless of their rank or job, asks the various groundies about their children, and the cookhouse staff if they're having a good day. I can only chat comfortably to the people I recognize, but the Boss will start a conversation with anyone. His enthusiasm is catching. He's one of the gang and always takes part in any practical jokes, but at the same time he commands ultimate respect. I think if he ever needed us to follow him into a certain-death mission, we all would.

'Thanks, Boss.' I still feel slightly unsure of my feelings, so I head to the computer room to write Jake an email. I don't tell him about what I've done, of course – I'll never be able to – it's confidential and I also find it so hard to talk about. I wonder if I'll have changed when I go back? If I'll look different, sound different; appear at ease with myself in the way I feel I always have been with him? I can't wait to hear his voice.

I tell him other stuff, talk about the foreign landscape that I still find so barren, burnt and angry; I long for the smell of grass, to see birds in the sky or to see bright flowers on a table.

I ask him about his work and family, for the latest gossip. I also pick up an email from Mia.

'Madison,' she writes. She's called me that since our time at CCF. It's a bit of a joke and feels entirely different to anything military.

'Now I've got some gossip for you.' She fills me in on all the latest scandal at home. An engagement, someone's new job, a rowdy birthday party when someone was sick on the way home, one of the beardos being disciplined after writing obscene things on a blog using his work email.

'So, of course I shopped him to my boss. It was *brilliant*. You should've seen his face. Anyway – it went straight to a final warning. I was seriously hoping he'd get the sack, but apparently he was quite remorseful. Weirdo.'

I picture her tapping away at her work computer and feel a sense of longing for home, worrying that I am missing out and that I really have changed. If only I could be that carefree again.

'Tuesday – know what that means?' Darwin asks.

'Of course! Shall we?' FOG says, closing his laptop and looking at his watch. 'We can go now, before lunch.'

'Yes, God forbid we get you to lunch late!' Darwin rolls his eyes.

We're sitting in the VHR tent, pretty much in the same positions we've been sitting in all morning: me lying on my bed reading my book (a Sophie Kinsella that Mia sent me), Darwin sitting in the collapsed chairs by the TV playing Nintendo and FOG sitting propped against his pillows using his laptop.

'Where's Nick?' asks Darwin, looking around.

'He's been darting between the VHR tent and the JHF all morning, trying to find a fight for us to go to,' I groan. I'm quite happy having some quiet time. 'He can't bear to sit still.

He'll be back to update us soon, no doubt. So, what does Tuesday mean?'

'Oh, it's the Jingly market,' says FOG.

'What?'

'Every week some of the locals are allowed to come on to camp to set up a market for the soldiers. They sell all sorts: rugs and fabric, knock-off CDs and DVDs, crappy clothes, jewellery, cheap fags . . . What else, Darwin?'

'All those supposed antique weapons and stuff. And watches, some pashminas, which my wife likes. All sorts,' Darwin says, standing up and stretching.

'Why "Jingly"?' I ask.

'You must have noticed all the locals' trucks,' FOG explains. 'What have they got all over them?'

'All that bling shit!' Darwin answers him. 'All those gold dangly bells and decorations. When they drive in, it all jingles.'

'Sounds good to me.' I'm keen for a change of scenery.

As soon as Nick gets back, we all pile into the Land Rover, with the usual disagreement between the boys over who drives. Darwin wins with the argument:

'We're on VHR! If we get a shout and *you're* driving we'll never get there in time. Fifteen miles an hour is too slow!'

'It's the speed limit, in case you hadn't noticed,' FOG replies, climbing into the back with me.

As we bump along the roads, the exhaust coughs out the usual black fumes and the airflow around the Rover sucks them into the back through the gap where the door doesn't meet the frame. FOG holds the door wide open with his foot to keep us from suffocating.

When he pulls up by the food tent, I jump to the ground and put my sunnies on. It's a gorgeous winter day, sunny and clear. The smell from the shit-pit isn't too bad either. We stroll towards the small, permanent coffee shop – the only shop on camp. It sells coffee, tea, two-week-old magazines and a few snacks. It's the same tea and coffee we can get for free in the food tent, but it feels civilized to pay for your drink and sit on the wooden benches outside.

I look up and see the market laid out, stretching away from us for maybe a hundred yards. The sellers lay their wares on the floor along two lanes. Brightly patterned scarves and pashminas stretch down one side of the market, and I can see Persian rugs at the far end. Their rich colours seem to sparkle in the sun, dazzling everyone with the unexpected splash of colour. I feel slightly dizzy looking at the rich shades after so much brown.

The closest pitch is stacked high with DVDs, all for $5 a piece. Some of them look like recent releases, and we gravitate towards them. Darwin peels off to buy cigarettes.

'Are these any good?' I ask FOG, picking up a copy of the latest *Harry Potter* film release.

'Some are perfect quality, others don't work at all. Bit hit and miss, really. But if you want movies, you should have just asked me – I've got hundreds on my hard drive,' FOG says proudly. 'You can always borrow it, you know.'

'Thanks, but I'm good with my book; it can't throw a fit and delete itself.'

We walk on through the market. I realize that the locals probably make a killing – everything seems really inexpensive but it's still probably ten times the price they can charge outside the wire. Most local Afghans are dirt poor and live hand to mouth.

On the far side are pitches selling 'real' designer watches, including 'Brightling' and 'Channel', and supposed artifacts from the war with Russia – old rifles and bits of tanks. From the prices, I doubt if anything is genuine. I see an 'I ❤ Allah' paperweight and an alarm clock in the shape of a mosque. The bearded seller sees me looking and comes running over to us, holding one in gaudy pink. He pushes his veiny hand into my face and presses a button on the top, and the tinny sound of prayer-calls comes out of the tiny speaker.

'No, no thank you.' I shake my head vigorously at him and we walk on. Darwin catches up with us, holding several two-hundred-packs of 'Malborog Lighs'.

FOG looks at them. 'You have no idea what they're putting in those; there could be anything in there.'

'You're joking, right? They don't grow anything in this country other than goats and opium. The worst that could be in them is goat shit.'

'Oh, yummy,' FOG answers sarcastically.

'But they're only $6 for two hundred. What a bargain!' Darwin says. 'I suppose I better get the missus another scarf – she really liked the one I brought home last time.'

I knew he was happily married, but Darwin rarely talked about his wife and kids, so I grab the opportunity to ask about her.

'How is Eva getting on without you?' I ask.

'Probably shacked up with Winston the gardener by now,' he says. 'No, she's used to it. She's really busy with the children – two kids under seven is never easy. I try and ring at least every couple of days, and she always seems to have a girlfriend around or something, so I guess she's fine. The kids drive her nuts, of course – I really miss them, but I wouldn't want to have them 24/7 either.'

'I can't imagine,' I say truthfully.

I don't know how anyone can go away on operations and leave children behind. I miss Jake and my friends so much; I can only guess how much, as a parent, I would miss my child. I wonder about the women working in the hospital a hundred or so yards away from me; so many of the doctors and nurses in there are older than the average soldier out here, so many of them must be mothers to children left behind. And it's almost Christmas, too – that must be an awful time to be away. Just as Darwin is bending to look at a scarf, the VHR callsign booms out of the Motorola radio.

'A shout!' screams Nick, ecstatic.

We run towards the Land Rover. The unspoken rule is that Darwin drives when we're in a rush, and we're on the move before FOG and I have fully climbed in. So much for shopping . . . I sit in the back, bracing myself against the bumping and crashing, and try to calculate what duty I'll be on next Tuesday.

While Jingly market is pretty good, mail day has to be the best day of the week in Bastion. However, like most things out here, it's pretty unpredictable, so you never know which day it will be. It's like turning the key to your front door at home and seeing on the door mat a shiny parcel wrapped in ribbon or a smooth cream envelope with ornate writing containing an invitation to the best party. Multiply that feeling by about ten and that's what it's like getting a delivery here; we all get stupidly excited every time. Even the most macho-looking men suddenly morph into hyperactive five-year-olds who have consumed too many E numbers.

One morning, when there wasn't much on to keep us busy, FOG and I do a walk-by recce of the mail tent and see hundreds of beautiful grey bags piled up outside, waiting to be sorted.

'Look at those babies,' I say, mentally preparing myself for at least two or three envelopes. Lots of sweets, some letters and – fingers crossed – the latest *Cosmopolitan Bride*.

'I'm guessing about two of those bags are mine,' FOG laughs.

From time to time, I get a bit of inside knowledge about the mail's arrival. Louise occasionally tips us off at the morning brief, because when she walks back from her night shift she can sometimes hear the C130 land. Everyone at Bastion knows what a C130 sounds like: sod the technical description; it's the sound of parcels and letters arriving from home.

We all find reasons to hang around in the JHF all day waiting for the signallers to come pushing through the dusty tent flaps, mail bags first, like rake-thin Father Christmases.

I sit in the corner trying to type up notes for a post-operational report the Boss has asked me to put together, but I'm distracted. You have to be fully marinated in boredom in order to do one of these properly. There is endless paperwork and form-filling, which has never been a strong point of mine. Rather than doing it, I find myself digging out my kneeboard – a Filofax containing military reference documents and a pad of paper which I attach to my leg – clearing out old scraps of paper covered in messy grids, a couple of sketch maps and the Viagra advert someone has obviously snuck into my stuff when I wasn't looking.

'So, who added this little something, huh?' I laugh, glancing at FOG, Nick and Darwin, who are all busying themselves with other tasks. They shrug, the corners of their mouths twitching.

The signallers come in before lunch and dump four bags on the tables. Immediately they are swarmed by soldiers vying for prime position near the mouth of the first bag. The letters, newspapers, parcels and presents spill over on to the map table; they're a positive cornucopia of happiness.

'Get off, you lot!' shouts the watchkeeper. His team try to get the mail filed neatly into the ammo boxes we use as pigeon-holes, but there are hands everywhere, shoving, pushing and grabbing.

The boxes are leftover 30mm ammunition shipping crates, about the size of four shoeboxes, and they make great storage. I grab a letter with my name on it and run away back to the flight tent.

It's my daily ebluey from Jake. If anyone is flying from Kandahar to Bastion, I can sometimes receive them four hours after he sits down at his computer. Sometimes I receive several days' worth at once if there's been a backlog for any reason, but today there's only one. I rip it open hungrily and read about his yesterday. He has been offered a choice of new jobs, so we are trying to decide which is best for both of us in terms of location and long-term goals. Thinking about mundane things like commute times, leave schedules and weekends off makes me forget about Bastion for a while.

After lunch, back in my tent, I lay out the day's spoils and decide which order to open them in. I've got four letters and a package. I decide to go for the letters first and leave the best, the package, until last. It has Jake's handwriting on the front and a drawing of a Christmas tree.

Three letters are Christmas cards from friends from uni. I proudly hang them on the line I've rigged above my bed with bungees. The fourth card is a long handwritten letter from a friend from Sandhurst who is sailing around the world. She has taken the time to send me a letter from Sydney. I think of her sitting in her skipper's cabin scribbling away and make a mental note to write to her when I have time.

I pause with the parcel in front of me, and then peel open the side of the laptop-sized box. As soon as there is a hole in the packaging, I jam my nose into it to try and capture any escaping scent of Jake, but I'm met by the saccharine smell of sweets and dusty cardboard.

I rip it open, and a handmade advent calendar stares out at me, complete with little 3D compartments holding presents. Every one of the twenty-five doors has a tiny picture of me and Jake on one of our holidays. There's one of me sunbathing, freckled and laughing, reaching up to grab the camera from his hand. Another one we tried to take ourselves, of both of us on a sailing holiday, and he's cut off my chin. It's awful, such a bad angle, but he knows it'll make me smile and tell him to burn it. A note tells me that, behind each door, is one of my favourite treats.

'Time to go, daydreamer.'

It's FOG, pulling on his boots and looking at his bedside clock, which is propped on top of an old water box.

We have an escort mission, which is one of our most boring tasks.

'Ugh. I fancy staying here and having a snooze, actually,' I say hopefully.

101

'Come on,' FOG says happily, looking as though he has all the energy in the world. I pick up my hated flying shirt and thin chamois-leather gloves, and we stroll slowly back up to the JHF along the designated walkways, discussing our mail hauls.

The Chinook crew, two pilots and three loadmasters, also known as loadies and responsible for passengers and equipment, wait for us. We go through our twenty-minute brief, discussing heights, speeds and the tactics we'll adopt if something goes wrong. Then FOG and I scrounge a lift from the signallers and climb into the aircraft with twenty minutes to go until take-off.

The boys on the ground are sometimes so short of supplies that they get down to one day's worth of ammo, so while we find these escort missions fairly routine, they're life-saving for our troops.

The Chinook drops off food, water and ammunition to troops based in platoon houses in the south of Garmsir, then zooms off back to Bastion at 140 knots. We have no hope of keeping up all the way, so once the Chinook is over safe desert, we slow down to a comfortable 120.

It's common practice to make a 'courtesy call' to any ground units we fly past in case they are in a contact and we can help out, but as we pass the northern tip of Garmsir, before I have the chance to get on the radio, I hear Widow Five Five.

'Ugly callsign, Ugly callsign, this is Widow Five Five. Are you on these means?' His voice is clipped and sounds urgent.

The boys down at Garmsir have been having a hard time. It's the most southerly point the troops have penetrated in Helmand, and everything beyond it down to the Pakistani border is unmapped Taliban land. The District Centre was set up in October 2006 and, since then, the Marines have been under attack 24/7. Far from gaining fresh ground, they are constantly forced to retreat into the old military barracks they're using as a base. The Taliban don't like us being in Garmsir one little bit. The area holds the key to their troops' entry from across the border with Pakistan, and the whole surrounding area is a gateway for the busy opium trade.

Once a bustling Afghan town, Garmsir has been deserted by the locals; they packed up and moved out long ago. It's now a ghost town, with only the sound of gunfire to splinter the eerie silence.

'Hello, Widow Five Five. This is Ugly Five Four. What's up?' I ask.

FOG is already turning back towards the platoon house location without us having to discuss it.

'Ugly, we've been taking sporadic fire for a while now,' he says. His voice sounds gravelly. 'It's really near, and we think it's coming from the only two-storey building in the area.'

'Stand by, we'll have a look.' I plug the grid into my keyboard unit and slave the sights to it.

FOG slowly wheels us around on top of the grid and, sure enough, we can see bright muzzle flashes from a tall, mud-coloured tower right near the grid.

Widow Five Five confirms the description and tells me that all the friendly forces are safely in the platoon house.

'I think we should Hellfire it,' I say. FOG agrees.

As we run in, I realize this will be my first missile in Afghanistan, the first one I fire in combat. My heart is thumping against my ribcage, pumping so hard it feels like it's only being contained in my chest by my LCJ. We've fired rockets and gun before now, but the Hellfire is in a different league. Its destructive power is terrifying. It can defeat all known armour. So tanks, cars, houses, compounds – you name it; it can blow it up with the squeeze of a finger.

I double-check the target details and slave the sight to exactly the right place as FOG turns the aircraft towards the tower.

'Four point eight clicks,' he says.

We need to fire at the right point; not so far that the missile will miss and not so close that the enemy could fire back at us. I aim to post it right through the window in the tower, so train the TADS on to it. It tracks it steadily.

'I'm a bit nervous actually,' I admit shakily to FOG. What if I screw this up? One of the pilots from the other flight fired a pair of flechettes completely off course on one occasion. They'd all had a right laugh at his expense and he was christened Elton, as in 'Rocket Man'. If I missed, I'd never hear the end of it.

'Loser, don't mess it up.'

I check all the switches are in the right settings and prepare to pull the cold trigger.

'Firing,' I say.

Loosing off the missile, I squeeze the laser like it's the only thing that matters. The flaming Hellfire hurtles away from us and we watch the impact in silence. It's awesome; the tower literally vaporizes before my eyes. One second it's there, and then it's gone. I make myself feel no remorse for the Taliban inside. After all, he had been trying to kill our troops.

'Check that out,' I say, full of relief. Not only have I fired a 'real' missile (I'm the last person in my squadron to do so), but the battle-damage assessment is amazing: there's nothing left down there except a pile of thick rubble and smoke. Hopefully that will put an end to the ever-increasing jokes about my being a 'peace-loving' female. I don't consider the true enormity of what I've actually done. Instead I feel like I've won the London Marathon because finally I've fired a missile, done the job I'm here to do. I'm on top of the world and have a big grin plastered all over my face. I have to focus on the task in hand, though, so I push my thoughts and feelings away, lock them under the trapdoor. There's no space in my head for anything else but the job at hand.

'Stop smiling so much, you'll get arrested,' FOG says. He's nonplussed, but he's done it all before and immediately gets on the radio to base telling them our ETA and fuel state.

Back at base, I know we have the usual tedious debrief to

get through but, to my delight, Sergeant Tucson, the squadron intelligence sergeant, is already tied up in a debrief with some crews who'd come back from a heavy mission in Kajaki an hour ago. I picture the grim look on his face when he finds out he'll have to debrief us as well. I have at least another hour of unwind time before I can possibly be trapped in the TPF (Tactical Planning Facility). I breathe a long sigh of relief.

Louise and I wisely spend our spare minutes looking at the Dessy website for bridesmaids' dresses and discussing colour schemes. She likes yellow; I'm already sold on green. Then we move on to dress styles, shoes, accessories – all the important stuff.

Sergeant Tucson emerges from the debrief, looking decidedly tired, with large purple bags under his eyes, sees me and smiles, then pinches his nose shut and screws up his face. I dive behind the computer screen to hide my laughter then turn to Louise.

'Sergeant T. reckons he can tell whether the returning crews have killed anyone just by smelling their breath,' I say.

'*What?*'

'He thinks it gives you "kill-breath", reckons he can smell it a mile off.'

Louise looks incredulous.

'He's been right so far,' I shrug. 'He says he has a 100 per cent success rate!'

He calls us in shortly afterwards. Thankfully, our debrief is short and sweet. Sergeant T. says it is the best battle-damage assessment he has ever seen from a Hellfire. I try not to, but can't stop myself grinning from ear to ear.

'Don't get too excited,' FOG says. 'That building was made of shit and sticks.'

I'm a bit disappointed to learn that my Hellfires won't always be so effective, but at least we'd got one more Taliban. That's one less to put a bullet in one of our soldiers.

Needless to say, I chew gum throughout the debrief to disguise any possible hint of kill-breath.

The following morning, I'm overjoyed to find even more mail spilling out of the APACHE PILOTS' ammo box; clearly a couple of extra bags from the previous day's haul.

'Woohoo! More post!' I shout to FOG when I spot it through the door of the tent. I drop my kneeboard on to the nearest surface and get down on the ground to look through the booty. FOG stands back to observe.

'Nope, nope, the Boss, nope,' I say aloud as I sift through the post looking for anything for Two Flight.

'One for Darwin.' I pull it out and set it aside.

'Ooh, me!' I spot a parcel with my name on it and, as I pause to inspect it, Nick bounds into the tent, muscles me aside and starts going through the metal box of treasure. He hands two eblueys to FOG.

'From my girlfriend,' FOG smiles, delighted. He's divorced from the mother of his children but his new girlfriend writes to him every day and her letters always put a smile on his face.

'See you later,' he says, and leaves, already tearing the flaps off the letters and heading off to find somewhere private to read them.

I sit on my knees in the dust. The parcel is huge, as long and wide as the advent calendar but much thicker. It has girly writing on the front of it and a couple of Snoopy stickers holding down the straining flap at the back. A gorgeous aroma, like that of an expensive face pack, emanates from the whole parcel. It looks delicious: it can only be from one person.

'Whatcha got?' asks Darwin, peering through the tent flap from where he is smoking a post-mission fag. I throw his letter over, and he catches it neatly.

'Parcel from Mia,' I say, then laugh as both boys look up from what they're doing, interested.

'Oh good, open it now. I've got nothing,' says Nick. 'She's the one who always sends you Haribo and biscuits, isn't she?'

'Yes she is, and no I won't. Last time there was nothing left by the time I got it back to my pod!'

The boys groan, knowing that I will be handing out any goodies eventually.

Back on my cot, I take my boots off – heaven – and as the air cools my hot, swollen feet I tear open Mia's package and let the wonderful perfume of it envelop me. I pick the card up and open it – it's dated three weeks ago.

Dear Charlie, I hope this gets to you intact. Last week I got a package back from the Post Office because, apparently, you can't send aerosol spray; I was trying to send you some Febreeze. Anyway, hope this makes the place smell better – I couldn't believe it when you said you live next to a cesspit. Hope the boys are being nice to you and you are OK living in your cramped tent.

Thinking of you all the time, love Mia x

P.S. My mum says hi.

Inside the parcel are three air fresheners, a bottle of my favourite perfume and the matching shower gel, two Champneys face masks, Guerlain chocolates, two bags of Haribo, a bright pink journal and a ballpoint pen with a pink feather on the end. I feel an unexpected pang of loneliness, which coils in my chest. I feel as if I might be sick, or maybe shed a tear. Having managed not to cry so far, I remind myself that receiving three Airwick fresheners really wouldn't be the moment.

Sunlight suddenly blooms into the tent as Darwin lets himself in through the back entrance, returning from his smoking deck. He takes a look at the loot on my cot.

'What the fuck is all that?'

'Some of us need more than cigarettes and a change of socks every week to feel human, thank you.' I give myself a quick squirt of perfume and sweep all my goodies back into the package protectively. 'I'm off to the computer.'

On my way to the JHF to use the internet computer, I pass FOG going in the opposite direction.

'Internet's down again,' he says, looking depressed. He wrinkles his nose. 'What's that funny smell?'

'Perfume. You're supposed to think it smells nice. What a bugger about the internet . . . Think I'll go and hang around anyway, just in case it comes back on.'

I make myself a lukewarm tea in the JHF and wander through to the bird table to see who's around. Louise is at her desk.

'Louise! I haven't seen you for ages.'

'I've been on nights.' She smiles and pulls her lower eyelids down with two fingers to illustrate how tiring it's been. 'Hopefully now I'm on normal shifts I might get some sleep – I never can sleep in the daytime. You smell nice.'

'Thanks.' I plonk myself down in an empty chair and start to fill her in on my package from Mia.

'Wow! That sounds amazing. Tom is quite good like that. Last parcel he sent me had some posh shower gel and a pair of fluffy socks.'

There's a flurry of noise as the VHR crew comes running in.

'Got to go,' Louise says, and dashes over to them to give them the latest brief.

I wander back over to the computer and – miracle of miracles – find the internet working. I look at the keyboard. It is a sick, yellowy colour and is so crusty I know I'm in danger of picking up something gross from it. Some of the keys are stuck together and the space bar is hanging off. I log into my email. It takes an age to load up, and I tap away gingerly with two fingers in the hope of minimizing my contact with the germs.

'Dear Mia, Thank you SO much for the package you sent me with all the smellies,' I write. 'I got it today, and I was feeling really in need of a treat. The tent absolutely STINKS at the moment – why are boys' feet so smelly? – so the air fresheners are great. It's really weird, being out here. None of the boys can stop talking about work the whole time. It's so boring. Have you got any decent gossip for me? Can't wait to come back and see you in March. Jake is organizing some kind of party for me. Make sure you're free! Miss you loads, thanks again for the parcel, Charlie xx.'

I press send and feel a wave of homesickness for Mia, Jake and everything English.

I walk back to the tent and unwrap two of the air fresheners, putting one under my bed to ward off the most offensive smells from all around. I take the second one and wander outside, carrying it into the next-door tent. I go into the shared men's/women's loos and prop the other one on the back of the toilet labelled 'GIRLS ONLY'. There's a man's muddy footprint on the floor and a copy of *FHM* on the cistern. The 'GIRLS ONLY' seems to act as a beacon to all the men; they know this is the cleanest, freshest-smelling place for them to come in and do their huge, smelly, dirty poos.

As the weeks pass, the tiredness starts to creep up on me but it's as if, when we're working, we're all completely programmed to ignore it. Every time the Motorola starts squeaking, I spring up out of bed like a jack-in-the-box, no questions asked. My brain is on automatic pilot, and my body follows. I throw my clothes on over my pyjamas and I'm running to the JHF before my eyes have even adjusted to being open. I chew gum instead of brushing my teeth, and a trip to the loo is a luxury I can't afford.

Thankfully, as Christmas approaches, the pace steadies. Winter 2006 kicks in and the temperature starts to drop; some nights it falls well below zero. With desert all around us, there's nothing to trap the day's heat, so the cold always feels extreme. Traditionally, this is when the fighting stops and doesn't start again until spring. The Taliban hate the cold and retreat back into their holes.

During one of our briefings, we get the low-down on Operation Glacier. We'd all heard the rumours that something big was on the horizon, and this was it – the most ambitious plan yet since our arrival.

All ears are pricked, and the men splay their legs a little wider in anticipation.

'The aim is to destroy the Taliban's main supply chain from Pakistan through to Garmsir,' our ops officer kicks off. 'They come over in their droves from Baram Chah, an opium-trading town on the border, and, from there, split up into small groups and travel north in Toyota 4x4s.'

After weeks of covert planning, five main locations have been identified. If we can punch a few holes in their network, then the Taliban would be up shit creek, at least for a while. It will take them time to rebuild the route, and time is exactly what this bigger operation needs. The boys down at Garmsir also need a break; they're having their arses whipped every time they move.

'It's going to be divided into two phases: quiet, then noisy,' the ops officer continues. 'Your bit will kick in during the noisy stage.'

The first stage will be a careful study of logistics: the roads, who comes and goes, how they travel, where they stop and the movements around their different centres. The men in Garmsir will snake their way into the Green Zone fringes recording everything they witness, from large numbers of enemy to snipers and sentries.

The operation is expected to take around two months. When it's complete, each centre is to be hit methodically, one after the other in a huge show of power.

'You will be tasked in a series of deliberate operations to help out, and it's going to take precedence over everything else,' the officer explains.

'And until then?' a voice pipes up, excited and eager.

'Until then, it's work as usual.'

The splayed legs return to their original positions.

*   *   *

By now, everyone is thinking about Christmas. The latest time-waster has been comparing trees. The best is clearly the four-foot beauty in the Crab and Archer, our squadron rest tent. It's slowly getting decorated in preparation for the party next week. All sorts of odd things are hanging from the branches, from paper snowflakes to string, kindly donated by a department store back home. An array of empty boxes wrapped in cheap paper bulk out Secret Santa's gifts beneath it.

My favourite tree is my own small effort, sent in another parcel by Mia. This little baby is a six-inch-high 'grow-your-own' which blossoms when you water it. Louise and I spend periods of time late at night enthusiastically watching it sprout. It's started to moult over the intelligence desk, but at least the sad scattering of pine needles looks vaguely festive. A few days after our heads-up on Operation Glacier, Louise and I sneak through the back entrance to her tent, which is almost always in total darkness, in order to accommodate eight other girls working on different shifts from us. There are no lights and no talking is allowed. Louise perches on her camp bed and I crouch beside her. She bends forward to avoid brushing her head against the mosquito net which forms a dome around her space. The six-by-four-foot 'pods' are lined up, four a side, against the sweating walls of the dark tent. It's pretty cramped; in my tent, we all removed the mozzie nets to give ourselves more space. Here they use them to guard their own small allotment of space. Being females only, at least it smells a whole lot better than mine.

Louise shows me the tiny illuminated tree her Tom has sent her. It casts a pink and green twinkly glow over her belongings as she whispers about her last package from him.

In hushed tones we compare notes on our plans – tiny, fleeting glimpses of what we still think of as normality.

'OK, I'm starting to plan and think about when I get home now,' I tell her.

'God, me too,' she says. 'I can't wait.'

'I'm thinking, at least a week of meals at home and cosy nights in front of the TV. I can't wait to get a good takeaway.'

'Me neither,' she continues. 'I think I may book a cottage for me and Tom. I can picture it now: log fires, long walks through the woods, pub lunches. Heaven. I just can't wait to see him.'

It isn't long before we each select a wedding magazine from the pile under her bed and start flicking through them.

After twenty minutes, I'm in a blissful state of civvieness, drifting through a world of wedding days, proper jobs and endless time with Jake. I'm jolted back to reality by a chorus of familiar voices and running footsteps.

'Where did she say she was going?' It's Nick, and the dreaded crackling of the Motorola radio.

Louise shoos me away. I throw the magazine under the bed, stand up and snag my hair in the zip of her pod. I tear my head away, then slide out into the blinding sunlight, swearing quietly and leaving a generous clump of hair behind me.

I stumble unseeing towards the sound of the squawking Motorola. It's always like this. The shouts never come when you're ready for them. When I'm in the ops room, in my flying kit, happily fed and watered and crossing my fingers for a shout, it never comes, but when I'm in the shower lathering up, the curtain stuck merrily to my bum crack, the all-seeing radio pipes up.

In between shouts the waiting is almost unbearable. It seems ghastly to yearn for a call-out – if we're needed, it's only because our troops are in contact or injured – but sitting staring at the radio for days on end induces extreme cabin fever. There are only so many times you can pluck your eyebrows.

Nick and I jump out of the still-moving vehicle at HQ, and FOG and Darwin speed off to fire up the Apaches. Inside HQ the mood is tense. The watchkeeper rattles through his brief as we run across the tent and grab our kneeboards.

'There's been a TIC at Kajaki. Two T2s and a T4. The

Chinny crews are already walking. Landing at Lancaster.'

Two seriously injured Brits and one dead. I feel the usual swell of nausea rising in my ribcage. I'm starting to think more and more about my own mortality. Being out here, you're forced to. I steer away from emotional thoughts about how something could hit the aircraft and make me spiral to the ground to my death, to imagining the impact my death would have on everyone at home, but in a totally practical sense. Who would come to my funeral? Would Jake cope? How would Mum and Dad be? The thoughts make me feel even sicker, but I can't stop them.

The Chinook crews will be airborne long before us if they're already on their way to the cabs and we'll have a hell of a job catching up.

We sprint to the aircraft, our feet pounding through the uneven dust. It catches in my throat and sits there; it feels as if I've swallowed sandpaper. I hitch up my outsized P-Diddy flying combats and try to keep up with Nick. The sweat is running down my face by the time I vault the angry barbed wire that lies in wait for the unwary halfway to the hangars. I've stabbed myself in the shins many a time coming back late from a night flight, but I'm clued up this time.

We wheeze our way through the REME office and they nod to confirm that FOG and Darwin have already signed out the aircraft. We bolt out of the side door, feet rattling against the corrugated-steel flooring. The groundie at my aircraft sees us approach and says something to FOG into his headset. He reaches up and secures my door in its horizontal position. I dive past the butt of my carbine rifle and drop my kneeboard and maps on to the cockpit floor, panting heavily.

'Kajaki.'

FOG's closed visor nods.

I try to catch my breath.

'More gym sessions for you,' the visor says. We compete in the running stakes, but I never win against FOG. He signals the groundie while I busy myself aligning the sights on the TADS.

We creep forwards so we can see Nick's aircraft around the blast wall. They give us a thumbs-up, then taxi and roll down the runway in one manoeuvre. We follow, and within moments we're airborne, only twenty-three minutes after the Motorola first crackled. Seven minutes to spare – not bad. I could have plucked my eyebrows again.

FOG and I take all the air-traffic-control radio calls, while Nick concentrates on the tactical nets. I call up Crowbar, the theatre-wide ATC (Air Traffic Control), to tell them where we're going and get the 'picture' – the details of other aircraft and activity in the area – as we lift from Bastion.

'Roger, picture clear,' they respond. 'Say again, what is your destination?'

I flick frantically through my kneeboard. I can't say Kajaki on the radio, so I have to find the codename. There's a pregnant pause on the frequency while everyone waits for slow-coach Ugly Five Four to get her act together. As I rifle through the pages, ham-fisted in my flying gloves, a laminated picture of a naked man surfaces. I find what I'm after, let Crowbar know where we're going, then tell FOG: 'I've got Rocco.'

'Yes!' he laughs. 'I thought he'd got lost – or that someone had procured him for their own personal use.'

Rocco has been on ops for a while now. I can't remember who started it, but it was bound to be someone on the other flight. A laminated picture of a hairy male porn star started showing up in the strangest places about six weeks ago. There are no rules: Rocco has found his way into pockets, kneeboards, helmet bags and underpants. Each victim simply passes him quietly on to the next. He has a habit of showing up when he's least welcome, but he always raises a laugh. I stash him away for later when I can sneakily give him to someone else.

The Chinooks are so far ahead we can't see them, even with

the TADS. As long as we clear them into the landing site with the JTAC on our secure radios, though, it doesn't matter.

Ten minutes later, Nick has done just that and on the insecure FM radios, we hear the Chinooks landing and collecting the casualties. As FOG reports that back to HQ, we receive the most annoying message possible:

'Ugly Five Two and Five Three, the TIC has now closed, you are to RTB.'

It's good news that the troops are no longer in immediate danger, but the sweat is only starting to dry on my back and I want to do something useful, like shoot some Taliban, especially the one that got our man, not return to base.

'Bloody hell,' I say to no one in particular.

I hear FOG breathing a deep sigh of frustration into his mike as he wheels us 180 degrees.

This happens fairly frequently. In an effort to save precious Apache hours, we're only allowed on scene if a TIC is ongoing. Sometimes we'll be called and run like crazy, start the engines and then shut them straight down again. While our flying hours have been upped, because we are a limited resource the powers that be want to keep us free for when the shit really does hit the fan. Coupled with this is the huge amount of money it costs for us to be in the air, chomping our way through expensive fuel and spare parts.

'Want to fly?' FOG says.

I normally take us back to Bastion to try and keep my hand in; it's so easy to sit in the front, buried in maps, kneeboards, water bottles, ammunition and a million bits of paper, but FOG makes a point of giving me the controls whenever he can. I don't mind; it's good to have the practice. I execute a bumpy landing on the strip and we taxi to the fuel bowser. Fifteen minutes later I bundle myself out of the cockpit and reach for the radio in my pocket. It's still on. I turn the volume up against the sound of the Chinook returning from the camp hospital. Just because we've got back, it doesn't mean the whole sequence won't be repeated any second now. I salivate at the thought of handing over VHR duty. All I can think about is heading back to my comfy camp cot and closing my eyes.

'Ah, great, you're all back.' The Boss's smiley face greets me and FOG the second we walk through the tent flap to the JHF. 'There's an Orders Group for Operation Glacier right now. It's next door in the briefing tent; go straight through.'

We trudge into the briefing room and sit in the back row. I spend the next hour struggling to pay attention to the endless stream of words about 'enemy forces', 'maintenance of momentum' and 'firepower'. My brain is busy replaying the mission, so my head feels as if it's filled with wasps, my arse is sore from sitting on it for so long without moving in the aircraft and my mouth feels so dry I can barely swallow.

'Nice quick orders,' FOG says sarcastically when we're finally released.

'No change there. I'm off to the tent to try and relax,' I reply.

'Captain Madison!' The watchkeeper bustles up and taps me on the elbow. 'There you are. You have a visitor.'

I look round. The JHF is noisy and frantic, and there are bodies everywhere. It smells like a mixture of must and sweat – clearly there is something kicking off.

'What? OK, send them back here where it's quieter, I'll grab a tea,' I sigh.

A filth-covered, bushy-haired man weaves his way towards me from the front of the JHF. His clothes are caked in dust, and he has several weeks' beard growth on him – he looks how I imagine British officers in the trenches during the World Wars looked. I silently motion for him to follow me and lead the way out of the back of the tent.

'Hi,' I say tentatively, confused that he hasn't started the conversation first to tell me what he wants. I'm so tired, my vision seems blurred. He looks more exhausted than me; he has three rows of bags under each eye.

116

There's a pause, then he looks directly at me and I feel slightly uncomfortable.

'Hi, Charlie.'

The voice is definitely familiar . . . the face is not . . . I rack my brains, then, 'Chris.' Fuck. The feeling of familiarity jars as my home and work life collide.

One of Jake's best mates from home, Chris has spent more hours at our house than any other of our friends. He has curly hair and a serious face, and his sarcastic sense of humour always means we have a good time together; but my memories of him all involve us sitting around a barbecue, drinking wine, painting our house or sailing in the Solent, not standing in a war zone expecting to talk about Apache capabilities or something. Usually, guys from the Forward Operating Bases (FOBs) spend their 'R&R' at Bastion in the temporary accommodation they're allocated; it's rare for anyone to make the effort to find their way to the JHF. I'm flattered.

'Didn't you recognize me?' he asks, shocked. His surprise at my lack of recognition smarts slightly. I feel awful but tell myself not to beat myself up over it – he looks at least two stone lighter and I can barely make out his features for hair and dust.

I remember seeing him in Portsmouth back in July 2005.

'Hurry up, you two, we've got to leave for the boat in half an hour,' I holler up the stairs.

Jake, Chris and I have been planning our sailing trip to France for months. We'll be taking the Royal Marines' forty-foot yacht from Portsmouth to Cherbourg, then spending a few days in the Channel Islands.

We're packing Jake's Land Rover with everything we'll need for our week on the water. The boys have, typically, organized everything with military precision and are taking the trip extremely seriously.

'Oilskins?' Jake reads down his checklist.

117

'Check.' Chris throws them into the car.

'Charts?'

'Check.'

'Bottled water? Gas canister? Euros?'

'Check, check, check.'

'Put a water in the front for the drive, mate,' Jake instructs Chris.

'Roger. This is going to be such a hoofing trip, Royal.'

'I know. Sailing is essence.'

Even after a year of speaking to Jake almost daily and spending time with his Royal Marine friends, I sometimes find it difficult to follow their conversations. I gather they are excited about our week away.

Twenty-four hours later, we're halfway to France, with no land visible in any direction.

Chris is also a Royal Marine and, like Jake, is physically fit and hugely practical. He's always tinkering with something and, now, it's with what looks like a GPS, a can of Fosters in his free hand.

He's standing casually against the railings at the back of the boat. Both he and Jake look divine in their tight T-shirts and oilskin trousers, like adverts for Musto sailing gear. Jake looks more relaxed than I ever remember seeing him before, leaning back with the wind tugging at his curly brown hair.

'I tell you what makes a change, Royal,' Chris shouts, 'and that is spending time with you without a damn paintbrush in my hand sorting out your house!'

We all laugh at this; it's true. Jake and I have a crumbling house in Nottingham, which for ever has bits falling off it and, in recent months, Chris has been there almost constantly helping us out.

'I've spent more hours fixing up your pad than I've spent asleep this year, I'm sure.' Chris throws the GPS at Jake in mock anger.

'I know, I know, we do really owe you, mate.'

*　　*　　*

Now, here in the JHF, I stare at him, ashamed that I didn't recognize him.

'Sorry,' I start, embarrassed. 'I wasn't thinking . . . I'm so tired . . . I . . . how are you?'

He gestures at his clothing and beard, 'Exhausted. I'm just passing through between patrols and wanted to see you. I told Jake I'd look you up and make sure you're not getting into trouble.' He smiles. His teeth look whiter than I remember, set against his dirty tan.

He's a slice of home; a piece of Jake. I want to hug him, like I normally would, and move towards him but, suddenly, with both of us in our combats, it feels inappropriate. I step back and smile.

'So how are things?'

'Yeah, good, you know, could be better. I think I need a shower.' He laughs, and I see the Chris I know; the Chris from home, the Chris that always stands with a paintbrush in one hand and a beer in the other, mouth wide open enjoying a joke with Jake. We chat for a few minutes about Jake, home and Chris's girlfriend before Chris excuses himself.

'I'm really sorry but I have to go – patrol leaves in ten minutes,' he says as he heads off.

As I walk slowly back to my accommodation, I wonder what he'll be doing tonight, what he's already done. I suddenly see him for what he is: a soldier, armed with a rifle and armoured vehicle, heading out to hunt down and kill other men and to protect his own. He will head back to his FOB and be in sole command of thirty other soldiers, all fighting for their lives. I'm shaken. I wonder if he considers what I've done, and what that makes him think of me.

As I approach the entrance to my tent, I see Louise just leaving it. Spotting me, she calls out.

'Charlie! I just came looking for you, I want to show you something.'

I feel my tiredness moving to the back of my mind and find myself craving her company.

'Cool. I'll come to yours; it's quiet there.'

We unzip the door to her tent, then crouch down to squeeze together into her pod. The net walls brush against my hair as I settle myself on to the floor. Louise lies on her cot with her boots hanging off the side and pushes a stack of brightly coloured magazines my way.

For once, I can't switch off, though. I tell her about seeing Chris, and how confused I was.

'I can't believe I didn't recognize him. He just seemed so out of place.'

'Tom's coming out here in a couple weeks, just after Christmas,' she says. I'd forgotten they would both be in Bastion at the same time. 'He's going to be in Bastion Two, the new, bigger camp across the road, so I won't be able to see him often, but I don't think I'd want to.'

'What do you mean?'

'Obviously I miss him like nothing else, but this is my time out here. I'm coping on my own and I wonder whether it will be weird seeing him – a bit like when you see your school-teacher on the high street and don't know how to act.'

'That's exactly how I just felt with Chris,' I agree. 'Jake was trying to get a job out here a while back, just to check on me. I was really against it.'

It's weird because, while I long to see Jake more than anything else, his being here would burst my bubble of self-sufficiency. When I'm with him, I allow myself to be looked after, emotionally as well as physically, but out here, I know I have to take care of myself. If Jake and I faced this together and I really told him my worries, fears, paranoia about the job, I'm frightened it might ruin things between us, destroy the delicate balance we've found.

One of the things that keeps me going is the daydream I have about him where we meet each other. I'm showered and made-up and looking casual, maybe in jeans and a strappy top and some high heels, like I haven't made too much effort (even though I have, and have thought about the meeting at least five times a day for the last eight weeks). I'd obviously have fresh breath, maybe I'd be chewing some Extra, and be laughing with the guys as we caught each other's eyes. In fact, they'd be wetting themselves at a hilarious joke I've just cracked. It would be like that scene in *Love Actually* where the soft music plays and I run into his muscly arms . . .

Louise snaps me out of my fantasy world.

'Er, Charlie, I'm off, I've got a briefing in five. See you later?'

'OK. Have a good one.'

I leave her tent and lie down on my own cot, close my eyes and try to ease myself back into my daydream, snatching at the thoughts of home and Jake as they run through my mind like beads on a string of pearls.

On Christmas Eve, FOG, Darwin, Nick and I are air-testing. There's only one flight that will get us back from Kandahar to Bastion in time for Christmas, and it's at 9 p.m. We walk into the terminal at 8.30 p.m. and book in, only to be told that there's a delay of at least four hours.

'Can we come back later then?' I ask, thinking about a last-minute dash for a cup of steaming tea and a large chocolate-chip muffin.

'No, now you've checked in you are most certainly not allowed to leave the terminal.'

It's already been a long day, and we've done a lot of flying. The four of us exchange grim looks. Actually, only three of us do; Nick never looks grim.

'At least we can finish that card game, huh? . . . Guys?' he says hopefully.

We stare back, po-faced and silent.

As I heave my bags on to the X-ray scanner, I wonder for the thousandth time what they're checking for. What could I possibly have in my bags that they wouldn't allow me to take? I imagine the same luggage going through Heathrow: 'Do you have any weapons, madam?' Yes. 'Knives?' Yes. 'Bullets, grenades, sharp objects?' Yes, yes and yes. I mean, even my rifle has to go through the machine.

The little RAF X-ray boy, who looks about ten years old, seems satisfied and I collect my kit and lug it into the corner of the enormous hangar. I sit at a wooden table and read my book for a while, looking jealously at all the guys who have bagged one of the wall-to-wall camp cots and are silently sleeping shoulder to shoulder.

After about an hour, the lights suddenly go out and the buzz of the X-ray machine dies. There's a brief silence. FOG's eyes narrow under the beam of his head torch.

'Power cut,' one of the soldiers next to me mutters. The power is run on generators and is always a bit temperamental.

Midnight arrives while it is pitch black, and someone taps me on the shoulder. It's Nick, wearing a ridiculous Christmas hat, holding his torch under his chin like a scary devil-Santa.

'Merry Christmas,' he whispers, smiling, then moves on to spread his greetings through the group. I re-open my book, feeling grumpy. It's freezing in here.

At 2 a.m. we're finally on the plane – forty soldiers wearing green ear-defenders and four Apache pilots wearing our flying helmets. We look silly, but it saves carrying around the combat helmets we're meant to be donning. I slide down my dark visor and try to sleep. FOG looks around the cabin murderously. As we fly high above the desert, I drift off. I dream that I've woken up on Christmas Day. My whole family – Mum, Dad, Seb and Aunt Margery – and Jake and Mia are all in the JHF with the squadron. I haven't bought anyone any presents. I jolt awake, sweating, as we make a bumpy landing back at Bastion. I stagger back to our accommodation tent half asleep, like some sort of zombie.

I wake up for the second time in my camp cot and think

about the day ahead. I've been busy organizing the Christmas party for ages. It's been great having something outside work to focus on, and I think most people are looking forward to it. I'm not flying, so I rush around making sure the decorations are up in the rec tent, the secret Santa gifts are safely stashed under the tree and the two-drinks-per-person are in place behind the makeshift bar. I'm excited.

In the afternoon, I stand in an hour-long queue for the phones, longing to hear my mum's voice. The mood as we wait is anxious; everyone is desperate to wish their loved ones a merry Christmas. By the time I get to the front of the line it's gone 6 p.m. – early afternoon, her time.

She answers straight away. 'Hello,' she says, unsurprised. It's like she always knows when I'm going to call.

'Mum,' I sigh. Her voice sounds like minced pies, woolly blankets and open fires.

'How are you? You haven't called for ten days – I guess you've been busy.'

'Mmmm,' I say. 'I've been really busy this week planning the squadron Christmas party. We've got loads of decorations for our rec tent, and a huge tree. I can't wait!'

'Sounds nice, Charlie. We're going to have lunch soon. Margery's here. I've done the full works. Sorry you won't be here to have any. Are they feeding you well?'

'Of course. The chefs do an amazing job. Don't worry about me, I'm fine.'

'And are you keeping safe?'

It's a loaded question, and I'm keen to brush over it. 'Of course I am, Mum. Don't worry, I'm fine.'

We spend a few more minutes talking and then I ring off:

'Speak to you in a week or so, Mum. Merry Christmas.'

'OK, Happy Christmas. I'm proud of you. Bye.'

I follow the same routine with Dad – he's in the States – he moved there a few years after my parents divorced, when I was seventeen. My brother is also there, having moved when he finished school to go and get a job doing IT stuff. He seems to have picked up my parents' ability to understand all things computer-based. They sound delighted to hear from me. It makes me feel horribly homesick and very alone.

I walk back from the phones in a reflective mood. Back at my tent, I grab ten minutes to open the final door in Jake's home-made advent calendar. Behind the last picture of the two of us is a big Hershey's bar wrapped in foil. Yum, I'll save that for later.

I hurry across the tented camp towards the Crab and Archer. As I approach, I can feel the heat whooshing out through the tent door into the cold night and can smell the incongruous whiff of alcohol fumes. I have a moment of displacement. The sounds are of a busy pub at Christmastime: clinking glasses, raucous laughter, 'I Saw Mommy Kissing Santa Claus' playing through big speakers, and the hum of cheerful banter. But underneath my issue boots is Afghan sand as fine as talcum powder, and poking through the open tent flap is the sinister barrel of a rifle, slung across someone's back.

I'm relieved I'm here with the whole squadron and not back at Kandahar. The Boss is very particular about having us all together like one big, happy family, and thinks it's a good idea to keep our spirits high. I push through the flaps of the tent, spy Louise next to the tree and rush over, relieved that she isn't on duty. We help ourselves to some vile white wine.

'Ugh.' Louise virtually gags. I agree, but we decide white-paintstripper-style wine is better than no wine.

The night is fun. We all drink our allotted two drinks, and everyone covertly produces their own secret supplies. Vodka is consumed from empty beer cans, wine is drunk from mouth-wash bottles. It isn't allowed, but everyone does it. We hide the booze from the Boss. Everyone gets tipsy, and the boys strip off to various states of undress. People sing tunelessly. Those returning from their shifts or flights boost the numbers;

others leave, reluctant and sober, to go to work. The secret Santa presents are all wrapped in porn, the most widely available paper in Bastion. Pages of *Playboy* and *Penthouse* are strewn around the room, and everywhere I look I see pairs of ginormous fake boobs and pouting women staring back at me. Prince Charles, the Army Air Corps' colonel-in-chief, has sent us gifts: Duchy biscuits 'for the boys' and cigars 'for the officers'. The soldiers smoke the cigars two at a time and dare each other to eat them. I choke on mine and pass it on. There's a food fight, and biscuit crumbs are greedily distributed all over faces and the floor.

I bring out my camera to catalogue the evening and snap away, then Louise and I sit in a corner and peer at the tiny screen to laugh at the photos. My favourite one shows me sandwiched between a couple of bare-chested guys with, in the background, a table piled high with posh-looking Duchy Originals tins, scrunched-up porn and empty beer cans. Peeking from the bottom of the rubble is someone's abandoned pistol.

The party has passed its peak by 1 a.m. when I see the Boss chatting to Nick in the corner of the tent. They both look serious; I figure they must be talking shop. I peer at them through the clouds of cigar smoke, trying to work out if this will affect me. Nick is nodding tipsily as the Boss walks out of the tent and then Nick scans the room before heading in my direction.

'Have you seen FOG and Darwin recently? You're going to love this. We're off back to KAF – tonight. 3 a.m. C130.' Back to Kandahar by Hercules. Nick looks distracted, his eyes trying to search out the others.

'FOG's probably sleeping. I'll go and find him now so I can pack.' I'm annoyed; I was looking forward to a night in my camp cot here, surrounded by all my stuff.

I walk quickly back to the accommodation tent and pause at the door. It's dark and very quiet, but I can just make out the sounds of gentle snoring. I reach through the tent flap and switch on the lights, steeling myself to deliver bad news.

'Oi, what are you doing?' FOG sits bolt upright and looks around. No one wakes up slowly here – you need to be ready to act as soon as your eyes are open.

'Oh, it's you, Charlie. I was sound asleep.' He doesn't sound as annoyed now that he's seen it's me, and I'm glad.

'Sorry to wake you, but Nick just came to find me and told me we're off to KAF. Umm . . . now.'

'*WHAT?*' Now he's annoyed.

'Yep. Boss wants us there tomorrow to air-test first thing.'

'Of all the . . . I mean . . .' FOG is snorting with pure fury. I decide the best thing is to leave him to it. I retreat behind my poncho-wall and reach under my cot for my kit bag.

It's not the best way to end the night, and I do feel a little peeved, but I smile, thinking that at least FOG is more annoyed than I am.

At 3 a.m. we're once again gathered together by the side of the airstrip waiting for the plane. It's cold, and we sit in a line watching our breath settle on to the ground. FOG hiccups grumpily, mutters under his breath and adjusts his carbine. We were all deemed sober enough to return to the armoury straight from the party and collect our carbines and pistols, but FOG's hiccupping was making Nick and me grin so widely I thought we'd be refused our weapons.

The C130 lands and we board under the silent direction of the loadmaster, the huge engines roaring over everyone's shouts. Darwin stuffs his iPod headphones under his helmet and shuts his eyes. FOG falls immediately asleep despite the noise, to avoid Nick's keen attempts to share his glossy *GQ* magazine with his neighbours. I close my eyes and think about how lucky I am to be in Two Flight and not party to any of the petty in-fighting that has plagued some of the other groups. I look around me and smile to myself. My first Christmas away from home hasn't been too bad after all.

Before the New Year kicks in, I start to feel really ill with a sore throat and headache. When I wake up one Sunday morning and my throat is bleeding, I know I can't ignore it any more. From the symptoms, it could just be tonsillitis, which I've had about ten times. I was hoping to keep on flying; I don't want to miss a day because I'm ill. And if I don't fly, someone else will have to fill my spot, and do their own work plus mine. I don't want to start making stupid mistakes in the air because I'm feeling rough, though, so I decide some prescription drugs are the only thing for it.

We have taken over VHR duty, so I take one of the Motorola bad-news radios and head off to Bastion's hospital.

Located on the far side of camp behind the cookhouse, it's a series of tents all connected together, with the staff coming and going through small flap doors. Casualties come in by helicopter and are wheeled straight to the wards. A doctor passes me as I'm peering into a window shut with Velcro, but when I turn to ask for directions, I'm stopped in my tracks. It feels as if my feet are glued to the ground, and my mouth is open in shock. I force myself to shut it. I must look like a complete moron. The doctor looks like a wax figure, incredibly pale, almost blue, and has a dead expression on his face. His white coat is barely distinguishable from his face.

'Hi, sorry, where do I need to go to see a doctor?' I ask cautiously.

He peers at me, then gestures with a nod of his head and leads me through an entrance I hadn't spotted before.

As we emerge into the gloom of the ward I suddenly feel absolutely ridiculous going in to be seen about a sore throat. Packed closely together, lying in hospital beds along both walls, are around twenty Afghan locals with various missing limbs, large dressings disguising their injuries. There's a soft humming noise.

I try not to look at them but, for a split-second, I catch the eye of an old Afghan man who's staring at me. The average life expectancy out here is in the forties, but he looks older. Lying on his side with his legs raised up towards his chest like a child, his long Afghan robe billows behind him. He has a full, unkempt black beard speckled with a few strands of grey. Most of his head is covered in a thick toothpaste-white bandage. His eyes look vacant and are sunken deep into his face. His cheeks are drawn and his lips slightly parted, as if he had been going to say something but stopped.

These are the unpublished casualties of the war: Afghan army personnel and civilians caught in the crossfire of our fight against the Taliban. We treat them for their injuries as part of our commitment to the hearts and minds effort, but sometimes it forces us to make interesting choices.

The Taliban are unlike anyone the British Army has ever fought. They first came to prominence in the autumn of 1994. Their leader, the one-eyed village clergyman Mullah Mohammed Omar, promised to restore peace and security and enforce sharia (Islamic law). The Afghan population, tired of the feuding of the mujahideen warlords, generally welcomed the Taliban and, initially, the future looked rosy. The Taliban stamped out corruption and lawlessness and established a base for commercial enterprise, and the areas under their control began to flourish. Soon after coming into power, they moved from Kandahar, where they had been formed, and took control of Herat, on the border with Iran, and then gained power of the capital, Kabul, eventually controlling 75 per cent of the country.

Then the really ugly stuff started. In 1998, they swept into the town of Mazari Sharif, and walked up and down the streets shooting; women, men, children and animals were fired upon indiscriminately, and a reported eight thousand people died in the butchery. They then forbade the locals to bury the bodies for six days, so they rotted in the sun and were gnawed by stray dogs. By 2000, the ruling factions had changed and the new regime tolerated no opposition; those who disobeyed were shot, stoned and publicly humiliated. The more prohibitive Wahabist attitudes (in which all things modern and western are deemed worthy of suspicion) began to prevail. The Taliban now wanted to take the country back to year zero and to create a strict Islamic state. Policies towards this end include the meting out of Islamic punishments such as the amputation of limbs for those found guilty of theft; the banning of television, music and cinema; and the requirement for men to wear beards and women the burkha. Girls are forbidden to go to school, and women are not allowed to work; to leave the house, unless accompanied by a male; to laugh – and they're definitely not allowed to wear high heels. If they are raped by someone other than their husband, it's their fault and they go to prison. In 1999, a mother of seven, 'Zarmina', was executed in front of 30,000 spectators in a stadium in Kabul for allegedly murdering her abusive husband. She was blindfolded when she entered the stadium so no one could see the pain and fear etched on her face. The first shot skimmed her hair, reminding her of her fate. She tried to crawl away, but the second shot, a single bullet fired by her brother-in-law, blew her brains out. She had been imprisoned for three years and *tortured* extensively prior to the execution yet, in a bid to protect her daughter, who was reportedly the real culprit, refused to plead her innocence.

After the events of 9/11, the Taliban refused to hand over the al-Qaeda leader Osama bin Laden, who was hiding in Afghanistan, which angered the international community and paved the way for a new war.

In Pakistan, along the Pashtun belt, many were sympathetic to the Taliban's cause and, in 2002, Taliban forces began a recruitment drive to launch a renewed 'jihad', or holy war. Small mobile training camps were established along the border in lawless havens, to train new recruits in guerrilla tactics and terrorist warfare. Logistics hubs then popped up, and the strength of the Taliban grew.

British officials have divided the organization into three tiers. Tier one consists of the most senior commanders, the ideological hardcore, including the leader Omar, who is still on the loose. Many of them are based in Pakistan, especially Quetta, and are unbending ideologues. Most work hand in hand with the drugs lords across the Pakistan border and exchange opium for money and arms. Tier two comprises the mid-level commanders and foreign jihadis. Most are young idealists from the schools of Pakistan, where they are taught about suicide bombing. They see their devotion to the cause as a divine mission, as their duty, and dream of the afterlife with Allah. Tier three is the rank and file, the dollar-a-day soldiers who go where the money is. One day they may be shooting at our troops, the next siding with them; they bat with whoever they think is the winning side.

Life is cheap in Afghanistan, and there are few alternative means to earn money. Most are farmers and, once they have planted and harvested the poppy fields from November to April, come summer, they are jobless and will do anything to feed their families. I glance around the ward; many of these injured Afghans could be Taliban. It makes me feel both angry and sad.

The zombie-doc leads me through the maze of wards, all filled with casualties, never looking towards any of the beds either side. It smells of antiseptic. I keep my head down and focus on the smooth plastic flooring. He delivers me to a nurse behind a folding trestle table who informs me sharply that I will have to wait. I take a seat on a plastic chair, turn up the volume on my Motorola in case I get a shout and, fifteen minutes later, another doctor greets me. If I thought the first doc looked tired, I was wrong. This one looks like he hasn't ever slept in his life. He can barely focus. As he leads me, without explanation, deeper into the maze, he mutters at me, telling me his name is Roger.

'You caught me on my first break since Thursday. We've had so many patients we've run out of room. We haven't stopped . . .There've been a couple of amputations, children losing their arms, one of our men lost both legs . . .' He trails off, lost in thought. I'm not sure how to respond to this devastating news. We all know awful things happen out on the ground but we also know what an amazing job they do in this hospital.

He starts up again: 'It's just so busy, we barely have time to rest ourselves and, with so much going on, it's impossible to switch off when you leave this place.'

I was at university with trainee doctors and know how they start to learn to take what happens in their job in their stride; they have to deal with illness and death every day, but this doctor has probably seen more than his fair share of death and destruction, enough to last a thousand lifetimes. I can't imagine having to break it to one of the young lads on the ground that they will lose a limb. Or lose a colleague. Or have to go home and leave their friends behind to fight this horrible war without them.

A radiologist told me soon after I arrived that, if you had to get injured, Camp Bastion was the best place on earth to do it. On average, every casualty wheeled in is seen immediately by two consultants, two anaesthetists and a team of nurses. Care is immediate and of the highest quality. Senior doctors and medical specialists who are also members of the Territorial Army frequently do tours here in Bastion, and they told me that the foremost neurosurgeon in the UK is working in the hospital right here on camp. I had no idea, and feel proud that we're able to offer all this to our injured troops.

Roger and I sit down in a brightly lit operating theatre. It must be the only place in the hospital that isn't occupied by wounded soldiers.

'So, you're a pilot then?' he asks, clocking my outfit. 'Lynx?'

'Apache.'

He raises his eyebrows in surprise. 'The helicopters keep delivering the casualties. The British ones we've been treating, then sending straight to the UK to be with their families, but every bed is still full with Afghan National Army soldiers and civilians. We've seen the worst injuries so far in the last few days,' he continues, then finally turns to look at me. 'Anyway, what can I do for you?'

'Umm, I have a sore throat,' I say lamely.

Roger is much kinder than he could have been. He peers down my throat and asks me a series of questions.

'Yeah, it's a nasty case of tonsillitis,' he confirms and sends me away with handfuls of painkillers and antibiotics from his drawer.

When I ask, he tells me that I can keep flying if I want to. I do.

As I leave the hospital I can hear another Chinook landing on the helicopter landing site with more casualties for Roger and his team. A handful of medics rush out. One of our men lies on a stretcher and four men run with it towards the hospital tents. Another follows carrying a drip. I see their mouths moving as they hurriedly fill each other in on his injuries. Their faces show concern. Roger turns to look at the scene. I feel so guilty for stealing his one chance for ten minutes off.

It's very strange being somewhere where you can't help but consider your own mortality almost every day. At home, it never crosses my mind; not properly. I try not to dwell on it here, but it's tough when we see the men on the ground coming into contact with enemy troops every time we fly. The number of mortally wounded men is creeping up, and it's starting to scare me. I try to detach from it, but the knowledge sits deep inside me and refuses to shift. It's always there. I discuss it with no one. I'm scared that, if I open the door to my emotions, I just won't be able to shut it. It might be like a tidal wave, and I would just drown in it, and I can't afford to lose the focus I've worked so hard to build up. It's the only way to survive.

132

Despite the Taliban's best efforts so far, they've failed to bring an Apache down in Afghanistan. But it's a different story in Iraq. Since 2003, twenty-two Apaches have crashed, so the odds aren't too healthy. Everyone going out on operational duty is advised to write a will, and we discuss in our flights what we would do if we were shot down and surrounded by Taliban: would we want to be shot or left to try and escape. For me, thinking about a situation like that opens up a whole host of differences in the risks a woman would face compared to a man. As a woman, it's hard to know what they would do with me if I was ever caught. To Afghans, women are 'only for making children' so a woman doing this job would be almost impossible to comprehend. Maybe they'd be confused, maybe they'd argue among themselves or maybe they'd shoot me on the spot. In any case, I'd want to beat them to it. I've decided I'd give it everything I have and then save the last bullet for myself.

I don't want to look at the man on the stretcher. I turn the other way and get the hell out of there as fast as I can.

We circle above Kajaki in silence, watching. I can see the tiny figures creeping along the dirt tracks, every now and again making a dash for cover to defend themselves against the gunfire I can't hear.

Operation Volcano has been going for a couple of weeks now. It's a British operation to clear a village – twenty-five compounds near the Kajaki hydroelectric dam – which the Taliban are using as a command and control node. It has been a site of regular insurgent mortar attacks over the last two months, and civilians have been forced from their homes, leaving the dam largely unserviceable. The clearance is part of an ongoing operation to create a safe zone around the dam and allow engineers to re-enter the area and bring it back up to full power. Once they have done so, the dam will supply power to 1.8 million Afghans. This is the second time my team has been scheduled to watch ground troops.

The Marines are clearing the north-eastern sector of the town. I scan the familiar landmarks, occasionally reacting to prompts from Darwin.

'Looks like some movement at Rabbit Warren . . .'

I line up the crosshairs in my monocle with the Warren, an area we know to contain a number of underground tunnels. I slave the TADS to my head. A zoomed-in picture, magnified 127 times, fills the screens in front of me. The Warren is about ten kilometres away from the area in which Operation Volcano is currently in full swing, but we know this doesn't mean the danger is contained. 'I can't see anything . . .'

'Moving south down the road.'

Darwin can see so much detail with just the naked eye. He's tracking a guy in man-jammies who's on his own and heading towards the fight. I squint into the sight, trying to see if he has anything concealed under his robes, but can't make anything out.

Darwin swings us around and we head east. I have one final glance at our man walking south before he disappears behind us.

'Nope, can't see anything on him, Darwin.' Local guy, I guess, someone's husband heading into town to gossip with his buddies. I try to remember the last time someone told *me* a really juicy bit of gossip. That's the problem with having so few girls around – all the men just want to talk about work.

Back on scene, we can make out a line of Marines lying behind an area of raised ground while their commanders decide what to do next.

Darwin and I peer into the target and report back.

'It's a U-shaped compound, open side to the east,' I tell Widow Six Five. 'It's surrounded by high walls. Looks like the only opening is on the south-eastern corner.' He needs this information to assess where the Taliban might be hiding and how he is going to break in.

'Roger Ugly,' Widow says. 'Any movement?'

'None this time. If you're happy there are enemy in there we can give you a Hellfire through the roof.' I want to make sure we incapacitate the opposition before our troops get too close.

There's a pause while Widow checks with his commander. 'No Ugly, we'll do it ourselves this time.'

'God, I really want to do something,' I mutter under my breath.

I focus my attention back on to the Marines, scanning the area around them. As I see them prepare to launch their assault, I'm reminded for the thousandth time how brave and physically strong these men are. I feel a surge of pride that I am part of the same army.

Four Marines suddenly set off at a run towards an outbuilding on the eastern side of the main compound. They throw themselves down, and the next four get up and run past. They repeat this well-practised 'salt and pepper' manoeuvre until they are less than fifteen metres from the outbuilding. We follow their every move.

Out of nowhere, I see a Taliban figure appear on the far side of the building. We can't fire – he's too close to our troops.

'Shit, they won't be able to see him!' I shout to Darwin as I stab at the radio switches.

I tell Widow, but he's with the commander, a tactical safe distance from the assault team.

It's too late.

My breathing shallow, I zoom in with the TADS as close as I can. I want to scream at them to get out, but I'm voiceless. The figures are now lifesize. I hunch down to block out the glaring sun. In slow motion, I see one of the Marines get up and sprint to the building. The armed, scared enemy fighter is metres away, around the corner, his ancient rifle to his shoulder. Everything seems frozen – our Apache hanging as if suspended in molasses – as the two figures stalk towards each other. In a heartbeat, the British soldier and the Taliban fighter close on each other and the Taliban shoots the Marine point blank in the face.

The breath is punched out of me.

'Darwin, Darwin,' I garble. 'He just shot him . . .'

Darwin is calm and collected, as always. 'Do we have a guy down? Tell Widow.' He's been looking out of the window at the bigger picture and hasn't seen what I've seen.

'Widow Six Five, Ugly Five Four. There's a man down, shot point blank. The platoon is taking the shooter out now. No further threat.'

I watch the dead Marine's section advance and kill the Taliban behind the building with practised efficiency. They cluster around their mate's body and pull him back behind friendly troops. It's over so fast but, like in a car crash, it feels as though I had all the time in the world to stop it.

The Marines continue towards the main compound and I force myself back into the sights. The cockpit smells stale, of old sweat and bad breath. I want to get out. I've been on station in the past while we took friendly casualties, but I've never watched it happen close up before. I feel like someone needs to tell all the soldiers that the war is over now and everyone can go home. Surely they need a moment to regain their composure and think about the horrific thing that has just happened?

But of course there's no time for that. The Marines reach the high walls of the main compound and I watch the first assault team race through the gap at the southern corner.

'I can't believe they're just carrying on . . . How do they have the strength to do that?'

Darwin is updating HQ, so he doesn't hear.

I leave the TADS trained on the main compound, but my eyes flicker briefly towards the tiny figures gathered around the motionless body.

We stay on station as the Marines search the compound. When they are a clear distance away, Widow asks us to destroy the building, so the Taliban can't use it for their own purposes.

I send two Hellfires screaming towards it. A giant plume of smoke spirals up from the building and chunks of concrete spin into the air.

I'm relieved when we're called back to base soon afterwards.

On the return flight from a big mission, we're usually laughing and joking, trying to return ourselves to a normal state of mind. This time, we're both quiet, lost in our own thoughts.

Darwin wants to know what happened. I rewind the tape, and we watch the miniature figures run backwards at double speed across our screens. I feel I have to check that it really happened; that I really didn't have time to intervene.

'Was it bad?' Darwin asks.

I don't know how to describe it, so I sit in silence, waiting for the right moment to press 'play'.

I punch the innocent little black button and we let the aircraft guide itself through the sky as we sit, our attention riveted to the VCR playback. It's every bit as horrific as I remembered.

'Jesus . . .' It's all Darwin can muster. 'Jesus . . .'

We don't say another word for the rest of the journey.

Back at camp, there is the usual debrief. We watch the tape again, accompanied by the OC, an intelligence officer and a Mission Planning Station (MPS) operator, before it's impounded. I feel helpless, like I could've done something. I feel like a child who's been forbidden to look through a hole in a fence but does it anyway, then witnesses something so horrible she wishes she could take it all back.

I have no time to let the incident settle in my mind. I park it in one corner, as if it's in a Tupperware box in my brain behind that trapdoor; like all of the awful things that happen out here: plastic containers piled on top of each other in neat stacks, waiting to be tipped over.

Flying through the woolly grey sky above the bleak Afghan desert, I see a blanket of smoke in the distance, smothering

137

the land beneath it. I can almost taste the electricity in the air. The cockpit is noisy and cramped. The consoles on either side of my seat push against my thighs in the darkness, and I get a sense that it's the calm before the storm; I can hear the *thud-thud-thud* as blood whirs around my head. Voices on the net – our communications system – are urgent and stressed.

Operation Glacier received the thumbs-up to go noisy just days earlier. The whole main supply route has been carefully mapped by intelligence forces; they've also located tunnel systems and ammo dumps. The aim is to complete the whole series of hits in a month, working from the south northwards. This is the second stage. The Apaches are tasked overhead in every offensive.

They're thinking what I'm thinking. This mission is different. This is gonna be big.

I can see the shadowy outline of Nick's aircraft a kilometre away. There's a strange comfort in operating as a pair, although in practical terms we'll always be too far away from each other to give any real mutual support. Nick radios in with the plan – his deep voice sounds fired up.

'You guys stick to the north of the fort, working directly with the head controller on the ground, we'll stay to the south where the troops are.'

'Roger.'

It's 4 a.m., and we're on a deliberate mission to cover the Royal Marines' attack on a compound called Jugroom Fort in Garmsir – a Taliban command headquarters for insurgent activity across the district that holds sixty fighters and a huge store of weapons. I can see the four watchtowers guarding the fort, just as our intelligence reported. The area has been under surveillance for months. They've watched how the cell operates – who comes and goes, what weapons and machinery they have inside, and located the entrances and exit points.

Now the time has come to strike.

As we approach, the sky is a hive of activity. A stack of

aircraft is already on the scene and engaging. American B1 bombers drop thousand- and two thousand-pound bombs, sending up clouds of dark grey smoke, choking our line of sight and sending shockwaves through our Apache's cockpit. Voices on the net collide inside my head. Instructions flood in from HQ as they watch images from the Unmanned Aerial Vehicles (UAVs) that patrol invisibly overhead.

From our earlier briefing, we know that, after the full-on assault by air, a platoon of Marines from Zulu Company is preparing to storm the compound at first light. They plan to plant an ISAF (International Security Assistance Force) flag on the ramparts, hoping that the symbolic message will draw out any of the bastards who've been hiding in the underground tunnels. They will then withdraw, leaving the Apaches to pick off the rest, piece by piece.

The Marines are already lined up in their armoured Vikings; ready to move across the river on the western side of the fort. Twelve vehicles hold over a hundred sweating, anxious, battle-hardened commandos. They vanish into the water one by one and emerge glistening into enemy territory on the other side. We were put into enforced rest the day before at four in the after-noon. I spent most of the time staring at the ceiling of our accom-modation tent, listening to the chorus of snores, farts and artillery explosions but, fifteen hours later, as we fly back to the action, I can feel the adrenaline starting to surge through my veins like a drug. I feel so alert; it's as if I could stay awake for ever.

The dawn light is rising, and the sky is beautiful – a swirling mix of blues, browns and oranges. It almost feels as if we're the only people in the world as we fly on towards to the battle scene.

The area around Jugroom is devastated; angry red fires flare across the landscape below us. Thick fingers of smoke reach upwards, grasping at the sky.

Darwin surveys the damage. 'Someone's been having fun. There's hardly anything left for us.'

The net is busy now, and so many TICs are going on that our controller decides to split us and our wing, Ugly Five Two – each of us working with two JTACs. It's chaos on the ground, and they need us both pulling the trigger.

A familiar thumping headache starts to build, caused by hours of hunching my shoulders to look into the TADs. I grab my water bottle and gulp as I dial in the first frequency.

A voice breaks through the stillness – a confident Brummie voice I have come to trust. I don't know Widow Eight Zero by sight, but he's one of the best JTACs out here. I imagine him tearing across the dusty earth below, surrounded by his platoon, plugged into his radio, summoning us. It's so strange to be able to trust someone that I've never actually laid eyes upon. I could pass him in the cookhouse and would never know – yet up here I feel I know him. I'll do anything he asks; give him any help he needs. Tonight he's controlling the whole battle, and he tells us to push straight to Knightrider Five Six who needs our help.

'Thank God he's on,' my co-pilot says. Glancing in my mirror, I can see Darwin's silhouette, and his smile gleaming in the dark.

Knightrider Five Six is on the move and gasping for breath. 'Ugly Five Four, thank God you're here huh, huh . . . we're taking fire from, huh, huh . . . the area of the southern towers.'

He gives me a grid, but I'm already looking into the sector.

'Both the southern towers are down,' I tell him. I long to reassure him or crack a joke to ease the tension but I can't waste time with anything other than the factual details.

He's giving me more grids, and I picture him running along with his 100lbs of equipment at the same time as trying to make a series of calculations from his map.

'Can you give me a talk-on from the south-eastern tower?' We both know where the tower is.

'We're being mortared from the large glass-roofed building in the courtyard to the north-east of south-east tower . . .'

We're flying north, and my sight is looking south-west . . .
so if I move my sight roughly downwards . . . There it is!

'Does it have a large tree at the . . .' I turn my head in the
cockpit, trying to orientate.

'South,' Darwin prompts through the intercom.

'. . . southern side?' I finish to Knightrider Five Six.

'That's the one!' he yells. His voice is hoarse from the dust
and from shouting; he can barely hear us over the gunfire.

My ears are ringing.

He asks us to engage fast. I'm soaked with sweat; it runs down
my face and neck collecting in a pool on my collarbone and
dribbling down my back into my oversized, greying M&S pants.
Despite the heat, I consider that, if I'd worn the expensive
Christmas knickers Jake sent me, maybe I wouldn't have a wedgie
right now. God knows what I think I'm saving them for.

Knightrider Five Six stops taking incoming fire after Darwin
and I wheel round and launch a Hellfire into the building, but
there are at least three TICs going on at any one time and only
two Apaches. We don't get a chance to draw breath.

Now Widow Eight Three is in trouble – the ground is a
terrifying mass of smoke and tracer fire and the Taliban have
swarmed the area.

'Ugly Five Four, can you see any enemy in the north-western
corner of the complex at grid 250835? We're taking fire.'

I know; I can hear the rounds punching through the air,
punctuating his words.

I see a white, man-shaped hot spot against the dawn-coloured
sand. Widow said there were no friendlies there. I let off twenty
rounds, and he rolls around on the ground, then another forty
at the five men in a nearby trench who move when I shoot
their sniper.

I move my attention away as Knightrider Five Six comes
back on to the net. 'We need a flechette at 41SPR28901055.'
I can hear him wheeze as he inhales.

The rocket has eighty six-inch darts inside it, and the results can be devastating. We know they're in trouble but, at just a few hundred metres, Knightrider and his men are too close for comfort.

'You're too near. I'll try and suppress them with gun,' I radio back, punching in the grid with bruised fingers and cursing the fact that I'm running out of paper to write these hundreds of numbers on. My finger closes around the trigger and a hundred bullets hammer towards the ground. It seems to do the trick, and there follow three minutes of silence.

Ugly Five Two fires two Semi-Active Laser (SAL) missiles into a building and a B1 bomber pulls into the stack above us, preparing to deliver another thousand-pounder. Widow Eight Zero pushes us west, over the river, to allow the B1 to drop it on the ruined fort.

'How can there be anywhere left for them to hide?'

'Ugly Five Four, this is Five Two, send sitrep.' I fill Nick in on what we've been up to, although he's listened in to Darwin's reports on the HQ net.

'Roger.'

I can hear the hammering of their 30mm in the background. 'We're *tat-tat-tat* engaging now on the eastern bank. Stay west.'

The JTAC is letting the Apache pair get on with it, deconflicting ourselves at the bottom of the stack; he knows us by voice and has more immediate concerns. We move further west so Ugly Five Two can dive and drop; a shockwave reverberates through the aircraft.

The Boss radios in and tells us that the VHR flight is coming to relieve us.

'Ugly Five Two and Five Three, this is Zero Alpha. I'm sending the VHR to you now. They will relieve you overhead Garmsir so you can return to base for fuel. I don't want to leave the troops with no cover while you fly back, refuel and return – that'll take almost ninety minutes.'

He's taken the decision now to ensure that Widow has constant Apache cover overhead.

Knightrider Five Six and his men are taking fire again. It's relentless.

'It's the building, at 41SPR24418302,' he says, rifle fire popping in the background. These men really are in hell. I locate the building, but I can no longer hear him. The radios out here are notorious for cutting out when the troops on the ground are on the move.

I call up the other JTAC. 'Widow Eight Three, this is Ugly Five Four, are you happy for me to engage on 24418302?' I'm shouting now.

No answer.

'Any Widow or Knightrider, this is Ugly Five Four.'

Nothing.

I can't fire until I'm given clearance. There could be friendlies or civilians nearby, or another aircraft moving in.

'Ug . . . Kn . . . krrrrrrrrrrr . . .'

'Knightrider, this is Ugly Five Four,' I holler. 'I need clearance on 24418302.'

Darwin winces and turns his volume down; he's on another call on a different radio.

The radio fills with noises of gunfire, and it sounds as though Knightrider is about to transmit something, but all I can hear is him shouting at someone else on the ground. My whole body is tensed, waiting for him to release his radio pressle so I can transmit down to him.

'No! Mate, just tell them to keep the fucking rounds going down towards the flashes. I fucking know! . . . Ugly?'

'Loud and clear,' I respond, and repeat my request for clearance all in one breath, scared of losing comms with him again.

'Cleared to engage, Ugly. Any leakers are all yours as well.'

My vision greys out as I curl my fingers once again around the trigger. It slams into the building. Huge charcoal clouds obscure the target. I'll come back and look later. Knightrider Five Six tells me the shooting has stopped, and that's enough for now.

143

The men on the ground have now been under fire for seven hours. Being bombarded like that for so long, each instant is like that split-second moment when you're driving along without a care in the world, radio playing, deep in thought and another car or a bike comes in front of you, or towards you. You swerve to miss it and everything goes into slow motion. Your heart leaps into your mouth, adrenaline fires through every vein, your mouth is so dry you can barely move your tongue. Your thinking is clouded with pumping fear, you can't quite believe it's really happening. And then the threat is gone, you've swerved away, or they have. It's over. I try to imagine this feeling of life-threatening fear and confusion lasting seven hours. I don't know how they do it. I'm sure I would expire in about ten minutes. The enemy must be stronger than we imagined. My fuel is getting low and I know that, any minute now, the green warning light will flash up. There's no sign of an end to this battle.

Ugly Five Zero and Five One arrive on station perfectly on cue. We hightail it back to Bastion, with just enough juice to get us home.

Ten minutes into our journey back, one of the radios crackles and we hear a distant conversation between the Chinook crews and the Widow.

'This is Lifter Three Zero. Confirm there are only four casualties. We were told it was five.'

There is a pause from the JTAC. 'Roger. Wait'

Just as the radios are petering out, we hear Widow again.

'Lifter Three Zero, this is Widow Eight Zero. Sunray just confirmed there were four casualties.'

The air is still cool when we arrive back at Bastion to refuel. I fling open the cockpit door and enjoy the feel of the gentle breeze as it licks my face.

The groundcrew rush to the empty aircraft, reloading us with ammunition and refuelling the tank.

'Do you think we'll go again?' I ask Darwin.

'I hope so.'

We're both wondering about food and a pee break.

One of the groundies taps on the cockpit door. It's only 7 a.m., but his face is already covered in a film of dust. 'Breakfast's up, ma'am.'

A flimsy tray is poked through the hatch: a piece of bacon, a sausage, some sweaty scrambled egg, a hash brown and some beans, along with steaming, watery tea in a polystyrene cup.

I feel like I haven't seen tea for weeks.

'Can I swap my bacon for your hash brown?' I ask Darwin.

'No.' He grins, a glint of grease around his mouth.

I'm desperate to go to the toilet – I know I'll find it hard to concentrate back on station if I don't. But time is short; we've been told we're off again imminently. I hop out of the cockpit. My legs feel like jelly as my feet land on the corrugated aluminium runway after four hours of near-paralysis in the cockpit. It wouldn't be the first time they've buckled under the weight of my kit. I run as quickly as possible towards the row of grime-covered grim-looking Portaloos at the side of the runway, my breathing confined by my tight body armour. I can practically see the stench surrounding them, like a halo around the ancient blue boxes. My pistol bashes the already bruised place on my hip and my aircrew knife whacks against the side of my boot.

Even though the Portaloos are far worse than they could be at any festival, in any Third World country or service station, I've come to the conclusion that they're still my favourite place at Bastion. They smell even worse than the cesspit at Kandahar and boast a selection of graphic porn taped to the walls, along with a slick film of urine, sweat and festering grime – but they do provide me with somewhere to be on my own. As long as I avoid the 'brown meniscus' as we call it, I can get a whole cubic metre of space to myself.

I rip off layer upon layer of clothing and drop them on the

piss-stained floor. I glance at my watch. The men get impatient when I take ages, and I don't want to annoy Darwin – but while the men just unzip two inches of material, everything has to come off for me to get to my all-in-one flying suit.

When I return, we get word on the radio that the VHR flight has everything under control. We close down the aircraft in record time, and I join Nick, Darwin and FOG on the pallets outside the REME hangar, where they're sharing two cups of lukewarm tea. I slot in silently and take one of the cups as it's passed around. We're all knackered. In England, a two-hour flight is considered enough to tire you out just because of the intense concentration required. Here, the flying is five times as tiring and it can last all day – there's more of it to come later today, I'm sure. My body is limp from the adrenaline tides, my head throbs menacingly and my vision is slightly blurred from focusing on the TADS.

We're all lost in our own thoughts for a while – I think about what my Jake might be doing at home; the boys are no doubt reliving the fight in their heads.

The calm scene is shattered as an engineer comes slamming through the heavy plastic doors of the hangar shouting for Nick.

'You're off! Launch asap! From Zero.'

We don't need to respond verbally; we immediately start running to the cabs, FOG thrusting the empty tea cup at the engineer. The groundies see us sprinting and follow us, trailing their comms leads in their wake.

'I wonder what's happened now?' Darwin pants as he straps in and reaches for the engine levers. It's clearly something major, or we would've had more information from base and more time to prepare.

The Boss updates us as we lift.

Knightrider Five Six's group was hit by a volley of machinegun fire as it moved towards the fort. They were forced to with-draw, as they had five serious casualties and it was getting light. That was the radio conversation we were listening to as we headed back to Bastion. But what we didn't know was that, as the men regrouped on the far side of the river, they discovered that one of the Marines, Lance Corporal Mathew Ford, was missing from the group of casualties the Chinook was meant to pick up.

Everyone knows the horror stories of what the Taliban do to dead troops or prisoners-of-war. Two weeks before, we had received intelligence that their latest plan, if they caught a coali-tion soldier, was to set up a live internet broadcast and skin him, or her, alive.

A shiver runs through me. I feel the familiar rush of adren-aline as the blood flies to my head, focusing every morsel of my attention. My mouth goes dry and I fight the urge to cough.

Every ISTAR (which stands for intelligence, surveillance, target acquisition and reconnaissance force, essentially acting as our eyes and ears in the air and on the ground) asset avail-able has been scouring the area for him, and now he has been spotted by the back-seater of Ugly Five One. He's beside the wall of the fort, a small S-shaped figure in the sights, motion-less but still giving off warmth.

Every resource available is mustered to get him back. A plan has been hatched to use Viking vehicles to retrieve him.

'God, I hope they're not too late. As soon as the Taliban get their grubby hands on him, they'll move him away as fast as they can so he's out of sight – we haven't got long,' Darwin mutters to himself

We fly as fast as possible towards Garmsir, but it seems to take for ever. The seconds tick past agonizingly slowly, like a metronome in my helmet. Darwin and I are quiet, tired and saving our energy for the fight.

As we come into radio range, we listen in to the frantic

chorus of voices directing and discussing. Face, the commander of the opposite flight, thinks there is a better way to retrieve the injured soldier. The most experienced pilot in the squadron, Face is a qualified helicopter instructor and polices us both on the ground and in the sky. He never misses an opportunity to assert himself and talks so much I sometimes hear his voice in my head while I'm on the loo.

'Of course, the way you did it worked but I, myself, personally, would've taken that shot this way . . .'

Face is short and petite, and his clothing and rig are always immaculate. On his starched flying suits he wears every possible badge to mark himself out – I wonder what the Taliban would make of him if the worst were to happen: I always end up with a mental picture of him talking them to a standstill by painstakingly explaining each and every badge. However, as it happens, he's earned every one of his decorations with hard slog. The one glaringly obvious exception to his perfect appearance is his curly mop of *The Simpsons'* Sideshow Bob dark hair, which grows upwards and outwards but never down. There's no doubt about it, though – we all respect his opinion and, as far as flying matters go, his word is law. He argues that the Viking plan may cost more men. It would also take almost two hours to prepare the equipment.

Face's plan is a bold one. He suggests landing within the enemy compound, strapping the injured man to the Apache and carrying him to safety; the rescue could start immediately.

I know Face won't have made the suggestion lightly.

A conversation ensues between Face and the Boss, who is back at base. The Boss is reluctant to risk the assets and concerned about the possibility of what may happen if it goes wrong. If they go down, it's the lives of four men on the line, not to mention £92 million's-worth of Apache.

But Face is resolute.

'Sir, the ground troops are nowhere near ready to cross. He

needs to be moved *now*. If I land, can I just confirm I will be disobeying a direct order?'

'Affirmative. You will be. You can't land both aircraft, you have no top cover.'

There's a long pause. The Boss trusts his team, but this is a tough call – the stakes are high. 'Don't do anything until the other flight arrives. I have no situational awareness, and you have the bigger picture. If you think it will work, you'll need permission from the ground commander.'

'Roger. Thank you.'

Minutes later, the Boss tells us the commanding officer on the ground has given them the nod of approval.

'Ugly Five Four, Ugly Five One has had approval from Charlie Oscar. Wait out for more details.' He's nervous; I can tell. Half his squadron are putting themselves right in the middle of the hornet's nest.

Face briefs his flight as we listen in. He sounds authoritative, but there is a tone of urgency in the pitch of his voice, which is higher and more breathy than usual.

'Ugly Five One, you and I will land together at the Marines' location – you follow me. Your back seat will get out, rotors running, and brief up four guys who are willing to come with us. Strap them on, two per cab, and we'll fly over the river and land on the southern side of the fort close to the casualty. They jump off, grab the casualty, strap him on as well, and we'll fly back. I'll ask Ugly Five Two's flight to give us top cover.'

We practised strapping men to the side of an Apache in training back in England, but it's never been done for real. The two helicopters will be extremely vulnerable while they're on the ground, which is where our flight comes in. As Face's flight lands in the desert to pick up the rescue party, Nick briefs me up. 'You take everything to the west of the river.' There are no enemy or friendlies there, just open ground and a small, deserted village.

'Provide covering fire as Five Zero and Five One fly in; try and draw the Taliban's attention to you.'

We are the decoys – a welcome distraction from the real action.

This is it Madison, this is your test.

I'm so glad Darwin is with me – I look into the rear-view mirror and feel reassured by his steady confidence. I see his face in profile, his jaw set hard as he surveys the area Nick has given us.

We start hammering towards the desert floor hard and fast. Face's flight lifts and I watch on the TADS as they cross over the river, just a fraction above the surface.

'Let's do it,' Darwin says.

We fly as low to the ground as we can, just on the western side of the river, while Ugly Five Zero and Five One land on.

Please let us get to him in time.

I can only spare a fraction of my attention for what the other Apaches are doing; we have enough on our plates flying at less than one hundred feet, with Darwin firing 30mm with his helmet sight and me keeping the TADS slaved to the area and watching for enemy.

As I glance quickly over on our third pass, firing gun into the hazy nothingness, I see something unsettling – a British soldier or a pilot running along the bank of the river, kicking up the dust with his heels. I see tracer fire flash metres from his helmet. He's heading deeper into the swathes of enemy territory.

What the hell? Who is that? Christ, this is all going wrong . . .

Then the radio booms into my head; it's Face's panic-stricken voice, loud and thin. It feels as if the cab has suddenly started to smell, of sweat and panic.

'Ugly Five Four, we need protective fire! We're sitting ducks, we're receiving fire. My back-seater's jumped out and I'm taking effective fire close range. He's dived out and locked the collective down – I can't move! Hurry! Get some fucking fire down!'

Shit. He sounds terrified.

Now I'm scared. Something has gone wrong. Vidal, the pilot who was flying with Face, must've got out with the four Marines, locking down the collective controls as he went.

I swallow hard. My mouth is dry and tastes sour.

Darwin is already flying over the river. I orientate myself, locating Face's helicopter and the nearest building where the most concentrated fire appears to be coming from. I steer the TADS across the devastated fort while my fingers move through the familiar sequence of button pushes to get our missiles ready. We go straight into a missile run without telling anyone on the radios – there's no time. Face is really shouting. He must be in a bad way.

'I'm a sitting duck, I'm a sitting duck.' His voice penetrates my skull, and I know I'll remember these radio calls for ever.

I fire two missiles at point-blank range into the room where the muzzle flashes are spitting from. They stop momentarily and we reset, just as Face tells us they have started again.

'They're firing again. I can't get them with gun.' The only protection he has is the cannon, which can fire at point-blank range through 90 degrees but no further.

One enemy RPG. That's all it would take.

I struggle to get the missiles off at such close quarters.

'Get some fucking fire down!' Darwin is shouting from the back seat.

I'm wildly squeezing the laser and the weapon trigger, willing something to come off the rails. I feel like I'm watching a video of myself on fast-forward. After sending another missile through the roof of the building, our final one slams into the adjacent window, and the firing stops.

There's a brief respite as we fly underneath the blanket of smog I'd been staring at that morning. It looks like a macabre cartoon of a warzone: rubble, smoke, tracer, tiny bodies and plumes of angry fire.

What a sorry mess. Only our rockets left now.

Darwin sets up for a run just to the east of where the two helicopters are still sitting on the ground, into a dense line of trees. I long to look at the two Apaches, find out what's going on, but I can't spare the concentration. We fire half our rockets, then repeat the manoeuvre just to the north. They come out in pairs, shooting forwards with their arses on fire. Suddenly an enemy RPG shoots past my Perspex window.

What the fuck? Fuck, help, fuck.

My head spins round, and I realize we're barely higher than the treetops. I can practically look through the windows of the nearby buildings.

As I send the final flechette rockets into the distance, Face's flight lifts off in a huge cloud of dust and grit. As soon as they're away, Darwin pulls max power and climbs away to the relative safety of two thousand feet.

Thank fuck for that.

'We're Winchester,' I tell him, with a huge exhalation of pent-up breath. It means we're out of ammo. (The saying dates back to the First World War: when biplane pilots had nothing left to fire, they reached for their Winchester Repeaters. No one has yet gone Winchester in an Apache.)

'Hello Five Two, this is Five Three pulling up, Winchester,' I tell Nick.

'Blimey. Not bad for a six-minute sortie.' He sounds as relieved as we do that the other Apaches are out of there.

The other flight is dangerously low on fuel, so we wait until the Chinook carrying Mathew Ford is on its way before we leave the station and follow Nick home.

I feel numb with exhaustion.

Back at camp, I know that a very lengthy debrief awaits me, but I'm just knackered. Eleven hours in the cockpit and more than nine of hard flying has finished me off, and I want to nip to the gym. I'm mentally exhausted, and I know it's the only place where I can be on my own with my thoughts and burn off some adrenaline while I'm at it. Then I'll crash out in bed and hopefully sleep.

Luckily for me, Face's flight is already tightly locked into the TPF, and the place is deserted, as every senior officer at JHF is discussing the rescue, so we have time to pause for thought.

News slowly trickles to us via one of the on-duty watch-keepers: Mathew Ford didn't make it. No one knows the precise details. No doubt there will be an investigation, but the fact remains that he's dead. The knowledge sits heavily with me and I fight the urge to shout and be angry. It just seems so unfair. I know Face's flight will be gutted; we all feel totally empty. At least the Taliban don't have his body – but every loss of life is one too many. I try not to think about what sort of man he might've been, or who he's left behind. I battle to try and think of him as just another name to be added to the brass war memorial on camp.

Another name.

I think of my loved ones – family, friends, Jake. I picture his smiling eyes and broad shoulders.

The huge metal doors clank shut as we enter the debrief room a while later. It's set out like a classroom, and the men sit with their legs wide open as we look through our gun tape and talk through our actions – where and what went through our minds when we fired, how we could've worked better, what we could've done differently.

I find out that the figure I saw running up the river was Vidal, one of the guys in the other flight. In the confusion, the two Marines had become disorientated and run the wrong way. Vidal, who got his nickname because of his slightly thinning bonce, had got out to help but had also become confused, and led two of the volunteers the wrong way, only realizing it when he came face to face with a group of rifle-brandishing Taliban. A typical Newcastle lad, he is definitely one of the boys, but in the air he is thoroughly serious. I can't imagine how terrified he must've been. They made it back to help strap Mathew on and get themselves out of there, quick-time. And, despite their unfortunate diversion, they executed the plan to perfection.

As always, I get a bit of a shock when I start to speak about my role. My voice, an octave higher than everyone else's, seems thin and ridiculous.

I fast-forward through what I did, giving short explanations, trying hard to speak with conviction. Everyone else seems to want to draw it out. I hate it – seeing bits of arms, legs and heads scattered across the battlefield. I'm sick of seeing dead people – our dead people, anyway.

I want to ring Jake, but I know I can't. 'Operation Minimize' is on, which means the satellite phones and internet are out of use until Ford's next-of-kin have been notified about his death. It's on loads, at least twice a week. It's just another sad reminder of what is really happening out here.

Vidal comes over during a break in the debrief, puts his arm around Face and slaps him hard on the back.

'I wasn't going to let my getaway vehicle go, like,' he laughs in his broad Geordie accent.

Face grins. 'You bastard.'

They're walking away when I hear Vidal shout my name. I look round.

'Oh, and ma'am . . . Face and I, like, we've decided your new tac sign can be Sniper.'

The hours and days after Jugroom Fort are confused. The new commanding officer, the Boss's new boss, has only been in the role for a couple of weeks, and flew over from Kandahar straight after the event to give Face's flight and the Boss a large

Me at Camp Bastion with a
typical mission load

Me in a Squirrel Helicopter
during flying training

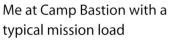

Desert/green zone between
Sangin and Gereshk

Apache carrying 16 Hellfire missiles

Chinook landing behind Apache at FOB Dwyer

An Apache firing at night

My Apache
as seen by
my wing man

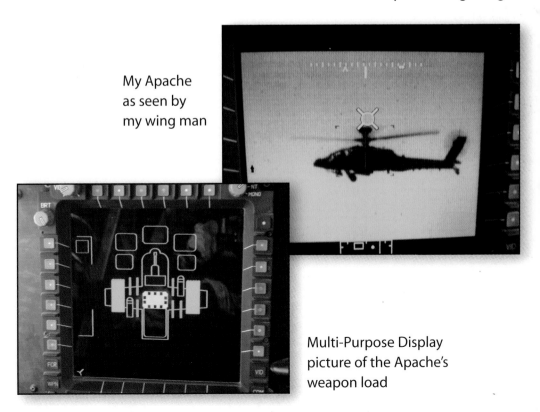

Multi-Purpose Display
picture of the Apache's
weapon load

Me conducting the daily walk round of my cab

Me with some un-put-downable reading material

Playing "kneeboard hangman" while waiting on Very High Readiness for hours

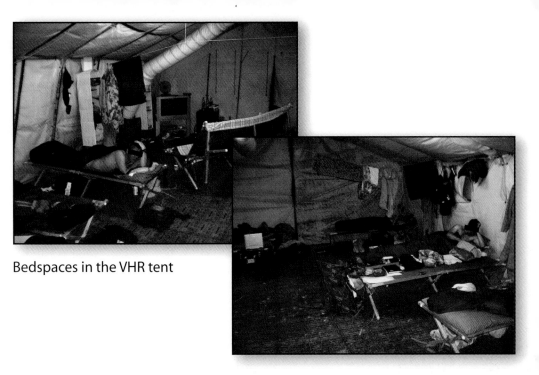

Bedspaces in the VHR tent

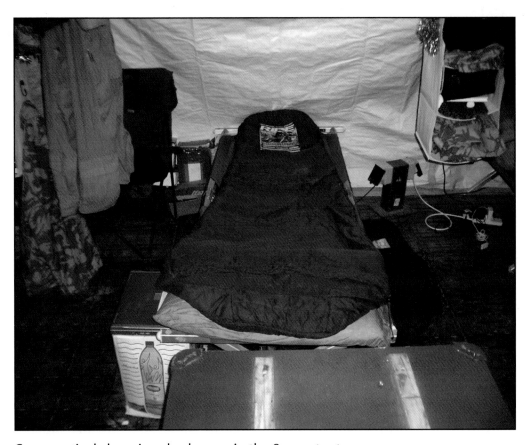

Comparatively luxurious bed space in the 8-man tents

Me with pistol, porn and illegal booze at our 2006 Squadron Christmas Party

The dusty gym at FOB Dwyer

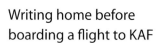

Writing home before boarding a flight to KAF

A Chinook, laden with soldiers, kit and mail

…and with the maximum number of troops

The memorial outside the Joint Helicopter Force at Camp Bastion

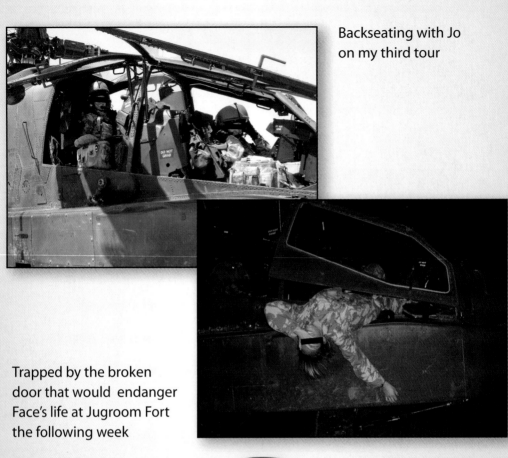

Backseating with Jo on my third tour

Trapped by the broken door that would endanger Face's life at Jugroom Fort the following week

656 Squadron Aircrew

bollocking, but his word is eventually overturned by the Brigadier. I find myself pondering on the deaths of Mathew Ford and the Marine all the time; when I'm on the loo, when I'm eating meals, reading my book. The only time I don't and can't think about them is when I am in the air and my brain is working too hard. The questions whir round and round and make me feel constantly sick. I feel emotionally crippled, but I know I can't let my guard down, and for that reason I just keep on, blindly, in my routine, trying to do the best job I can.

There's a mountain of paperwork to get through, as is the case with any mortality in theatre: the pilots who landed on the ground are interviewed and the Boss writes a long statement. We all wish that, just for a while, it could all be kept secret, giving Mathew's family time to grieve, but just twenty-four hours afterwards, it's in every British newspaper and on TV news programmes across the world. After minimize is off I receive a flurry of emails from friends asking me if I was involved. The day after the mission I have emails from Mum, Dad, Jake and Mia saying they'd seen it in the news and was I involved? Am I OK? What happened? We watch the gun tapes again. The FLIR had picked up a heat source for Mathew throughout, and the group spends a lot of time reassuring each other that everyone made the right decisions, took the right actions. We also sit through the feed from the Nimrod, which was patrolling above throughout, and see the scores of Taliban, up to a hundred of them, hiding in a long drainage ditch down the eastern side of the fort. Darwin and I watch our gun tape again, and I'm shocked to see how many RPGs and volleys of tracer fire miss our aircraft by inches. It's a small miracle that, of all the aircraft that left Bastion that day, not a single one came back with a bullet hole in it. No physical damage was sustained, but the emotional battering was enormous.

We are put on enforced rest, and the boys talk over and over the incident. There's a lot of back-slapping and hand-shaking.

I shake so many hands I'm sure I clutch the same ones at least three times over. I hate the fact that I'm forced to relive it over and over again, yet elated that I was part of a team that did well; that I have truly been accepted as one of the gang. I allow myself to be swept along with the compliments like a leaf in the wind. But in other ways, I feel so tired of it all. I'm exhausted.

A week after the rescue, I walk into the squadron rest tent and the TV is on. A few people are crowded around watching. I join the throng to see what's on. It's a documentary about the lives of some of the Marines out here. The camera follows them as they go about their everyday lives as they train for war. Suddenly I recognize one of the stars of the show. Despite the fact that the documentary mentions the date and place of his death, it takes me a while to cotton on to the fact that the lively, funny, healthy-looking man on the screen is the man who died in an instant, before my eyes, behind a dusty outhouse. The realization dawns on me like a punch in the stomach. I long to reach into the TV screen and pull his smiling, brave, handsome face out. Nausea rushes through me and I want to scratch at my skin. I feel horribly unsteady on my feet. Suddenly the credits are rolling and I am walking away; I have to get out of there, into the fresh air.

I emerge blinking into the bright sunlight at the back of the tent and fall into a nearby chair. Resting my head in my hands, I tell myself to hold it together. I concentrate hard on my breathing until it slows and my vision comes back into focus.

I tell myself to stop thinking about it. I can't let it get me down, affect me in this way, or else I'll never make it through the rest of my time here. I shake myself off, get up and head back to my accommodation tent.

FOG is sitting on his bed watching a film on his computer and listening on headphones. He waves and points towards my cot.

There's a package on my pillow. It's from Mia. I open the note and pull out a wedding magazine, a new book by Marian Keyes and some Haribo.

Madison, I've been thinking about you a lot recently. How are you? I'm still thinking a lot about what I read in the paper. I know you might not be able to talk about it, but just let me know you're OK . . .

I've got great news. I got the job. Woo hoo! Showbiz, here I come! My first interview is in three days with David Hasselhoff. I've got him for an hour – and it's in a hotel. Eeek! Was it you who still has your childhood *Knightrider* duvet? Any ideas what I should ask? Mum says hi. How are your folks? Hope all is good. Miss you xxx

I open the magazine. It's the perfect distraction in my confused and morbid state of mind. I touch the glossy paper and start flicking . . .

The following day, I'm more relieved than ever to be getting out of Bastion. The flightline looms ahead of us in the grey morning, the tall, dusty hangars containing, among other things, the squadron's most valued possession – the ping-pong table. Beyond them, the two runways stretch across the horizon like two long, grey tongues reaching out to lick the mountains in the distance.

Darwin and I trudge up towards our destination, our leaden legs tripping over the uneven, coffee-coloured ground. I can't wait to get to Kandahar; I can already taste the fresh fruit that awaits me in the expansive American dining facility.

'It's just too bad we have to take all this stuff with us!' Darwin says when we finally arrive at the hangar, which contains all our kit. He gasps as he unloads his locker and begins weighing himself down with bags. I'm too busy struggling with my carbine sling to comment. I've got my long black issue grip bag on my back, which has ammunition, rations and water in it and weighs about 50lbs. My helmet bag digs into my shoulder; it bulges with maps, flight reference cards, my kneeboard and various other bits of kit. My go-bag is on my other shoulder, packed with more ammunition and water – damn heavy, but you never leave home without it. I pick up my LCJ with one free hand; and with the other I grab my pistol, body armour and combat helmet, then slam my locker shut with a toe. I bend over very slowly to retrieve my carbine from the floor. As I crouch down, my fingertips stretch slowly closer to the carbine's metal grip and I feel my heavy load starting to shift off centre. I try to snatch myself upright to catch it all, but it's too late. My helmet bag slides off my shoulder and my pistol swings around to crack me in the shin.

'Bugger! I don't know how the soldiers do it,' I say to Darwin, not for the first time. They carry this amount of kit around all the time, in every situation imaginable. God knows how – they must be superhuman.

The watchkeeper tells us the Chinook might be too busy to take us, but we're prepared to wait on the off chance; the Chinook crews normally just throw us in the jump seat when they're full, because we're pilots. We need the break in Kandahar more than ever and there's not another flight going until the wee hours of tomorrow.

Fully loaded, we make our way carefully towards the Chinook flightline. It's to the north, towards the edge of the airfield, and the going is difficult. Large pebbles trip us up all the way, and by the time we finally get to the HLS, I'm sweating big time. Darwin sits neatly on his Bergen, looking soldierly, and lights a cigarette.

I collapse in a heap on top of all my kit and pant. Three minutes later, the Chinook lands in a hurricane of dust and aviation fumes, and the loadmaster pulls up his helmet visor and beckons us on board. Darwin stamps out his perfectly timed cigarette, I grab my kit as quickly as possible, and we struggle up the ramp into the Chinook's belly.

As my eyes adjust I understand what the watchkeeper was saying: the helicopter is stacked from floor to ceiling with equipment – Bergens, grip bags, ammunition, water and mail destined for the FOBs in the region. Thirty-odd soldiers are squeezed down either side of the mountain of kit, sleeping or trying to listen to their iPods over the roar of the engines. Everyone is waiting for us, so I dump my kit at the ramp and start climbing over the piles of equipment towards the only seat I see free in the murky darkness. I spin myself around on top of a box of rations and wedge myself backwards into the webbing seat, feeling its metal edge dig into my backside. Finally in, I tighten my body armour and rest my head back on the wall of the helicopter, glad to be on board.

Twenty minutes later, the Chinook begins its abrupt descent into our first drop-off location. My stomach turns in a not unpleasant, fairground-ride kind of way with the sudden drop in altitude then, before I know it, we slap down hard, and the loadie shouts, 'Lash,' prompting five or six soldiers to rouse themselves from sleep, unwedge bags from the mountain as if it were some sort of game of Jenga and stumble out of the back into the FOB at Lashkagar.

We do another two drop-offs, but both times I'm asleep for all but the final landing bump at each location. I drift off even as lines of laden soldiers march out over my tired legs, carrying with them various items salvaged from the piles of equipment.

At Kandahar, Darwin and I stay on board while the remaining passengers disembark, and I snooze for another five minutes, dimly aware of the sound of the massive rotors slowing to a stop and then the engines closing down. In the silence that follows I rouse myself, rub my eyes and throw a loose ration box at Darwin to wake him. We join the loadies stowing the rest of the kit in the Chinook aircrew Land Rover at the bottom of the ramp. Finally we shove our bags on top of the mound and jump into the trailer.

The drive across the flightline here is now mundanely familiar; a huge desert of white concrete stretches in both directions, radiating dusty heat and packed with Chinooks, Lynx and Apaches, as well as Black Hawks, Kiowas, CH53s, Halos and dozens of other types of helicopters. From here, the fixed-wing dispersals are out of sight, but the whole parking area spans almost two miles.

We hitch a ride to the JHF building and jump out, then nip inside.

'Air-testing at 3 p.m.' The engineers look expectantly at us. We smile sweetly back, groaning underneath our breath. Admin done, we thank the Chinook guys and drive ourselves to the coffee shop for a bagel and a cappuccino. Heaven; life's good here.

The next day we're air-testing again – and by 10 a.m. it already feels like lunchtime. My dust-sodden clothes feel coarse against my body and I have that itchy, dirty feeling you have after a long-haul flight. As Darwin and I walk out to the aircraft for what seems like the million-and-oneth time I can feel the sweat running freely down my back into the seat of my knickers – or glowing freely, or whatever it is women are supposed to do. Either way, a long bath and some fresh clothes wouldn't go amiss.

We reach the aircraft just in time to see the engineers packing their tools up in preparation for our next air-test.

'How's she looking?' Darwin asks.

'I have a good feeling about this run, buddy,' replies the mechanic. I cross my fingers. The finest adjustment to the aircraft can make a huge difference between us having a horribly bumpy ride and one that's totally smooth. A 'track and vibe' air-test like the one we're doing today is a painfully frequent occurrence. If a pilot notices a vibration while flying, or if the engineers change anything to do with the rotor blades, the cab will need up to eight hours' flying and several days' engineering time.

We do a quick walk-round; everything looks good. I'm careful not to touch anything with my bare hands, always keeping my oil-saturated gloves on to avoid scorching myself on the hot

160

metal airframe. Darwin checks the gun. In the UK, the REME don't work on aircraft if they're armed, but here we always fly with the gun loaded – especially on air-tests. These test flights are considered fairly risky, because we have to fly short, predictable patterns around the airfield.

We climb in, and I plaster my *Little House on the Prairie*-style cloth hat over my hair so the greasy strands won't get yanked back into a Croydon facelift as I pull on my helmet. We start up the engines and I run the first few tests on the kit the REME have plumbed into the front cockpit. Darwin busies himself with pre-taxi checks as the air-con finally wheezes into life.

'Let's get going. Don't want to miss scoff!' Darwin speedily reverses us out of our bay. He's a safe pair of hands.

As we sit waiting for clearance on to the runway, ATC is busy and I can't get a word in edgeways. I drum my fingers on the cockpit dashboard and Darwin whistles tunelessly. Seconds tick by, and the radios buzz with voices.

'Mayday Mayday Mayday, this is Death 23 Death 23 Death 23.'

An American man's voice booms over the radio, and the first three words make everyone listening freeze. Mayday is a call only made when the aircraft or the crew is in immediate peril, and everything stops to ensure the safety of the stricken crew. To have a Mayday emergency in a hostile environment is a crew's worst nightmare.

'Shit,' we say together, reaching in tandem for our radio volume dials so that we can hear every word. I can practically feel every aircraft within a ten-mile radius listening in.

'Death 23, this is Kandahar Air Traffic, your Mayday call is acknowledged. Send your position and type of emergency,' the calm voice of the girl in ATC replies immediately.

Darwin and I hold our breath for the details. My heart beats against my harness straps, imagining if I was one of the crew inside Death.

'Roger, stand by.' Death's voice is clear and slow – he doesn't sound as stressed as I'd be.

'He sounds chilled out, doesn't he?' Darwin notices.

'Well, it's all recorded, isn't it? You don't want to sound like a Wiener when they listen to the tape at the Board of Inquiry, do you?' I stick up for Death. We used to sit around on bad-weather days on the pilots course bragging about the radio call we'd make if we were ever speeding towards the ground in a flameball. There was a famous tale of a fast-jet pilot who'd fatally crashed into a cliff, and just before impact he radioed his base with: 'Better cancel the hot lunches.' It was legend with all baby-pilots.

'What kind of aircraft is Death anyway?' I ask Darwin.

'Beats me.' He's distracted, waiting for details.

'Kandahar traffic, this is Death 23. We have suffered an engine failure after take-off. We are currently 500 yards east of the 27 threshold. We are on the ground, repeat: on the ground.'

'Roger,' ATC responds. 'Can you confirm that you are still inside the wire?' If the aircraft is inside the safety of the barbed-wire fence around the Kandahar base, then it's not as bad as it sounds, I think. If not, it's the worst news imaginable.

'Death is outside the wire,' the voice drawls back.

'Why the hell is he so relaxed about it then?' Darwin says loudly. 'Shall we?'

'I know,' I say, as the idea comes simultaneously to me. 'I'll offer to go into overwatch.'

We are armed and scary-looking; we can hover over the scene of the accident as a deterrent until some ground troops can recover the wreck and the crew. It works overhead Kajaki, so there's no reason we can't prevent an enemy attack here too.

'Kandahar, this is Ugly Five Four,' I transmit.

'Stand by,' ATC cuts in.

She's not happy with my interruption. She radios Death and urgently asks for his coordinates; he tells her to wait. He's clearly in no rush, whereas she is now starting to sound worried.

'Kandahar, Ugly Five Four can lift immediately and cover the accident. We are armed.' I transmit this in one long sentence so she can't cut me out.

'Roger,' she responds, then swiftly relays our offer to Death. There is a pause, and then, unbelievably, he declines.

'That won't be necessary,' he calmly tells ATC.

For some minutes, we repeat this exchange with increasing levels of urgency. Death is outside the wire, unprotected. At least the crew seem to be fine. I keep telling ATC that we can be overhead in less than a minute; she keeps suggesting it to Death, Death keeps refusing. My mouth is dry and my heart is beating so hard it's as if something is kicking me from inside. Sweat starts to form in beads on my back and shoulders but I feel strangely cold.

ATC is getting into the swing of things now and asks Death whether they have any injuries on board.

'Negative. No pilots or crew onboard,' Death replies.

'Ha! No wonder he crashed, with no pilot,' shouts Darwin. I'm confused. What the . . .?

ATC is confused too.

'Confirm NO crew?' she repeats.

'Affirm, ma'am. Death is an unmanned aerial vehicle. I'm talking to you from my office.'

I can't believe I wasted heartbeats on him. I look at Darwin in the mirror. He looks back, shaking his head. Nothing needs to be said, and I can hear him chuckling into his microphone. Thank God for that.

Our stint in Kandahar lasts longer than usual. We spend six days fixing one dodgy cab. I hit the treadmill every day, max out on cookies to reward myself and ring Jake at every possible opportunity.

Back in Bastion the rota is reshuffled and other crews cover our duties. Operation Glacier is completed. The Boss tells us over the phone that the site of Glacier 3 has already been vacated and, by the time the troops arrived, the enemy had cleared out with their tails between their legs. This is a good sign. Glacier 4 and 5 are ground assaults launched from Garmsir DC to the south. Marines, backed by Afghan National Army and backed up by air, leave the Taliban nowhere to run.

Flight by flight, the rest of the squadron pilots join us at Kandahar, all ridiculously excited about going home. We spend our time packing, repacking and discussing how we'll spend our leave. I'm breathless with excitement at the thought of going home but strangely nervous about seeing all my friends. It feels like so much has happened in my life, and I wonder whether I've missed anything at home, whether something might have changed.

High above Europe, I manage to kill at least twenty minutes making a long list of all the things I plan to do. It reads: make raspberry cheesecake; get a facial, massage and manicure with these gel tips I've heard are amazing; go for full colour, cut and blow dry at first possible opportunity to rid myself of the dreaded roots; go for a long walk with Jake somewhere quiet; do some more wedding planning and finally have a long bath with bubbles in it and a glass of wine.

Early on a Monday morning, our Tristar touches down at Brize Norton. I feel disgusting from the long flight and desperately in need of a shower and some clean clothes. As I look at the familiar faces of my squadron as the men climb wearily down the steps of the plane, I see tiredness on every face – they all look ten years older than when we left, and in need of some under-eye concealer. They also look comforting in the unfamiliar surroundings at Brize, and I feel an unexpected pang at the thought of not seeing them all over the coming weeks. Waiting for my bag, I get dizzy watching the carousel going around and around. I feel as if I've been awake for seven years, and my mouth feels like a bowl of salt.

Against my wishes, Jake has asked to meet me in the arrivals terminal, and I quickly brush my teeth in the loos while I wait for my bag. I wanted to travel back to Wattisham with the rest of the squadron on the coach, have a shower and put some make-up on before Jake sees me, but he wouldn't be deterred.

I'm unaccountably nervous about seeing him; I wonder whether I have changed too much. I've got so used to him being a voice on the end of a phone that I no longer yearn for a hug or any physical contact the way I did the first weeks in Bastion. As I round the corner to Arrivals, my heart is in my mouth and I'm holding my breath. I'm also aware of the rest of the squadron walking behind and around me; they are all intrigued to see Jake and I know they'll be watching our greeting. I feel under pressure.

We see each other at the same time, and he breaks into a huge grin. He looks gorgeous and is carrying an enormous bunch of lilies. As he weaves his way towards me through the throng, I notice he's wearing the jeans I always say I like, the ones he says are too tight on his balls for comfort. I smile more broadly at the thought that he spent time choosing what to wear.

'Hi, gorgeous girl,' he says, and puts his arms around me.

I'm enveloped in a cloud of his shampoo, deodorant and washing powder – the Jake smell, with overtones of lily. I'm transported to another life and relax effortlessly into the embrace.

'Hi, J,' I say, my voice muffled by his shoulder.

We head out of the terminal hand in hand, me trying to ignore the stares from the soldiers as they observe the scene.

In the car, I don't know what to say – it's too big a topic to get started, so I opt for basics instead.

'Where are we going, then?' I ask.

Jake doesn't let go of my hand as we drive out of camp, instead awkwardly doing everything one-handed, that big grin still plastered all over his face. He tells me we're driving straight to my mum's house for the night. I stare quietly out of the window at the familiar but too-green scenery. The light outside is almost too bright and the different greens are blinding. It's like I've been living in a sepia-tint film, and now the colour has just been switched on.

Everything looks and sounds alien yet ordinary at the same time. As we whizz down the motorway and cars accelerate past, they make me jump, and even the sight of so many other women around – driving cars, walking along the roads, sitting with friends – strikes me as slightly strange. I inhale, and everything smells like it's just fallen out the laundry. Yet even that – something I'd dreamed about – is not as comforting as I'd hoped.

I've been planning these first hours at home for months, how I'll feel so relaxed, like a weight has lifted from my shoulders. I'll feel triumphant at having proved myself. I'll stay up all night talking to Jake face to face at last, I'll fill my family and friends in on every detail of my tour, showing them photos and explaining each one. But instead I don't even want to think about where I've been, what I've been doing. I want to pretend the last four months haven't happened. I just feel overwhelmingly, unbelievably knackered, like my body has nothing left inside it. I want to go into a dark corner and collapse into a ball with Jake holding me.

When we arrive, I see that Mum's put balloons up all the way down the street. She looks elated when I climb out of the car. We go out for dinner and I try and catch up with my mum, dad – who has come over to the UK for a brief holiday – and Jake as best I can through my tired brain-fog.

'Was your flight nice, dear? What was the food like?'

I can hear my mum's voice filtering into my brain as if it is coming from three years away. I can barely bring myself to respond, either verbally or by moving my body. They seem to not pick up on my lack of energy; I guess they think I just need a good night's sleep. The questions go on: what was my tent like, how was the food, were the people nice? These are the things my parents genuinely want to know most and, luckily, they are easy to answer. It's easier to sit totally still and think of nothing and keep my answers minimal. For now, I know I can get away with it; it's my first day back. I hope this feeling of numbness passes before I'm not allowed to behave oddly any more. For today, though, the hard question comes later, in bed with Jake.

We lie in the dark, and he asks if I feel different. I consider slowly, before saying truthfully, 'Yes, of course I do, but . . .'

I tail off, unsure what to say, or how to process what I've been through in my head and put it into words. I don't feel ready to talk about it, or open up to anyone, even to Jake. I want to slot back into my old life, as if I've just been on a long holiday, and I'm terrified that my experiences won't let me be the same person I was before.

'I'm really tired, Jake, I can't talk about this now.'

Jake rolls over and gives me a tight, long hug. 'I can't believe you're home, it's like a dream having you back.'

I close my eyes and breathe in his smell.

Back at work the following afternoon, it's almost as if we haven't been away. All the boys look odd in their green combats after three months of my seeing nothing but desert shades, and Dishforth is as quiet as usual. We all potter around the squadron, moving back in and checking emails. A few people need to fly in the simulator to keep their hours up, and the rest of us just drink tea and try to pass the time until we can go home at five. Just one week of work to get through, and then we're all on leave.

Jake has come to live with me in the mess and spends the working days in York, running errands with some of the boys' wives and girlfriends. He calls it the WAGs group. I've been put in charge of organizing a dinner for the regiment to celebrate our return, and Jake buys corsages, table decorations and coloured napkins while I tread water at work.

The dinner on Friday night goes smoothly. It's designed to thank the wives and girlfriends for their support during our time away, but all the speeches end with, 'And now please be upstanding and give a toast to the wives and girlfriends . . . and Jake.' I cringe every time, but Jake takes it graciously in his stride, confident enough in himself to smile his gorgeous white smile. I love him even more.

A few days after I get back, I decide to do something about my hair. It's not been cut in over three months and looks dire – I've got roots and the ends are all ratty.

I book an appointment at a local salon; somewhere totally anonymous, so I can just relax and not talk to anyone. It's one of those brightly lit neon places and makes me feel slightly nervous but, as I ease down into the padded chair to have my hair washed, I start to relax and feel the tension ease from my weary limbs.

By the time I'm having my hair coloured, I'm starting to feel vaguely normal; I'm doing what normal girls do once every couple of months, I tell myself.

The girl doing my hair has peroxide-blonde, spiky locks and heavy make-up. She looks about eighteen – and is dressed in tiny shorts and a white shirt. She makes me feel really old.

She works silently for a few minutes, methodically stroking colour into my hair. Then she tries to strike up a conversation.

'Wow, you've got a great tan. Where have you been?'

'Oh, I've been in Afghanistan.'

'What, on holiday?' she asks. I'm completely thrown by the question.

'Er, no,' I reply, thinking there are a thousand places I'd rather go to get a bit of sun. An all-inclusive holiday in Helmand doesn't quite cut it for me. 'Work.'

'Oh right.' She looks a bit confused. 'So when you next going on holiday?'

I can't quite summon the energy to blow my fuse. But it does make me think. Do people not realize that we are fighting a war over there? Everyone seems to know what Jordan and Peter Andre are having for supper . . . Why doesn't she know that thousands of our men are risking their lives in Afghanistan?

It's three weeks later, and my emotions are still very fresh. I continue to feel slightly overawed and uncertain when faced with the unlimited choices and bright luminous lights in the thin aisles of Tesco's. I find it impossible to believe no one is staring at me in the street and I find it very hard to talk to anyone about what Afghanistan was like. I avoid the subject totally, deliberately isolating myself from it – and myself from my friends as a consequence. I know they think I'm cold and distant but I find it easier to just withdraw completely. Jake read my diary from cover to cover when I returned – I've always written a diary but this time I wrote it with him in mind. I feel that, this way, we don't have to discuss it. I don't ask him how he feels.

On our third weekend together since my return, we travel to central London for my friend's engagement party. Jake and I are running late; we caught separate trains to London, me from Dishforth and him from Somerset, and met up at our hotel. All I want to do is have a long soak in the bath, get a takeaway and spend some time together, but if we gave ourselves as much time alone as I'd like, we'd have no social life at all. I'm already in the shower when he pushes through the door with his suit carrier; I'm busily drying my hair while he's shaving and we've barely exchanged weary hellos when we join hands and leave the hotel to find the bar.

My friends are all on good form – they dance, drink and joke, but I can't get into it. I feel deeply tired and somehow separate from everyone in the room, almost as if I'm looking in on myself. I feel I desperately want to talk to someone about everything, but I know there's no way I could find the words. I dutifully coo over my newly engaged friend's ring and listen to the gossip.

Jake gets heroically drunk, still on a high from having me safely back, and we leave fairly early to try and get some sleep. As we walk through the streets looking for a taxi, Jake sings drunkenly by my side, hanging on to my arm. I am bone-weary, exhausted to the core. It seems as if my brain is struggling with the simplest of tasks, and I feel a familiar panic and incandescent anger building inside me. Why are there no black cabs? How dare Jake get so drunk? Why can none of my friends see that I need to talk?

Jake and I spend a week in France, and then the squadron reassembles back at Dishforth. I clock up the hours flying in the simulator, and most of the other pilots busy themselves with air-testing.

We have another routine exercise coming up, so I spend hours fiddling with the logistics of that. As part of the exercise, someone has thought up a fake 'enemy scenario', but I can't make myself be interested in it and palm it off on the intelligence sergeant to perfect. Other than a deep tiredness, I feel like Afghanistan was just a dream.

Louise's wedding is on a crisp day in May, and I huddle closer to Jake to protect myself against the chill in the stone church. The rows on our side are packed with all Louise's friends and family and there is an excited buzz of chatter.

'I can't wait to see her,' I tell Jake, rubbing my hands together furiously in an attempt to warm them up.

'It can't be that much of a surprise though? I'm pretty sure you planned most of it with her!' Jake sounds slightly tired of wedding chat. 'Mind you, Tom does looks smart.'

I look up over a cluster of hats and see Tom waiting nervously at the altar. He looks every inch the model officer: his buttons gleam, his uniform is spotless and a sword hangs down by his side. His eyes flick repeatedly to the church doors every time there is a noise. He runs his hand through his thick red hair, whispers to his best man, who is standing to his right, and faces the assembled rows of guests.

'She always takes ages to get ready,' he says loudly, pointedly looking at his watch again. Everyone chuckles.

Then the organ starts playing and the heavy wooden doors bang open. Tom's face whips around again and his expression changes to pure delight; his eyes widen and his smile looks as if it might break his face apart.

I turn slowly around, preparing to savour the moment. Louise is utterly gorgeous even in her military uniform, and I know she's going to look incredible today.

Her dress is just as we discussed it – it's a flowing, ivory, A-line gown scattered with pearls. Her floor-length veil is edged with crystals and pearls to match. She is clutching a bouquet of ivory roses. Her tiny frame looks impossibly delicate and beautiful, and as I catch her eye, I feel my breath stick in my throat as I realize what today really means.

She walks past, arm in arm with her dad, and a band of yellow bridesmaids follows.

'It'll be us soon,' Jake whispers, squeezing my hand.

The ceremony is perfect: everyone sings the hymns with gusto, the readings are suitably poignant and, as Louise and Tom look into each other's eyes and make their vows, there are hankies and Kleenex being pulled from handbags and pockets all around me. I even give a little sniff, and Jake looks over at me in surprise.

As the couple walk out of the church, some of their guests from the military raise their swords in a guard of honour, and they walk through the arch like two parts of a human jigsaw.

Champagne corks are popped and everyone cheers. I can tell that the ibuprofen I packed in my bag will come in useful in the morning; military weddings tend to be an extreme version of civilian ones. It's the 'work hard, play harder' mentality:

virtually everyone gets blind drunk, and at least three of the wedding party end up naked by the end, without fail.

At the reception, I find the opportunity to speak to Louise. Her cheeks are red and she is slightly breathless from being bombarded by photographers and friends.

'Charlie!'

I give her a huge hug – she feels tiny, like I could wrap my arms round her twice.

'It was amazing,' I tell her. 'Is it the best day of your life so far?'

'Oh Charlie, I can't tell you . . .' She tails off as the photographer asks her to smile for a shot with her mother. 'It's just wonderful. I must be the luckiest person in the world.'

In an attempt to reconnect with the outside world, I throw myself back into my previous existence. I go through the motions of weekends away, parties and barbecues, but I still feel as if I'm living on the edges of my old life.

In June, I go to a hen party for one of my old school friends. We're renting a cottage just outside Bath and have come into the town centre to have dinner before heading to a nightclub, losing the bride-to-be's mother and mother-in-law on the way.

When we arrive at the family-oriented Italian restaurant, we're ushered to the back by two very Italian waiters.

'Ah bella, bella, this way,' they gesture as we pass the families and couples dining by candlelight.

We're seated alongside two other large groups: another hen party and a gathering of young guys who claim they are not on a stag do but clearly are.

During the starters, they pipe up.

'Oi you, Barbie,' they say, pointing directly at me. 'And her,' they continue, singling out a girl from the other party. I try to shuffle behind Mia, but there's no hiding place.

'We want you to do a dance-off. Go on, to see who can dance the best.'

I can't think of anything worse.

The singling out reminds me of being in Afghanistan but, here, I am cosseted by my gorgeous female friends. On weekends like this I feel as if I'm bouncing on a warm marshmallowy pink cloud of girliness, and I love it.

The men start jesting with some of the others too, so I feel less picked on. We all start rolling our eyes, joking that we are clearly a higher calibre of hen than the neighbouring table of girls. We nickname them the 'battery hens', and give ourselves the status of organic, free-range corn-fed hens. The battery hens can't possibly win, but they tease us back while everyone slowly gets drunk.

When the men suggest for a second time that the other girl and I take to the dancefloor, the hen comes up with what I'm guessing she thinks is a fantastic idea.

'I know,' she tells the stag party. 'One of you lot can armwrestle her and, if she wins, we get a bottle of wine.' She laughs, tossing her perfect blonde hair and looking angelic.

She knows what they don't – I am really strong. I've always hated my over-muscly arms, but tonight I've curled my hair and put on an extra dollop of lip gloss, so I'm guessing the boys probably haven't noticed. I'm slightly hesitant, but then the chanting starts and I know I can't back out.

The guy in question also looks slightly hesitant and a bit embarrassed, but soon the hollering has become so loud he has to go for it too. Even the battery-hen mothers are giving it some welly.

The chanting is almost deafening.

'Charlie, Charlie, Charlie, Charlie.'

I'm trying hard to concentrate and not to snigger. What started out as a bit of fun has turned a competitive corner, and I'm battling him with all my strength, even though it's the last thing I really want to be doing.

I don't want to let my friends down. Most are crowded round the wobbly, plastic serving table we've hijacked for the competition, but some are standing on tables so that they can see over everybody else. Mia is in the middle, shouting the loudest of all. It seems we've drawn quite a crowd. The Italian waiters look on, a little bemused.

The guy's fingers feel fatter than Jake's, and he's pushing hard. I struggle to keep my elbow down and I know my biceps have popped out like a man's. I don't catch his eye but instead concentrate on a vague spot on my forearm. Our arms stay resolutely stuck at 90 degrees, despite all the pushing.

'Look at her arms!' one of the men kindly notices. I cringe. It's starting to hurt. Both of our knuckles are white as he slowly pushes me off my axis towards the table.

I'm stuck between wanting to lose, like the weakling girl should, and wanting to just get this over with and go back to my wine. I push with all my might. Slowly but surely his arm eases backwards and touches the table.

The room explodes.

'Woo hoo!' All the girls are screaming and hugging me – including the battery hens.

The man looks ashen-faced and shuffles towards the bar. My group of hens starts shouting: 'Ha, ha, you picked the army chick! You didn't even know!'

He comes back and hands over our bottle of wine, our prize, seemingly having lost his sense of humour on the way.

The group of men start singing:

'Billy is a girl, Billy is a girl,' followed by a loud and raucous version of 'We're in the Army Now'.

Another three weeks later, and I'm back in Middle Wallop. I take another look at the flying programme board just to make sure, then dive out of the double doors and dash off in the direction of a different building, smiling.

I burst through the doors to the instructor's office, see Jo and rush over to her desk. She's an instructor and is completing a tour here before she goes out to Afghanistan for the first time. She has thousands of hours of experience, and everyone tells me she is an exceptional teacher in the air. She's in her mid-thirties, athletic, always happy, and I can't wait to fly with her.

'Have you seen the flypro this morning?' I grin at her.

'Sure have. Can you believe it? I think this'll be the first ever Apache flight with two girls,' she answers, while deftly sweeping her flying kit up off her desk.

We start walking back to the main building for the morning brief in the midst of a gaggle of pilots.

'You can finally tell me what you were going to say about . . .' I lower my voice, seeing the guys all trying to earwig, '. . . well, you know what,' I whisper conspiratorially.

'Oh, yeah, I forgot about that!' she says, and we burst into giggles.

Since my tour in Afghanistan, I've flown a number of exercises through England and Scotland, and now I'm finally going to share the cockpit with a female, someone whose sense of humour is the same as mine and who will instantly understand if I say I'm questioning myself for the millionth time about my flying, someone who won't think it's tedious and unnecessary to gossip during the flight. I know it's going to feel like a fun roadtrip with a friend – the ones where you laugh all the way to your destination and when you get there you feel nauseous from travel snacks and hysteria.

Jo will be looking forward to it just as much; we've always joked about how great it would be, and how much fun the men must have just basically flying around with their mates. We both get on with all the boys, but it's never going to be quite the same flying in a mixed crew. However, until now, the 'powers that be' had not seen fit to grant our wish to be crewed together.

An hour later, we're trudging towards our aircraft via the office, to sign for the cab and pick up the keys. We push through the narrow door, our kit wider than the door space, still breathless. We laugh that we'd better not crash, as when they listen to the black box they'll hear our gripes about our other halves, our Top Five If-You-Had-To list and a few rounds of 'Shoot, Shag or Marry?'

As soon as we walk into the REME office, we notice that there are substantially more people in there than usual. And they're all looking expectantly in our direction.

'What's up?' I whisper to Jo. She shrugs and dumps her kit inside the doors.

A lab-coated civilian walks over to us from a group of four others. He has wiry grey hair and NHS-style specs: a proper cartoon mad scientist. He is holding a handful of wires and a small plastic box.

'Are you ladies here for the trial?' he enquires in a thin, cracking voice.

'Er, not that we know of,' Jo sighs, the relief that our girly flight isn't ruined evident in her voice. She signs for the aircraft and jingles the keys. 'Ready?'

The mad scientist has been conferring with the six REMEs and his four civvie pals and is being pushed over in our direction again.

'Ah, I think I need to get you ladies prepared for the trial. You're the only ones flying today, and the OC promised us we could get some more data before we leave tonight. He even gave me your names.' He shrugs apologetically. We grumble.

I also dump my kit on the floor; it's becoming evident we're going to be in here a while.

'What's the trial then?' I ask, curious to know what we are getting ourselves into.

He explains that his team are researching the levels of noise and vibration which military pilots are subjected to. He needs to wire us both up with earbuds and a recording mike that fits into our helmets. We'll also need to sit on some sort of vibration-measuring seat pad, but that's not what catches our attention. It's something else he says.

'Did you say everything we say will be recorded?' Jo's eyebrows are raised.

'Yes, but don't worry, we record everything on a graph and we'll only listen to what's going on when there is a peak in the noise. You know, like a loud bang or a particularly loud radio call.'

'Yeah, or a loud screech from one of us at a good bit in the conversation,' I say to Jo as soon as we're out of earshot. I can just see the scientists clustered around their seismograph-style machine excitedly pointing out a peak in the noise and cueing up the tapes only to hear our thoughts on the Boss's arse.

We've been kitted out with our earphones and vibration cushions now, and are all too aware of them as we do our daily walk-round of the cab and climb in. We lift from the concrete dispersal and climb high over the barbed-wire fence protecting the cabs, and spend the next hour practising airfield manoeuvres on the grass runway in the thick fog. The weather is only just legal for flight and, as well as concentrating, we are both almost ridiculously silent, wary of saying anything that will make us sound silly.

I enjoy my flight anyway; Jo points out my mistakes in a kind way and encourages me to do better. It is so unlike the male version of the instructor, who is far more forceful and generally teases you to try and improve your technique.

When we land on, instead of feeling battered and embarrassed from having my errors highlighted, I feel more as if I've been for a coffee with one of the girls. We yank off the earphones, pulling out little bits of hair as we do so, and the engine compressor stops running and we climb out. I sigh, thinking what it would be like if all Apache pilots were female – it would be an idyllic Athena-like state, where chocolate and Carmex lipbalm were compulsory flying accessories, along with twice-daily showers. The men could fetch the coffees.

*   *   *

The weeks pass, and I know I'm going to have to return to Afghanistan at the end of August. I have so many nagging doubts about this next tour that I don't know where to start even thinking about it. I don't feel that I've properly reintegrated into my home life yet; it's been harder than I ever imagined, and going away again will only make things worse. On the other hand, I'm almost looking forward to being back in a landscape I understand – no pretending to be 'normal', no trying to brush over what I've done. The short tour I'm going on has been planned for ages; there aren't enough Apache pilots in my regiment to deploy without all of us going out again, so we have all volunteered for various slots during the summer. I feel more confident this time, though; I know what to pack, what to expect and, most importantly, that I'll be able to do the job.

'Do you know who you're flying with this time?' Jake asks one day.

'Wiggy. Should be quite fun, really. I'm mainly really excited that Bertie is going to be out there – it'll be amazing having a girl around all the time.'

Wiggy is the squadron prankster, and has an incredibly juvenile sense of humour. From all accounts, he spends every exercise wheeling out the 'What do you call a donkey with three legs?' joke. He has giant hands that gesticulate wildly, almost like when someone else is pretending to be your arms and hands. He also likes his booze. I wonder how he'll cope without it. Probably much the same way I'll cope without my mascara – not particularly well.

And the only person, I hear, who can probably drink and banter more than Wiggy is Bertie, who has only recently completed her Apache training. I already envy her ability to blend seamlessly into a group of men, and her jokes are funnier than all of theirs put together. Both Wiggy and Bertie are pilots I've seen around and exchanged the odd 'hello' with; Wiggy was in Afghanistan during my first tour, but we never flew alongside each other. I'm really looking forward to getting to know them better. And after my flight with Jo, I can't wait to have another female Apache pilot to offload to about the men's stinky feet, constant farting and boring helicopter chat.

It seems I'm getting better at goodbye every time Jake and I do it, and as he drives away from Wattisham, where he's dropped me off, I shed a few tears in my room and mentally add up how many sleeps there are until I see him again. I pack my things while trying to soak up as much reality TV as possible and, by the next morning, I can feel myself switching back into work mode. I arrive at the squadron laden with heavy kit and refuse all offers of help, trying to get used to the idea of coping on my own for the next couple of months and focusing on survival. By the time we board the coach that will take us to the airport, I feel ready to hit Bastion running.

I walk out on to dispersal in the stifling morning heat, following Pete's tall outline; he looks far more graceful carrying all his hefty kit than I do mine. We do our walk-round in anxious silence – it's always slightly daunting getting into the cab when it's been a while, and out here it's much worse. It's time for me to stand up and be counted again.

We're doing our 'famil' flight – to familiarize ourselves with all the changes that have taken place since we left. Even in a short space of time, I am told, the ground in Afghanistan can change unrecognizably: new patrol bases; new enemy firing points; fresh nicknames for the scattered buildings, deep wadis and dirty alleyways. When we are called to our first TIC, we need to know exactly what we're looking at.

The cab is filthy, covered in oil, dust and grease. By the time I've finished checking my side of the aircraft, my hands are slimy. I wipe my itchy nose and accidentally smear hydraulics on to my face.

'Dammit, I'm all gross already and it's only eight o'clock!' I say.

'Well, let's just get this over with, and then we can come back and clean up,' Pete replies, practical as ever. He's all textbook, like an Eton schoolboy; tall, blond, slim, neat and professional. If there was a pamphlet somewhere on how to be the perfect officer, it would have his face on it.

My new flight – Pete, Wiggy and JB – are all good guys and trying hard with me, but I still can't budge the slightly homesick feeling I have for Nick, FOG and Darwin.

Wiggy reminds me of Johnny Vegas; he's heavily built, blond and always has a bit of banter at the ready. His lame jokes never end. It seems he has met his match in the humour stakes with JB though. They're already as thick as thieves. On paper, JB's the sort of person I would be really scared of: he's done about a million Special Forces-style jobs in his career, and lots of other things he doesn't speak about. He always has a fag hanging out the side of his mouth, and he hates the gym, saying it's 'for losers', but in every fitness test he leaves us for dust. Scottish and naturally fair, he loves the sun and will find a patch of UV everywhere we go, so he's always a bit 'Brits-abroad-red' around the face. But I'm really warming to him. Happily married – a big surprise when I found out from the Boss, as he seems very much 'one of the boys', and never mentions his family – he is viciously funny and not remotely condescending towards us less experienced pilots, as I'd expected him to be.

I hear an eruption of laughter filter over the blast wall that separates my aircraft from Wiggy's, and look over to see JB standing up by his radar shouting something down to Wiggy and howling.

'Some dirty joke, no doubt,' I say to Pete, who just raises his eyebrows as we put on our LCJs.

The cockpit floor is caked in mud and smells like hot woollen upholstery. I put my helmet on, and the liner smells reassuringly like me: honey shampoo and a little bit of sweat – a comforting recipe.

I start the APU just as I hear Wiggy starting his.

It feels good being in the cockpit again. I passed my check ride to become an aircraft commander as soon as I returned from Afghanistan in the spring, and it means I can now sign for an aircraft and take it where I like, with full responsibility for safety, navigation and piloting. It means I'm mostly in the front seat, and that always seems like the high-pressure seat. You're lower, so you can't see as much, and that saps your capacity before you start. Also, the burden of radio calls, navigation, initiating the challenge-and-response flight checks and all major tactical decisions fall to the front-seater.

I sit in the back, carefully running through the back-seater checks – I'm in charge of the aircraft's 'health', is the way I see it. I look at the engine pages to check temperatures and pressure, set up the aircraft's radar and configure the radios and weapons to take the burden from Pete. I plug in our route for today and check that the settings are all how I want them.

I double-check everything I do, aware that I'm more used to front-seat checks these days, and I can sense that Pete is monitoring my actions as well.

'Oil pressure's rising there,' he says haughtily. He's only making certain I'm paying attention to it, but I feel slightly offended by the superior edge to his voice, which I know is a bit silly, but I'm trying hard to impress them all.

We start our engines, and I look across at JB's aircraft to see that he's taken the cue from our rotors turning and started his. We lift from the runway and I suddenly feel like I've never been away. I smile and automatically make my call to Zero to tell them we're wheels up.

First we're off to the south, and we cruise high above Garmsir, Lashkagar and Gereshk, reacquainting ourselves with everything and talking to the new JTACs on the ground. The dusty villages and compounds look fascinating, like brown and snaking labyrinths scarring the desert. I know the novelty will wear off in a couple of days, but I think again how this would be an interesting country to visit on holiday if it weren't perpetually at war.

The district centres are busy with men and children pushing wheelbarrows through the busy markets and squatting in doorways. Women and the smaller kids roam freely around inside the compound complexes, hanging laundry, tending cooking fires and feeding animals.

We cut north-west over FOB Price, marvelling at how large it is now compared to the tiny desert HLS it used to be. We approach Now Zad from the south, flying high at 2,000 feet. We do a quick flight over the town, but don't linger. The intelligence picture wasn't favourable and we didn't want to get into any trouble on our first flight back in country.

'Not much changed here,' Pete says.

'Nope. Same firing points as always, by the looks of it,' I sigh, feeling weary.

We sit in silence for a few seconds, then I hear this strange clicking sound. I figure it must be Pete.

'What are you doing?' I say, at the same time he asks: 'Is that you?'

We both pause for as long as it takes to realize that the weird, popcorn-like noise is coming from outside the cab.

'Ugly, this is Widow Eight Zero, I can hear heavy machinegun fire over in your direction. Confirm you can see the firing point?' The JTAC is straight in.

'What the fuck?' Pete's head is swinging from side to side in front of me as he looks for the firing point.

'That'll be the big gun the IntO mentioned, then!' I yank the collective to full pitch and reposition so that we can turn in for a better look.

'Widow Eight Zero. Ugly Five Two, we can hear it but can't see it. We're expediting out,' he replies. I take his cue and spin us around to head out of town.

'Ugly Five Four, this is Five Two. We've just taken incoming, can you come and do a visual inspection?' he radios to our wing.

'Roger, en route.' The reply is immediate, emotionless and professional. I look north to see Wiggy's cab swinging back towards us as we rocket out of the Green Zone. They fly once around us, then over the top and underneath us.

'Nothing seen. We're scanning the wooded area,' JB reports. Pete acknowledges. The intelligence officer told us there might be an anti-aircraft weapon – a DHSKA – in the woods on the eastern side of town.

'I guess it must have just been missing us; we must've heard the rounds going past the rotors. Close call,' Pete concludes, his head still down in the sights trying to identify where it might be coming from, but he can't see anything.

Eventually, his head pops up from the TADS and he looks into the rear-view mirror, smiling.

'Well, lucky first flight. Hopefully that's our brush with death out of the way for the tour.'

I hope so. I report back to base and imagine the signallers writing it all down word for word in their radio logs and reporting back to the Boss.

An hour later, we're on the ground and back in the JHF, with intelligence asking us for every detail. We're not very helpful though, as it's not like we even heard it very clearly and we certainly couldn't see anything.

It's almost a mark of pride to bring back an aircraft with holes in it, so part of me is almost pleased to have been shot at already. Every time you survive hostile fire, it feels as if you're reducing the probability of being shot at again. I know this is nonsense, but it's not just me either – during my first tour I witnessed two of the boys having a stand-up argument about who was last to fly one of the cabs when the REME found a massive hole in the rocket pod.

However, it's also very serious. In May, Flipper Seven Five, a US Chinook, was shot down by an RPG in Kajaki killing all seven soldiers on board. This says a lot about the Taliban's developing tactics. They use RPGs on low-flying aircraft such as Chinooks. More worryingly, there is possible evidence that they have acquired shoulder-launched surface-to-air missiles from Iran, which have a range of more than a mile and could drop most aircraft out of the sky. We hear they are more determined than ever to get an Apache – in their eyes, a 'mosquito' would be the ultimate prize.

Everything dies down within a few minutes, and it's back to our normal routine. My ears are still burning from all the radio traffic during our flight, and my head swims with all the new information we've taken in. We spoke to twenty-odd ground callsigns on the radio, plus the other aircraft on voice and data throughout the flight. It's strange reconciling my chats with the JTACs – so professional and grateful for our help – with the guys here at Bastion, who crudely wolf-whistle and jeer at me. I can't believe they're the same men.

I sneak out of the JHF and go for a run in the sunshine, pushing all thoughts of work and war from my head. When I get back, I find that Wiggy and JB are back in the tent playing Extreme Nerf, their favourite stress-buster. They strip down to their shorts and throw the Nerf, a styrofoam miniature rugby-ball-shaped toy with a hard plastic tip, at each other. They stand at opposite corners of the tent and chuck it with all their strength, and it produces a whistling noise when it travels through the air. I'm pretty sure this is one of Wiggy's ideas.

I push my head through the tent flaps to be greeted with a familiar hissing noise.

'Oof, that hurt, you bugger.' It was JB's voice.

I hear scuffling noises as my eyes adjust to the sudden gloom and relative cool of the tent. I can hear Wiggy sniggering, and I can just begin to make out his naked torso against the far wall of the tent. JB is clutching his balls through his shorts and feeling around under one of the camp cots.

'Got it!' He waves the Nerf. 'You're in big trouble now, mate.'

The main rule is that the throwee can't move; you have to stand still and take it. The other rule is that, at any point, the throwee can end the game and take the Nerf for themselves. They then reinstigate the game at any time of day or night by throwing the Nerf at another unsuspecting member of the flight. It's painful. Cluedo is much more up my street.

JB takes a short run-up and hurls the Nerf across the tent. Wiggy squeezes his eyes shut as the whistling toy hurtles towards his chest, then he doubles over.

'Right in my nip, you fucker!' he says, clutching the left side of his chest. 'Right, that's enough, this is mine now.' He tucks the Nerf away under his bed, and I make a mental note to be nice to Wiggy until further notice.

I think it's funny that the Nerf makes a sound like an incoming rocket. Although we hear rockets landing frequently at Kandahar and don't react, if we hear a similar noise here at Bastion, our flight is learning to be perfectly conditioned to dive immediately for cover.

It doesn't take long before I'm back into the swing of missions. It's the usual mix of escorting Chinooks on resupplies, helping out on TICs and the odd fighting patrol. The British are building and moving into more patrol bases and FOBs all over Helmand. This means a lot more escorting duties for us, and there are more mouths to feed in terms of rations and water, and the Chinooks are delivering it all.

The part I was most nervous about – getting back into VHR – turns out to be a breeze. By the second day of our first VHR stint, my new flight already has it down to a fine art. The phone rings three times, JB answers it, gives us one or two fingers to indicate how many aircraft are going, and we all jump up and scramble for the door. Wiggy and Pete dash on foot to the JHF for orders while JB and I bundle into the Rover and burn rubber to the flightline. By the time Wiggy and Pete make it to the cabs with instructions, we're up and running on APU.

We're also having a good time as a flight. Wiggy and JB are huge practical jokers; you can't possibly be serious while they're around. Pete looks on disapprovingly and I join whichever camp suits me at the time.

One afternoon, I'm lying on my camp cot after an escort mission. JB has gone for a cigarette, and Pete lies at the far side of the tent on his cot, reading a military biography. I hear a noise next to me and half-open one of my eyes, to see Wiggy smiling widely to himself and creeping towards JB's empty cot.

'What on earth are you doing?' I ask, sitting up.

'JB should have known better than to leave this out!' Wiggy says ominously, picking up JB's flying shirt.

I watch as he ties a knot at the end of each sleeve, then starts filling every pocket with JB's stuff. He's enjoying himself immensely, shoving pants, toothpaste and sand into every available area of the shirt. One ill-timed nap around here, and anything can happen; if JB is called to go flying in a hurry, he'll be taking his toothpaste with him.

'Wiggy, that's not funny.' Pete's voice floats across the tent.

'You don't think anything's funny.' Wiggy finishes by setting JB's alarm clock to 3 a.m. and stands back to survey his work.

Thirty minutes later, JB, freshly showered, sits on his bed wrapped in a towel and chuckling. Wiggy is snoring quietly in the bed next to me.

'What?' I whisper to JB.

'The little bastard – look at my flying shirt!' JB whispers back.

Then, as if in slow motion, JB stands up, sweeping his hands under his pillow and retrieving the Nerf in one fluid motion. He takes two running strides across the room and releases the Nerf. Pete hears the noise and immediately curls into a ball on his bed while I satisfy myself that it's not headed for me.

The Nerf slowly spirals its way towards the sleeping Wiggy,

and as I back towards the tent door, I see the impact of the Nerf as it hits Wiggy's prostrate backside.

I readjust my position, lying flat on my back on the gravel. There are red-hot stones poking into the backs of my thighs, and when I reach for my bottle of water it tastes like warm miso soup. I give up trying to find comfort, tell myself it's all in the name of beauty and pick up *Heat* to read the last few pages.

I'm lying out sunbathing on the two-metre-wide stretch of gravel between the back of the accommodation tent and the HESCO wall. It's a complete heat-trap, but it's also the only place I can take off enough clothes to sunbathe without feeling like I'm lying on a strip-club podium. The tent flaps rustle behind me and I hear the zip opening; I prop myself up on sweaty elbows and peer into the gloom of the tent as Bertie emerges, smile first, with a huge 'Hiya!'

'Hey dude,' I answer happily. 'Did you bring suncream?'

'Nah, I need to go for the burn,' Bertie says, spreading out another skanky roll mat on the gravel. I'm amused to notice that we're both wearing our gym shorts and a crop top to avoid being overly revealing; no bikinis in sight.

We've been back out in Afghanistan for almost two weeks now, and I'm fully back into it. I've kept my routine exactly the same as last time, my bed is the same, the food is the same . . . the one huge difference is Bertie. She arrived just after me, and it was the nicest feeling in the world. Louise was wonderful last time, but this is better – Bertie does the same job as me. I feel as if I'm seeing myself from the outside: she goes off on these hardcore missions, for which all the boys respect her, and then comes back and stresses that her anti-aging moisturizer is running out.

Bertie doesn't only make me laugh; she has the boys doubled over too with her dirty jokes and has a full, gravelly cackle. She reminds me a bit of Lily Allen – the mouthy girl who men would love to go for a pint down the pub with and the women would love to go shopping with for her honest critique. She went to Sandhurst straight from school and flew Lynx before converting to Apache. I'd been aware of her, but it's only, finally, out here that I get to meet her properly.

'How long have you done?' Bertie asks, arranging her long chestnut-brown hair into a plait – her trademark style.

'Fifteen minutes each side. I wasn't going to bother sunbathing today, but the boys were just talking incessantly about work, so I thought I'd escape.'

'God, I know,' Bertie sympathizes. 'At breakfast this morning the Boss sat down with my flight and talked shop for about twenty minutes; he wanted to rehash some points from yesterday's mission. Again.' She does a fake snore to demonstrate the tediousness and settles into position on her mat. I'm starting to realize that she's just as girly as me, with all the same reservations I have about our job.

'Anyway,' she continues, 'then my girlfriend from Sandhurst – you know the one – sat down as well, and we were chatting about what we want to buy when we go shopping at home again.'

'Mmmmm . . . shopping,' I cut in, thinking lazily about my own purchases-to-come list once I get out of here. I turn my head to face her and squint against the bright sun.

'Exactly,' Bertie goes on, now lying with her eyes closed and gesturing meaningfully with her hands. 'Great conversation topic. But the Boss said, "This conversation has certainly taken a turn for the worse. I'm off," and left in a huff. Do they have no idea how dull it is for us when they chat about work all the time? Or tits? I mean, that's all the boys ever talk about.'

'No, I don't think they do realize.'

I reach for my water-soup and take a swig. I gag slightly then lie back again with my eyes closed.

'It can be really lonely being the only girl, even when you're

188

surrounded by the whole squadron,' I say. 'I mean, we've both been "the only one", and it's harder than people think.'

I pause. 'You can be with your flight for two months solid, eating, sleeping and showering with them, and think you're closer than family, and then some female Chinook pilot comes out and you immediately feel a closer bond with her than you ever could with the boys in your flight. It's weird, but you know another girl will think how you do, worry about the same stuff, and stress about little things the same way.' I look over at Bertie again. 'Bertie?' I say.

She's asleep.

While I do enjoy the odd sunbathing session, as the weeks go on and the heat starts rising, even I find it unbearable; even though it's early September, most days it's between forty and fifty degrees. It smacks you hard in the face and takes your breath away. It's like being in the blast from a giant hairdryer.

I'm trying to have a lie-in. Delicious in principle but, as soon as the sun rises, the tent heats up to thirty degrees. After several minutes of tossing and turning, I give up, pull out another copy of *Heat* from the stack Jake has sent me and fill my brain with the latest Posh and Becks drama while pretending I'm lying in a Turkish steam room in an expensive spa.

I hear the boys stir about ten minutes later, so I grab my dressing gown, sunglasses and shower kit and bolt before the dawn farting chorus gets started.

I brave the catwalk past the gym area, the groundies' accommodation and the firemen's tent in my PJs. The sunglasses are a must for covering the I-just-woke-up eyes, especially for mid-morning starts like this when everyone else has been up for hours. All the guys in the squadron area are used to seeing me wandering around, so I never really get a hard time walking to and from the showers, but it pays to be prepared.

As I unzip the flap, steam billows around me. The luxurious

air con in here rarely works. I dump my stuff outside the best shower – the one at the far end – and stroll to the loos on the opposite side of the room. I've burnt my backside a number of times on no-air-con days – the metal loo seats can reach sixty degrees – but today I'm ready to deploy my well-practised hover technique.

Twenty minutes later, showered and changed, I sit on my cot and wait for Wiggy, Pete and JB to finish doing whatever it is they do when they say they're 'just nipping out for a quick shower, won't be a moment'.

The four of us eventually head out to lunch.

The staring is much worse today. I make sure I've zipped my flies, haven't tied my boots together or somehow forgotten to get dressed at all, but everything feels fine. Wiggy and Co. don't seem to notice anything, so I put it down to paranoia.

As I walk in through the greasy flap of the cookhouse door, someone behind me in the queue says loudly, 'What, her?', and points. I turn to see a gaggle of twenty-something soldiers conferring and laughing.

'Do you want me to do something?' JB fumes.

'No. It's fine.' It'll only make me look stupid, I think. I try to smile and laugh it off, but I feel my cheeks burning with anger and embarrassment.

Head bowed, I try to make myself invisible as I survey the hotplate.

'Oi, ma'am!' the voice rings out, and heads turn.

I now have a choice: I can go and see what he wants; or I can pretend I haven't heard, which would precipitate another summons from laughing boy. Ignoring won't solve anything; everyone is looking, and it would be cowardly.

I put down my tray and weave my way across the room, a hundred pairs of eyes burning a hole in my back and two hundred more in my front. I can't ignore them, however much I wish I could. I'm close enough for them to see that my T-shirt is stuck to my boobs with sweat.

I finally reach the speaker. 'Yes?' Everyone in the room is looking.

'Never mind, ma'am.'

Laughter erupts around me.

I walk back to collect my tray, head high and expression blank, trying to look as if I'm completely unaffected. My head explodes with a chorus of 'Ohmygod, ohmygod, how embarrassing'. My eyes dart from side to side, trying to see Wiggy and Pete so I can just go and sit down with them. I daren't look up. I go to the buffet, throw some random food on a tray. Just as I'm about to slink away, someone taps me on my shoulder.

'Umm, is it true?' It's a young soldier, maybe only eighteen. He looks sheepish, as if he's been put up to this.

'What?' I'm annoyed now.

'Well . . . umm . . .' He seems to change his mind at the last minute. Someone prods him in the back. 'Were you top in your pilot school?'

'No,' I snap. I start walking away.

'Do you fly jets too?' the lad asks. I can hear his mates whispering.

'No.' I stalk off.

I see JB waving me over, and I slide with a huge sigh of relief into the seat next to him.

If that's what they do dare ask me, what gets discussed behind closed doors?

'You all right?' Wiggy asks.

'Let's talk about something else,' I say quickly, afraid I might cry. No one but Jake can see me cry.

As we leave the tent, my eyes are cast down. I just want to escape as quickly as possible.

Pushing through the tent flaps, JB says testily, 'Charlie, do you want me to say something to them?'

I look up.

'All that staring,' JB says, 'what do they think they're doing? Want me to say something next time?'

191

'I just wish they wouldn't do that calling-me-over thing all the time! Next time there's a TIC I'm going to ask whether anyone down there has ever taken the piss out of me before helping them.'

'No, you won't,' JB says.

'No, I won't,' I sigh again. 'I'd do anything to help those guys. We all would, and we all know it.'

It's the middle of the night, and I am nearing my first stop-off in Farah, on the border of Afghanistan and Iran. I'm so tired my vision is blurred, but I know I have to concentrate to land safely here.

We arrive overhead to discover that our landing pad is minute; from the air it looks like a pencil dot. We don't have the power to overshoot if I mess things up, and there are Chinooks either side of my pad. I can barely see on the FLIR, and it's too dark for the naked eye.

As soon as I lower the collective to start the approach in our heavy aircraft, we're committed. My breathing is shallow.

'This is totally bloody different from the diagram . . .' Wiggy's nerves are frayed too after the two-hour flight here.

I'm running on empty as well; I can't raise the energy to respond. My palms prickle and my vision starts to tunnel; I'm really scared. I leave it to fate and my training as I fly down the glide path to the dot marking my landing point, and in the final few metres I struggle not to squeeze my eyes shut in panic.

We make it on to the ground but I have the full-on shakes while I shut the engines down. I concentrate on my breathing; I count each exhaled breath. *Pull yourself together . . . We haven't even started the mission yet.*

I'm on duty ops, but things have been busy, and every pilot in the squadron has been called to fly in the last twenty-four hours. I've been awake for almost eighteen hours, but there'll be no time to get my head down; the plan is to refuel here and head straight out on the mission.

I'm desperate for a wee so, as the aircraft is being refuelled, I hold up my NVGs like opera specs and look for a likely location. I hop out and disappear behind my pre-selected Italian Mangusta helicopter. It's still desert-dark, but I'm painfully aware that there are almost fifty soldiers around me also wearing NVGs. Too bad if they glance this way, I guess. I emerge from the Mangusta's tail rotor adjusting my flying suit and trying to look nonchalant and stroll back towards my parked Apache.

In my distraction, I almost stumble over a group of shadowy figures. It's only at the last moment that I realize who they are. The dark, monk-like figures are hooded and cuffed pris-oners-of-war. I see one of them being led, his head bowed and hands tied tightly behind his back, from the helicopter to the holding compound. It's deadly quiet; the prisoners aren't allowed to communicate, and none of the soldiers talks either, for fear of giving anything away. I feel I've seen something I shouldn't and turn and run back to the relative normality of my aircraft. Someone passes a bagel through the cockpit door. I'm too tired to wonder where it's come from and almost too tired to chew.

Wiggy returns from the orders group.

'We've got the go-ahead to launch. As briefed, we're heading to the border to intercept a Taliban leader driving back from Iran; they reckon he's pretty high up the pecking order, too, so it's the one we've been hoping for.'

I know from our intelligence brief that, if this is our best-case-scenario man, he's in charge of hundreds of militant fighters in Helmand. Capturing him would be a huge blow for the enemy. We don't know whether there are going to be other vehicles escorting him, or if he'll be accompanied by body-guards. As usual, we're flying into the unknown, so the only thing that's certain is that the job is an important one.

We lift from Farah as a four-ship; two Apaches and two Chinooks. The Chinooks carry fifty soldiers and officers –

enough to surround and capture the suspected Taliban leader.

I shake my head to try and clear it as I pull power in to take off. The dust clouds billow around us in the night. I lose sight of the other aircraft and concentrate on the fact that I know there is a mountain immediately to the west, the way I'm heading.

As my Apache clears the eight-foot wall surrounding Farah, with three helicopters on my wings and the mountain looming, my FLIR picture vanishes. My system has broken and I'm blind. Talk about bad timing.

'Blind!' I shout. Wiggy grabs the controls as we veer off, and I scrabble on my helmet for my NVGs.

'Just as well I'm here, eh, Charlie? I'm a lifesaver too . . . not just a pretty face,' Wiggy pipes up cheerfully.

'Not even that,' I retort, clipping on the goggles. 'Give me the controls back; I don't trust you front-seaters at all.'

The flight to the border is altogether calmer, though I'm still half blind. Forty-five minutes out, and we find two cars about a kilometre from where we were expecting them.

'Which way are they heading, Ugly?'

The JTAC is in the back of the circling Chinook trying to decide where he wants the ground troops to land. Together we need to select a suitable ambush site.

'The road bends to the north-east then goes through a village,' Wiggy says.

We decide to wait until the cars have cleared the village – we don't think the locals will take kindly to being woken by a Chinook at four in the morning.

Wiggy gives the other Apache directions: 'You track the second car; we'll keep our eyes on the one in front.'

He follows the leading vehicle with his TADS as it makes its way through a collection of ramshackle houses on either side of a dirt track. Everything seems to be going to plan. But as it exits the village, it abruptly comes to a halt.

'Widow, this is Ugly, you need to get wheels down, and quick. The cars have stopped . . .'

We watch the target, our eyes straining to make out the slightest detail. From this far away, the car is just a speck, a pale-green ant against a dark green background.

Suddenly, there are even smaller ants bomb-bursting out of it in all directions. It takes us a split second to work out what's going on, then the radios explode into life.

'Five Two, this is Five Three; we've got three leakers.' Our wing aircraft updates us as Wiggy transmits.

'Widow,' Wiggy yells, 'the Bravos are on the move.'

We have a problem. There are four pilots up here and at least seven leakers now, and we don't know which one is our target. We try to follow as many as possible, but our attention is divided. There's a 70mph wind fighting me, and Wiggy is struggling to get a word in on the radios.

The Chinooks land in a field, and the soldiers swarm around the vehicles.

They radio us: 'Ugly, the Bravos are all on the move and the cars are full of weapons. Request you deny both vehicles when we're clear. Where are the leakers?'

We update them as best we can, and they catch a handful of the enemy. It appears that the main target got away; we chose the wrong guys to follow. We don't think about that yet; there's still work to do.

As the soldiers and prisoners load back into the Chinook, I steer into position to fire a missile into the car we've been told to target. The wing will stick with his vehicle and take it out when we're clear.

The Chinooks move safely away, and Wiggy looses off a Hellfire. It moves like a dart towards the ground, locked on to the target. The car erupts in a blinding flash, like a miniature atom bomb. It's a bigger explosion than any we've seen so far; it must have been jam-packed with explosives.

Ugly Five Four denies his vehicle moments later. Their fireball pales in comparison to ours and we remind ourselves to gloat about it later. We watch the cars smoulder for a while, then follow the Chinooks back towards Farah. I'm absolutely whacked.

By the time Wiggy and I have refuelled, had a quick stretch and climbed wearily back into our cab, we've been away for almost twenty-five hours flying missions all over southern Afghanistan.

We head back in almost total silence as the sun comes up dead ahead of us. I squint into the bright sunlight and wish I had my dark visor instead of my NVGs on my head. I think back over everything I've done today . . . about getting back to camp . . . how much I want to sleep . . . my bed . . .

'Whoa, Wiggy!' I wake with a start.

'W–what?' He sounds jumpy.

'I think I just fell asleep flying.' I'm shocked at myself.

'Oh shit, me too,' says Wiggy. I see him slapping the side of his face in the front cockpit.

'Oh well, nobody died,' he adds, chuckling.

I know we're both mortified with ourselves, which is more effective as a deterrent than any bollocking. We sing annoying songs to each other for the next half-hour to keep awake, and by the time we are in radio range of Bastion, we can hear another flight involved in heavy fighting in Helmand.

'Welcome home,' I say.

Two days later, and we're on our way back from an uneventful TIC in FOB Inkerman. Based in the Upper Sangin Valley on the edge of the notorious Green Zone, around two hundred soldiers live here. They go out on patrol defending the area and restraining the activity of the enemy forces to the north and south of the base. The area is a hotbed of Taliban resistance – so much so that the troops have nicknamed Inkerman 'FOB Incoming'. The troops there are in contact more than anywhere else in Helmand, and Apaches fly out to assist most days.

The TIC today had already died down by the time we arrived, and we couldn't see any of the little bastards hiding nearby, so we were called back to Bastion after about twenty minutes by the current boss, Chris James' replacement. I hate leaving when the guys on the ground want us to stay, but the flying hours are tight and the boss has to allocate hours where they are needed most.

I'm flying with Wiggy, and I listen as he changes frequency and tells Crowbar we're inbound. They acknowledge.

Crowbar is like air-traffic control for the whole of Helmand province; at any one time there could be more than a hundred pilots and crews listening. They know what callsigns are flying, where, why and with what weapons. It's a great service, but I'm always aware of how many people can hear when I transmit. Everyone knows who the Ugly callsigns are and, seeing as I'm one of only two women, if I screw up, they'll know it's me. I try and keep it short and to the point.

Wiggy and I are in the lead, and Pete and JB are behind. Their cab is faster than ours – this sometimes happens, depending on how good the engines are – so as we race back they keep overtaking us, just to remind us they can. I see them again now, Pete's smug face leering out through the canopy. It's slowly dawning on me that Pete and I don't see eye to eye. It's not anything hostile, or even awkward; we just wouldn't ever spend time with each other given the choice. Being in such close confines makes you ultra-sensitive to the other person's annoying little habits as well, which makes the situation so much worse.

This week, my biggest gripe is Pete's feet. He has the most incredibly stinky feet I have ever come across. I simply can't imagine how someone who showers every day could possibly smell so bad and, on top of that, how they could then appear not to notice the stink. I spend a disproportionate amount of time dwelling on this topic. It's ridiculous.

Anyway, every day, Pete walks into our pod when he finishes in the JHF tent and I try to angle my face and nostrils pre-emptively away from the impending assault. When his boots are off, his feet seem to smell at me actively, willing their stench towards my cot. I usually have to leave; otherwise my countermeasure of shallow breathing makes me dizzy.

I can tell I irritate him as well. He thinks I'm ditzy and pointless, and because I know he thinks this, I worry when I'm around him. Then, because I worry, I forget things or say stupid stuff. It's a self-fulfilling cycle of panic and muttering self-reassurance. I know I'm doomed as soon as he raises his eyebrows at something I'm saying.

I'm thinking about the day before, when we were trying to get out of Kandahar in a hurry. I left my hat in the cookhouse and Pete had to drive me back so I could rescue it. He was annoyed, I could tell. Then, after we got back to the accommodation, we had a shout almost straight away. When we ran out to the Land Rover, in my rush not to be last, I left my flying shirt behind. He was seething, and I found out from the guys in the car that he'd said he 'couldn't believe anyone could be such an air-head'.

I can't shake these thoughts from my head as we fly back towards Bastion. I'm attempting to coach myself on how to be less like a moron and more like a professional when the radio crackles into life.

'Ugly Five Four, this is Five Four, do you fancy doing manoeuvres for the photo shoot?' Pete sounds jolly.

He's been playing with his new camera for the past few weeks, getting video clips of life out here to take home. He's got some really good shots, but he wants more of us flying.

'We talked about this on the way to the cab,' Wiggy tells me over the intercom. 'He wants something other than us just flying straight and level.'

I can imagine Pete thrilled, planning the shot. I see them slowing in anticipation.

I'm on the controls in the back seat, so I pull the collective up to max torque and push forward on the cyclic, watching us gain on them for the first time today. I start with a couple of passes in front of Pete's cab and then fly over the top of them. I sneak around behind them and fly quickly past, then duck down underneath them and emerge next to their windows.

'Pull up really fast,' suggests Wiggy.

I grab the stick and pull back, flaring the helicopter backwards. The world disappears beneath me and all I see is sky through all the windows, and I imagine Pete getting a great shot of the helicopter's monstrous black underbelly.

Crowbar frequency crackles. It's Pete: 'God, that was so good I think I've just come in my pants!'

Wiggy and I look at each other in the mirror, stunned.

'Did he . . .?' I start at the same time as Wiggy says, 'Was that . . .?'

'Yep,' I confirm. 'Sounded like Pete to me!'

I am elated. Finally, a small crack has appeared in the otherwise smooth, professional shell. He was so excited about videoing that he'd left his foot on the radio transmitter and broadcast when he'd just wanted to speak to JB in the back seat!

The whole of Helmand had borne witness to Pete 'coming in his pants', and we'll be able to tease him mercilessly.

The final ten minutes before landing pass in a blur of wanting to find out what Pete has to say about it. We land on first and they draw up behind us.

Wiggy starts typing: NICE WORK ON THE RADIO. It is met by silence. Interesting.

We both taxi for fuel and begin the daily race to see who finishes first (the fuel lines are different speeds).

After parking in our bays, we all hop out of our aircraft. Pete avoids any eye contact and goes to sign in his aircraft. Wiggy and I head for the lockers to dump our stuff.

When JB finally rounds the corner into the locker area carrying all his kit, he can barely keep a straight face to tell us what happened.

'Oh man, it was funny, I nearly died.' He's giggling like a girl. 'When I realized he'd said it over the radio, I thought I'd crash laughing.'

We hear footsteps coming towards the lockers and smother our smiles as Pete emerges.

'Shall we stroll back?' he says, deadpan.

He may try and sweep this one under the carpet, I think, but I'll be dining out on it for weeks. I can't wait to tell Jake.

A few days before I head home, Major James arrives back in theatre. I've barely seen the Boss since he arrived a few days ago, because he's been snowed under by the handover avalanche. The first, and only, proper chat I have with him is in the cookhouse over a greasy breakfast.

'I see the "Afghan Plan" has gone to pot then,' he says, sitting down and eyeing my sausage sarnie.

'I've been very good, actually.' I tell him I've been to the gym loads.

'So, how do you feel about not coming back here for a while? I mean, you won't have to deploy again until next Christmas,' he says. That's more than a year away.

I feel another surge of gratitude and happiness, as I remember that the Boss has promised to keep me in England until my wedding. I can't thank him enough.

'I'll really miss this place . . .' I start.

'Really?'

'No!' I say. 'Of course not. I'm so pleased to be out of here I can't describe it. I wouldn't care if I never saw this place again.'

'You might feel differently when you get home,' he forecasts.

'Maybe,' I say doubtfully and tuck into my breakfast.

Coming home after this tour mirrors my first time back: I'm apprehensive about slotting back into my everyday life, feel out of the loop on my friends' lives and, most of all, I want to talk about my experiences but I'm not sure what to say. In a slightly weird way, and true to the Boss's word, there are things I miss about Bastion – mostly, the people; the fact that they understand without you having to explain.

As I walk into my house, everything looks the same: the deep blue sofas where I am so used to snuggling up in front of trashy TV; the smooth dark wood of the grand piano I inherited from my great-grandmother; my double bass sitting regally in the corner. Everything looks the same, yet something fundamental has shifted in my life. I feel I am off axis and I'm struggling to realign and get into the rhythm of being back.

I tell Jake to read my diary again. I leave him to digest it, and we don't talk about it afterwards.

During my two weeks' leave, I try to sleep and sometimes manage eleven or twelve hours a night, yet tiredness still gnaws away at me. We try to make the most of my short time off and I move in with Jake in the officers' mess in Linton, in Yorkshire.

In the early hours one morning, I spring out of bed, my heart unsteady with urgency. As I swing my legs down, searching for my flying boots, I feel unfamiliar carpet under my feet and hands around my waist. Then I hear Jake's voice asking what I'm doing.

'I have a VHR shout, I have to hurry.' I'm groggy, confused and panicky. 'What are you doing here?' He says nothing, just embraces me as my hammering heart slows.

When I'm fully awake, I'm embarrassed. Jake smiles and says, 'Don't be. You were very fast on that shout,' and hugs me tighter.

As Jake settles back to sleep, I lie thinking about my vivid nightmare. It was very dark outside the stuffy cockpit; the weather horrible. There was something very urgent I was trying to do; lives at risk. I started to drift into uneasy sleep and I had a gun slaved to my head – everywhere I looked, the crosshairs were lined up, ready to attack. I'm a jack-in-the-box, ready to spring at a moment's notice. My heart is still racing as I fall back into my nightmare.

Back at work, it's more of the same: air-testing, simulator and more simulator. In addition, my squadron has picked up orderly duties, so we cycle round counting pants for the man who looks after the stores. It's mindless and boring but just about right for my cloudy state of mind.

A few months later, and I'm in London celebrating Mia's birthday. She picks me up during rush hour at Liverpool Street station. I smile at everyone in a friendly way and they look at me like I'm a weirdo. People rush past, their briefcases smacking my legs. It feels alien. As we make our way to a bar in Shoreditch, I constantly have to jump out of the road as the traffic speeds past. I'm only used to the slow-moving vehicles of the military world. I'm cold too; and while Mia wears a skimpy dress, enjoying the early signs of spring, I'm freezing in jeans and a jacket.

I'm thankful the bar isn't too crowded. We sit on low leather sofas, our drinks to hand. A lot of my friends from home come, and it's good to see more familiar faces. People do ask me about myself, but I don't really know what to say; I smile and move the conversation on to the latest gossip – engagements, new houses and holidays.

On the way back in a taxi to Mia's flat in St John's Wood, I'm quiet. I'm also tipsy from one too many drinks and have a wave of courage. I think, if anyone can understand, Mia will. I know she'll try.

'I know, I know, I'm sorry,' I finally answer when she asks for the tenth time why I'm so quiet. 'It's really weird, you know. I spend so much time thinking about Afghanistan, but I don't feel it's appropriate to talk about it. I try not to think about it but I can't help it. I *want* to talk about it, but I can't imagine that anyone would understand. And I don't want to make it more real by discussing it.'

She looks at me, attentive and surprised. We've been friends for over ten years, and she knows a moment like this is rare.

'You can talk to me about it. I know I may not understand. But I can try, Charlie, and I really will.'

The problem is that the whole thing is so far removed from

everyone else's life. I know she'd try, but it would take so much time; I'd have to start from the very beginning.

She starts again, looking at me with willing eyes: 'You can talk to Jake, can't you? I'm sure he'd understand. I mean, he's been in similar places – Bosnia, Iraq. He must see the sort of things that you have?'

'No, I don't ever talk about it. Killing people, I mean. I think it might ruin it – our relationship. I don't want to be that person back home. I want to be me.' I don't catch her eye and stare through the taxi's windows. Neon lights shining from kebab shops and bars pass in a blur.

'OK. Listen – we can talk about it. Don't bottle it up, Charlie, please.'

But I feel like I've said too much. I feel marginally better, though, and I change the subject.

'Can we go shopping tomorrow? I want to check out Karen Millen. I've seen a killer pair of heels in there.'

'Yeah, let's do it.'

She knows me too well and so doesn't press me further.

I hope, with time, these horrible feelings will pass, but I know that for many people they don't. One of Jake's best and oldest friends came back from Afghanistan an unrecognizable man. He'd seen the dead bodies of his comrades coming in through the gates of Bastion too regularly and just couldn't make sense of it. He stopped sleeping and turned to religion, to intermittent violence, then succumbed to complete madness and was sectioned for a time. He was discharged from the Marines with no investigation or medical assistance. Another of Jake's friends talks of nothing but his Afghanistan experiences, also trying to make sense of them. And Jake struggles with his own monsters: memories of burying his close friends in Iraq. No one is unaffected, yet when you get home you're expected to join in all the barbecues and parties with the energy and innocence you left with.

The truth is that, while you're away, all you can think of is getting home and getting back to normal, but when you get home, you realize that normal doesn't exist any more. The demons come home with you, and the knowledge that the confusion will continue while you're at home fills your dreams with anxiety and dread.

It also feels as if no one will, or can, understand.

Two weeks later, and I've got the weekend off again – this time, I'm with my family in Oxford for my mum's birthday. I always plan my time off carefully so that I see people – I'm anxious that, when I'm away, I may have missed out, so I'm eager to catch up.

The mood is playful, chatty and cheerful. We're out having a sumptuous lunch, and I feel the usual warm glow at being surrounded by all my family; so many people I love in one room. Dad couldn't make it over from Chicago, but I'm getting back into the swing of normal life and work. I'm still extremely delicate on the subject of injured soldiers, post-traumatic stress treatment or our political reasons for being at war, and try not to be drawn on any of those topics, despite people's constant assumptions that I will be, and should be, interested in discussing them.

A package sent by Dad hasn't arrived in time and this sparks off a conversation about the Royal Mail and the price and efficiency of the service. A friend of Mum's, Julie, turns to me and asks what I think of the group of mothers who successfully lobbied for permanent free post to Afghanistan and Iraq this Christmas. It was a long battle and I was overjoyed when they won.

I don't even pause to think, knowing everyone will share my viewpoint anyway.

'I think it's well overdue, obviously. I mean, the thought of so many families, some who really can't afford it, paying through the nose just to send socks, pants and food to their sons in the FOBs is unreal.'

204

Julie nods thoughtfully. There's a pause while we continue to eat and drink.

'Well, I think it's scandalous,' spits Aunt Margery, putting down her glass firmly.

'What?' I ask, bemused.

'It's pardon, not what,' she says automatically, 'and I think it's ridiculous that the taxpayers should be paying so that parents can send their kids treats.'

I'm confused, and not sure where she's going with this. I start to feel that creeping anxiety in my tummy I get whenever there's an uncomfortable discussion about the war.

'Margery, it's not just treats they're sending, it's things to make life bearable out there. And why shouldn't they send treats – do you have any idea what the boys go through?' My face is flushed.

Jake has gone quiet, leaving me to rant. He's very sensitive about this too, because of friends of his who have suffered. He squeezes my hand as a warning under the table.

'Anyway,' I continue, 'you should be grateful to be only paying the price of a few stamps if it shows support for the armed forces. You should support them. Us.'

'Why should we? You're not out there for us, we don't want you there,' says Aunt Margery, and takes a bite of her pie.

I'm gobsmacked. The table is silent for a minute or more. Julie changes the subject, and soon everyone is chattering happily about the unusually sunny weather for February. I try to forget what Margery said, and we finish the meal amicably.

Afterwards, we all pile into our cars to head back to Mum's. Jake and I collapse into his Land Rover and I burst into tears.

'My own family doesn't even understand!' I scream. I'm so angry, and stunned.

I thought that, of all the people in the world, my family would 'get it'. I've always sent long, descriptive letters home, telling them about what we go through in Bastion and, more importantly, what life is like for the men who do the dirty work: life in the FOBs and out in the Green Zone. There's never any need to ham it up, the boys have it tough, and I thought everyone appreciated that – and the fact that they're not doing it for the good of their health. It's their job, and they do a bloody good one at that. These boys joined up young to fight for their country, and it's not their fault, our fault, that the government has sent us somewhere so controversial.

'If Margery can say something like that, to our faces, then there's no hope with people who have no direct connections with the military,' I sigh, beaten.

Jake leans across the car, squeezes me and gives me his hankie. It smells of Imperial Leather and pocket fluff. I snivel into it.

'There's nothing we can do about it apart from keep going out to these places and doing our best. Cheer up, gorgeous.' Jake smiles and I feel the anger melting away. It doesn't help to be so furious, after all.

'Now, can we go to your Mum's so I don't miss the cake?' Jake asks, laughing. He's making light of it all, but I know he feels it too; it's just so hard facing the critics over something that we're not in control of.

I sigh and agree. I know we'll be having this conversation again.

I spend hours with Mia in the next few months planning every detail of my wedding and hen party; it is this, more than anything else, that helps me back into normality. In some ways I find it easier than the first time round, because I know what to expect, but in other ways I don't. I feel desperately tired, even after weeks of ten-hour sleeps, and of course I'm still thinking a lot about everything that happened on both tours, trying to make sense of it all. Mia and I visit wedding-dress shops together and try on everything from Vivienne Westwood specials to second-hand Oxfam numbers. I'm finding laughter, girly conversations and diversion the best antidote. And as every girl who has planned a wedding will say, even if you try not to become a Bride-zilla, somewhere along the way, the big monster starts making an appearance.

Work continues at a frightening pace, considering this year is supposed to be the squadron's recuperation year. We have back-to-back training exercises to plan on top of keeping all the pilots in the squadron competent. I fly to Duxford and show children around the cabs, the Boss and I fly to Blackpool as night training and draw a huge crowd for take-off. Memorably, in front of this crowd, I forget to remove a crucial pin before starting rotors and the Boss insists on shutting the whole aircraft down before I go and retrieve it. All eyes are on me as I unstrap, open the door, climb out, crawl one metre along the side, remove the pin and retrace my steps. The Boss thinks it is hilarious.

All the squadron pilots spend time in the simulator trying to keep our weapon skills up to scratch. We fire at tanks, trees and ships – anything the sim can invent – and as new information filters back from Afghanistan, we practise new techniques and procedures too. There is one sortie – the 'Hot & High' – where a simulated aircraft is loaded up to the absolute max, then the temperature is cranked up to the fifties, leaving us with almost no power. We then have to fly over tall buildings with no run-up, survive engine failures and hover. I'm rubbish at it at first, but bit by bit we all get better, and I feel like I'm at least keeping up my skill level.

One wintry day, the Boss and I are hovering stealthily in our Battle Position (BP). We're on the forward edge of a Scottish hill, over a dark-coloured field; perfect for concealing the dark shape of our helicopter from above.

It's the last day of the annual Tactics Instructor course at RAF Leuchars in Fife. The students are being tested on everything they've learned, and our two Apaches have been asked to try to simulate shooting them down. We've chosen the location carefully; it's on their route home, so they'll be starting to relax, thinking it's all over.

I scan the sky for the packet of helicopters.

'There they are!' the Boss shouts soon after.

I slave the TADS to where he's looking and, sure enough, a line of helicopters comes into view. Just right.

I action the missiles and engage the auto-track on to the first one.

Our wingman is behind us and about a mile to our east. I pass him the details of their location and some instructions: 'You take the first helicopter and work backwards, I'll start at the last one and work forwards.'

I track from the final cab – a Puma, the little icon flashes on my MPD. I'm waiting for the exact moment to spring the ambush . . .

Now!

I pull the triggers and hear the simulated missile leaving the aircraft. I count down the seconds until the missile would impact if it were real, announce 'Impact', and move the sights on to the next helicopter, a Chinook.

For real, the Puma would now be a burning mass heading for the ground but, of course, we're only playing, so they have no idea. I track the Chinook and repeat the engagement, announcing 'Impact' again when the missile hits.

We have time to take out three of the helicopters before they are out of my sight, and I hope that our wing has swept up the rest.

Forty minutes later, I sit with a mug of milky tea in my hands and try to concentrate on staying awake; this debrief has been going on far too long, and it's all very self-congratu-latory. Thirty-odd students and instructors sit on plastic chairs facing the front of the room, the students waiting to find out whether they've passed.

The chief instructor is a man called Nicky-J. He is a loud, likeable guy, but obviously fancies himself a lot. He is just finishing up debriefing the final stages of the trip he's just led, giving a blow-by-blow account of how well his aircraft did. He was in the Puma at the back of the pack, and I smirk to myself.

Nicky-J gives a toothy smile and sums up: 'Overall, a big success, so a huge "Well done" to all the students. You obviously had a great instructor.' I start to perk up, knowing what's coming. 'Anyone got any points?' he asks.

My time has come; I stand up.

'I have,' I announce, and hit 'play' on the tape player. A video picture fills the screen at the front of the room, and I tell everyone exactly where we were sitting in our BPs and when. Understanding dawns on some of the faces as I talk through our 'secret' mission to shoot them down, given to us by the instructors' boss.

Nicky-J looks crestfallen.

He stands up and starts to address the students: 'Don't let that detract from the success of the mission, guys.'

The Boss breaks in: 'You all got shot down! That would detract from anyone's day, I should think.' Then he deals the final blow: 'And I doubt that's the first time Nicky-J has been shot down by a girl.'

The room erupts, and Nicky-J goes red and sits down. The laughing takes a long time to die away.

In between the flying, there is always other stuff: adventure training, days on the ranges, meetings and briefings, and annual survival-training exercises. Two months after my success at Leuchars, we're travelling down to Felixstowe for a 'sea survival' day. This is something all the squadron aircrew do every two years or so. We have a few lectures in the morning to remind us of the basics if we are ever to crash over the sea and have to stay out there until we're rescued, then we drive to the coast and get on to a large tugboat-type thing and change into our immersion suits. These are full rubber suits made specially for each one of us, with watertight neck and wrist seals. We wear them whenever we're flying over a large expanse of water, just in case, with as many layers of warm clothing underneath as we can fit. Once in the water, we reacquaint ourselves with the logistics of deploying our single-man life rafts and bob around for an hour or so to remind everyone how cold it gets and how nauseous you feel.

After a period of time, a Sea King helicopter comes and winches us out of the sea and we get dropped back on to the tugboat. Then we have fish and chips and drive home via the pub. So, you see, it all sounds fine, but not if you hate water like I do.

By the time we arrive at the harbour, the boat has been prepared. I board and struggle into my 'bunny suit', a ribbed woollen all-in-one that goes underneath the immersion suit, looks like a giant furry condom and makes me look like the Michelin man. Then I pull out of my bag my secret weapon – a second bunny suit. I borrowed this from one of the guys who isn't here – I intend to keep the cold, and the water, out. I am huge and immobile by the time I stretch my rubber suit on, but very smug. I totter out on deck and we all help each other with the zips at the back, then glance around looking for the sea-survival instructor.

'OK, you lot. Time to get your LCJs and helmets on. Come grab one.' He gestures to a pile of sopping-wet kit on the deck. He looks extremely pleased with himself standing there in his North Face puffa jacket and Oakleys while we look like overgrown Quality Streets.

I clip on my LCJ. Usually, it holds survival beacons, water and flares, among other stuff, but this one is just for show – and for the winching carabiner on the front. I don my bright yellow safety helmet, wondering not for the first time how it is that we're allowed to go flying around Afghanistan but still have to wear a safety helmet to jump into the Felixstowe sea.

I see the Oakleys instructor waving everyone towards my end of the deck, away from the back, then hear a loud bang and a grinding noise. The most extraordinary thing is happening: a section of the deck has detached itself from the rest and is sliding back, like a sun roof in the floor. As we watch, mesmerized, a speedboat is revealed on a hidden deck below. As it rises up to meet our deck, I suddenly feel like I'm a Bond Girl and consider rushing to get my camera, but then remember what I look like in my rubber playsuit and stay where I am.

Oakley grabs two of the other instructors, jumps in, lowers himself into the water and reverses out in a spray of icy-cold seawater and cheesy grinning before any of us has moved an inch. It's all very cool.

'Right, stop staring at our new toy,' one of the other instructors shouts. 'Get yourselves in the water, sharpish.'

We all make sure the plastic boxes containing our one-man life rafts are firmly attached to our LCJs and prepare to dive in. There is a scrum at the back of the boat as the boys rush to be off first. The Boss tries a backwards somersault but comes up spluttering in the choppy water. Wiggy and I wait until last and then gingerly hold our noses and plop in as gently as possible, drawing a huge chorus of 'Looooosserrrrs' from the water.

Out of all twenty-four bodies in the water, I can only see Wiggy's head and one other now that we are in the huge, terrifying, rolling waves. I start panicking but tell myself to keep calm. I'm petrified of water, but I know if I keep busy I'll be fine. I occupy myself with getting the plastic life raft box the right way up and yank the red string on the side.

A pause; then there is a hissing noise and the plastic box comes open, revealing a bright orange mass of thin plastic. As the hissing continues, the orange thing self-inflates into an adult-sized floating papoose. It's like a sleeping bag with a back rest, and it's on an insulating, floating floor. As soon as it's inflated, I scramble eagerly in with the grace of a baby seal, and do up the Velcro across the top. There is a hood with a clear plastic face-shield which I also Velcro shut – now I'm enclosed and safe. I stick the antenna from my LCJ's radio through the hood as I've been taught and glance at the floor to take stock of the equipment provided: a pump to inflate the papoose manually, a sponge, some water, a 'drogue' for keeping your raft pointing downstream and a water pump, which I get busy with straight away, bailing out all the water I scooped in with me on entry. I finish bailing and deploy the drogue.

Task complete, I scan the horizon for the others; it's important to stay together. I see Wiggy already making his way over, so decide to paddle his way to halve the distance. I rip open the Velcro to my raft, the cold wind biting my face, stick my arms out and into the water and start paddling furiously towards him to warm myself up. Once we're within a few feet of each other I throw him my drogue and he ties us together. One of the other pilots joins us breathlessly a minute or so later.

We joke and talk about what happens if the helicopter doesn't show up for another ten minutes, and are joined by another two pilots. We all Velcro ourselves back into the warmth and safety of our own rafts and clock-watch.

'Can't believe the Boss isn't here yet,' jokes Wiggy from inside his plastic hood. His voice is muffled. 'He can never resist a big bunch of people to talk to.'

We all agree, and then I look over on to the crest of a huge wave and see another tiny orange thing moving our way.

'That'll be him now,' I tease Wiggy, but then I squint into the sun and see that it really might be.

As he draws closer, I can see that the Boss is pumping hard, against the current. As a raft of five, we're too big to paddle, so we sit still and shout encouragement, like 'You'll never make it!', to him.

Just as it looks like he's treading water and will never make it to us, a massive swell propels him into our group. The front of his raft hits the side of Wiggy's papoose at high speed, but everyone just laughs and starts tying the Boss to our growing floating gaggle.

'What's that noise?' asks Wiggy seconds later, and the concern in his voice quietens us.

There's a hissing noise, like air escaping.

'Oh my God! I'm sinking,' shrieks Wiggy suddenly, and we all look over to see that his raft is indeed losing air. The inflatable hood is now empty plastic dragging down over his face. He struggles to free his head from it but in doing so speeds up the air loss from the rest of his raft. The inflatable floor has sunk under his weight and the whole thing is wrapping itself around him. He's sinking fast.

We all struggle back out of our Velcroed-in shells and grab at him, trying to tug him and the massive weight of his water-filled raft on to the top of our human life raft.

'What happened?' one of the others asks as he grabs at Wiggy's feet.

I glance up at the Boss. His raft has ended up on the far side of us. He can't reach Wiggy to help, but he wouldn't be able to anyway – he's immobilized with hysterical laughter.

I turn to see that, now that the immediate danger has passed, Wiggy is also laughing himself silly.

'You bloody murderer!' he shouts.

'I didn't . . .' the Boss starts, then just laughs harder, which sets Wiggy off again.

I start to understand what has happened – the Boss punctured Wiggy's raft when he careered into us earlier.

Wiggy lies, soaking wet, across the top of all our rafts. After thirty minutes, he's starting to get really cold.

'Where's the damn helicopter?' I ask, becoming impatient. The immersion suits never keep all the water out, and there's only so long you can happily sit in a plastic coffin with a wet arse.

Finally, I hear the familiar and very welcome sound of helicopter rotor blades beating the air. We all poke our heads out of our orange hoods and try to see the Sea King first.

'There!' someone shouts. We all follow a shrivelled finger up into the sky and see the tiny dot of the approaching freedom bird. God, I know where I'd rather be.

'Now we just have to hope it comes to us first,' shivers Wiggy from his floating throne.

The helicopter gets louder and closer, and the relief on Wiggy's face when it slows down to a hover above us would be comical in any other situation. The noise of the rotors is deafening, and the water is now chopping and spraying violently in the helicopter's downwash.

'You go first!' the Boss shouts to Wiggy over the roar. He nods, frozen, and looks up to where the winchman is being lowered expertly to our group.

When I spot him, I'm immediately reminded of Kevin Costner playing a rescue swimmer in *The Guardian*, a film that was still on my mind days after watching it. I gaze at his strong hands and wonder how many lives he's saved.

He comes to a stop about a foot above Wiggy and beckons him to sit up. The winchman wears a warm, red suit and is already drenched from the spray. He looks ridiculously pleased to be down here, dangling on the end of a thin wire attached only to whirring rotor blades and a fuel tank, but we're as happy as he is.

Wiggy's LCJ is attached to the end of the winch, and he wraps himself around our rescuer. They slowly ascend into the air, the helicopter holding a rock-solid hover above us. Wiggy makes time to look down and give us two fingers before disappearing into the side door of the Sea King.

'Bastard,' says the Boss. 'And we let him go first!'

In the lull before the winchman descends again, the James Bond boat suddenly screeches up, covering us in more water.

'Oi, where've you been?' someone demands. 'We've been here almost an hour!'

Oakley instructor smiles and explains, 'It wouldn't be very good training if we plucked you out of the water straight away, would it?'

The Bondmobile is here to pick up the orange papooses once we've been winched to safety. In a real-life sea-rescue operation, they would just be discarded in the water, but for training they are used again. Probably why there were so many leaks in mine, I think, shifting my wet backside around.

One by one, we're plucked from the water; I go third.

When I sit up in my raft, the wind is freezing on my face and arms, and the winchman's beckoning hand looks miles away. He lowers himself another fraction and clips his safety carabiner on to mine. I'm then lifted bodily from my life raft. The wind is biting into me, and I feel a sudden rush of vertigo as the winch creaks and starts to raise me high above the sea. It feels like a long way to the Sea King's door, but about halfway up I can feel the flaming heat of the engines on my face.

We reach the door without incident and I pile unceremoniously on to the floor, stiff with cold and too many clothes. A second crewman pushes me towards the seats that line the sides of the helicopter's belly and I buckle in, dripping all over the floor.

Wiggy and one of the other pilots are sitting opposite me, grinning and taking photos. They'll not be for the family album, I think.

Once everyone has been picked up we head home, and within minutes we're hovering above the tugboat and the side door is re-opened. The winching procedure is reversed, and we're lowered with surprising delicacy on to the deck.

I feel frozen but triumphant as I head for the below-deck showers. I didn't drown. I descend into the gloom below deck and climb into one of the stationery-cupboard-sized shower cubicles that line the sides like lockers. I struggle out of my kit and throw it out of the door before turning on the hot water; it feels amazing. The only problem is staying upright; the tugboat is pitching and rolling and the shower floor is pretty slippery.

I hear Wiggy laughing to himself in the next-door shower as the boat heaves again, and I grab the soap dish for support.

Five minutes later, I emerge, bruised but warm.

It takes almost another two hours for everyone to be winched to safety and showered and for the boat to get back to Felixstowe, but the mood on arrival is jubilant. We all pile into the minibus, drive to the fish and chip shop and then home in a seawater and salt-and-vinegar haze.

Thankfully, life reverts back to a series of extremely boring training exercises, which allows me to focus on enjoying my final months as a Bride-zilla without distraction.

I get married on a crisp November morning. Our wedding day is every bit as perfect as I hope it will be. Not normally one to love the attention being solely on me, today I relish it. As Jake and I walk down the cathedral aisle hand in hand, our cheeks aching already from smiling so much, tourists with rucksacks and dodgy camcorders slung round their necks take pictures. I continue to grin.

Twenty of our military friends, who are all wearing their formal dress, gather at the entrance to form a guard of honour. They raise their swords into the icy air to make an archway and we walk through to applause.

From there, we follow the marching guard to a local hall we've hired for the reception. It's been transformed into a winter wonderland: a forest of real trees fills one side, fairy lights are strung from the ceiling and a band plays jazz as everyone gets slowly drunk on mulled wine and champagne. We try to get around to speak to our guests – on my side, from my American relatives to my university and Sandhurst friends. Louise and Tom look blissfully happily married; she tells me she feels more content than she ever imagined she could be. The Boss has even forsaken a day watching *High School Musical 3* with his kids to join the celebrations.

I can't help snatching a few moments to think about my life, though; how Afghanistan has changed me and how it's brought Jake and me closer together in a way that other couples could never imagine. A wedding is so far removed from what is happening there, so when I look at my work colleagues, I have moments of dislocation; yet I know I'm as settled as I can be into my old life.

Just as we think it's time for the wedding breakfast, Jake ushers me outside. All our friends follow, and everyone forms an L-shape along two sides of the front lawn.

He's organized a performance by the military drummers – we've seen them at formal balls before and he knows I love them. As they drum, march and move in perfect synchronization, I watch with a smile which I know is making me look goofy. But I can't stop. I feel like a princess in my own fairytale.

In the run-up to our first married Christmas, Jake and I spend ages picking the right tree, or rather, like on a shopping trip for a new pair of shoes, I find one and he agrees and then I decide it's not right – with the tree, it's either not quite tall enough, or bushy enough, or the right shape. Eventually, on about tree 143, we find 'the one', which we lovingly decorate. Various family members come to us, and we spend the days eating, cooking, walking, trying to stop the dog eating the left-over turkey, and relaxing in front of bad-film re-runs.

During the merriment, thoughts of my return to Afghanistan are always present. January the first looms like dirty water seeping into my mind. I try to push it out and plug the hole, but it just returns, the flow even heavier than the time before. I know I only have a few days left at home and, while I'm consciously trying to eke out the time, I also want to get on my way so that I can start counting the days until I'm back.

As soon as my family leave, I go to the local hairdresser and ask her to cut my hair short and dye it brown. I want to draw less attention to myself back at Bastion. When I see the result, I'm happy – I think I look a bit like Audrey Tautou. I'm less happy when Jake tells me I look like the weird girl next door, but I know he's joking.

There's also always the very real chance I won't come back. I try not to dwell on it but, in practical terms, I make certain decisions: I won't spend the John Lewis vouchers we've been given as wedding gifts and don't buy anything new. Just in case. I write letters to the people I love: Jake, my mum and dad, Mia. It's hard to know what to write, but I want everyone to know how much I love them. This is my third time making the necessary pre-deployment preparations, but these important letters need rewriting each time I go away to make sure they're relevant and up to date. As I write to Jake how much he means to me, I find tears in my eyes when I think of the pain it would cause him if I didn't return.

It's been over a year since I was in Afghanistan last, so the memories of my previous trips seem distant figments in my mind. I know I've blocked a lot of it out anyway, as part of my post-Afghanistan survival technique, and, as when I try and dig around for scraps or highlights, I come up blank. I start to question whether I'm actually going to be able to do the job. I've also started mentally to disengage with the military – I know this is my last tour of duty and that, after that, I'll be free. It's my first chance to escape because I have served the minimum time to allow me to leave. I'm due to become a civilian as soon as I get back to the UK this time. I can't wait. The next move, the next course, the next posting; none of it bothers me any more.

This time out I have a new role – as the Boss's right-hand man, the ops officer. I'll be in charge of scheduling people to jobs and making sure they're briefed properly. It's a big promotion, and I hope the mountain of paperwork and other tasks will keep me busy and make the time pass faster. I'm looking forward to making a difference to the way the squadron is run.

I've the won the toss, as far as Jake is concerned. It's always worse being the person left at home. He'll be in his usual rhythms, with nothing to distract him; he won't know why I can't call on some days and, when we do speak, I won't be able to tell him the specifics. When I get home, I know from experience that I won't want to tell him what I've been up to, so he'll never really know.

Everyone says you feel different in yourself when you're married, and I do, I feel more confident. It's as if a warm, comforting blanket shrouds me, protecting me from the outside world. I guess the slight nerves I have before this next tour are normal, but my anxiety is mixed with a sliver of relief that, at least to some extent, I know what to expect out there.

New Year's Eve is spent reservedly sipping champagne and watching a somewhat extreme horror flick to take our minds off the fact that I'm going. When Jake drives me to the station in the morning, I open the door and fling myself and my kit out while the car is still on the move.

I don't look back and I don't cry. I'm determined to keep it together this time.

The next day, as the whole squadron travels up the M25 towards Brize Norton, I stare longingly out of the coach windows at the other cars on the road: Fiestas full of squealing teenagers and 4x4s heading west with small children asleep in their car seats. I'd rather be anyone but me right now, I think.

As I descend the plane's metal steps in Kandahar, the smell of faeces from the cesspit hits me hard in the face – it's the most powerful sense I have of this vast place; it brings me back the same way a pack of waxy crayons takes me back to kindergarten. The difference now is that it no longer smells gross; it's just Kandahar. There's dust everywhere, and as I inhale, the warm air shoots up my nose into my mouth and eyes. The

Bastion bogeys have started already, I think. All sorts of things come out of your nostrils here; it's a hazard of the job. As we stagger towards the hangar with what amounts to pretty much all the possessions we'll have for the next few months, the wind kicks up spirals of grit. My eyes scan the scene: there are people in civilian clothing, some carrying doughnuts, Starbucks cups and takeaway boxes.

'Why can't we live here, with all these doughnuts available?' says Stu, my new back-seater. He reminds me of Tintin in every way. He is small with a blond quiff and a cheeky ever-present grin, and he's always up for mischief. He joined the army as a soldier and was in the signals, which is great, because I know I'll be able to blame all the radio problems on him.

'Tell me about it. Apart from then we'd all get fatter out here rather than thinner,' I point out, prodding my muffin tops.

'Yep,' Bertie agrees. 'Get me on the Afghan Plan.'

'I agree. I had noticed you two were getting a bit portly,' Stu chips in. 'Not like me, I'm a picture of perfection, don'tcha think?'

I can tell he's taking the piss, so I just snort and say, 'Yeah, well at least I don't look like a balding albino.'

'Shut up, look at me – tanned and ripped. I bet my muscles alone weigh 200lbs!'

I look at his normal-sized frame and know we're going to get on.

We're taken into the accommodation block. Bertie and I glance at each other with wide-eyed glee. In the time we've been away, ten new two-storey, semi-permanent accommodation blocks have been built. They're like Portakabins stuck together, with tiny rooms; each has two beds with plastic mattresses. I'm on an all-girl corridor with female-only loos and showers just two doors down. No sharing with boys! It feels like the Ritz of Bastion.

I test the bed out – the metal springs protest and my sweaty hands slip on the plastic mattress, but it's luxury compared to a camp cot.

'Couldn't get away with much on these, could you?' says Bertie, giving a dirty laugh and bouncing on her mattress.

'Not that there's any chance of that,' I say, eyeballing the male Afghan cleaners in the hallway.

When I left the previous time, there were only a handful of locally employed contractors helping out around camp; now there are more than two thousand, and most of them appear to be in our corridor now, shamelessly devouring our uncovered arms and heads with their eyes.

Helmand has changed so much as to be almost unrecognizable. Thousands more troops now occupy FOBs across the region, but many are virtually pinned down, as each time they set off on patrol they are attacked with home-made bombs and mines. The area is vast but the enemy more so; they could fight us for a thousand years and still have replacements trickling over every border. They're lawless, ruthless men with no sense of the 'gentleman's war' the British like to fight. At Christmas, our troops donned Santa hats and sat around the scorched earth singing carols; far from abiding by the ceasefire, the enemy surrounded the FOBs and commenced bloody attacks.

The 654 Squadron guys we're taking over from are, of course, overjoyed to see us. As we walk into the JHF for the first time, a chorus of 'Nice to see you, mate', 'Finally, you're here' and 'Right, it's all yours, you fuckers. I'm off' greets us – the last from Wiggy. He was recently posted to 654 and has been doing the job I'm about to take on.

I go on a famil flight with one of the pilots who's finishing his three-month stint. Things change so quickly here that my two previous tours are almost irrelevant in terms of knowing where we'll fly and where the troops are now concentrated.

221

I feel out of touch, and my back-seater's voice seems muffled when it filters through my brain. The sun's too bright and there's too much to learn, but I try to relax into it and soak up the new info.

'Nad-e Ali is a real hotspot,' my back-seater is saying. 'We come here to fight on an almost daily basis.'

I'd never even heard of Nad-e Ali on my first tour; the enemy has changed its dispositions radically. As we continue our circuit, I stare down at the thousands of tiny compounds, at the occasional white car weaving between the dunes; I aim the TADS into villages and see dogs teasing goats and women inside compounds hanging out the laundry. I start thinking about my little house in York and of Jake at home trying to work the washing machine on his own . . .

My back-seater's voice jolts me back: 'And here in Sangin we sometimes use Lynx as well as Apaches to escort the Chinooks in.'

Now Zad, where I did so much fighting in the first tour, is now the responsibility of the Americans and apparently the Brits never go there. We don't go to Kajaki or Garmsir as much either. Musa Qal'eh in the north is very busy for the Apaches though, as are loads of the new FOBs scattered around the region.

I arrive back at Bastion, my brain befuddled, and sit down immediately in the debriefing room to write down as much as I can remember.

As a part of the final handover, the Boss and I watch reams of gun tape; we need to know where it's all archived so that, when we give briefings to the guys on the ground, we show them the relevant stuff.

'You OK, Charlie?' the Boss asks.

'Fine,' I reply. I am looking away from the TV screen, out of the window. 'It's just a bit full-on watching this, that's all.'

We've been in here for about an hour and it's all kill TV – bodies being thrown through the air, lying in heaps, burning.

Nausea washes through me and I wonder again why I don't get as excited about it as all the boys – they can't get enough of it. To them it's like a drug.

I'm feeling nervous about my first killing on this tour – the situation sounds macabre and it is. It's complicated by the fact that the rules of engagement have changed dramatically, mainly to avoid civilian casualties. The first thing we're told is that we can't destroy whole buildings indiscriminately, even if they are clearly being used by the Taliban, because if we destroy someone's house, the British government might end up paying out, and the hearts and minds effort is starting to become expensive. But the biggest reason is that the detrimental effect of a village member's house being destroyed far outweighs the temporary military advantage of the bombing. After all, the Taliban will just move to the next house along, but the innocent owner of the destroyed house – and would-be supporter of the British military – is turned against us for ever.

We have to wait until there is a gun pointing at us or at one of our troops to be allowed to retaliate; it's the same rule that applies to any member of the public in the UK – self-defence. I know that we'll be carefully scrutinized, as always, after each engagement. It's not to catch us out – the Boss has stated many times that he trusts us all implicitly – but because it is a legal requirement.

I also feel as if I've had time to think about what's going on out here or even come to terms with what we're doing, and it's all very real now. I think all the pilots who are returning after a long break feel similarly, although none of us has actually spoken about it. The new pilots remind me of my first tour: they're just doing this automatically, like in the simulator, lining up the sights, pulling the trigger and moving on. For me, it's more than that now, and I'm not sure if I can actually go through with it. Being married to Jake, planning our future family, has made me realize what is at stake here – what I am taking away from someone every time I pull my trigger.

I'm also apprehensive that the more deeply I allow myself to be immersed in life here, the longer it will take me to reintegrate back home.

I laugh harder as I try and get the Fruit Shoot juice bottle to balance on my helmeted head. The cyclic digs into my leg and tears roll down my dusty face when I catch sight of Stu in the rear-view mirror; he's laughing almost as much as I am as he attempts to hold the camera still. I can't remember why we thought this would be a good photo, but it's passing the time nicely. It's already 7 a.m.

We have slotted straight into the twelve-day cycle; our lives are no longer about seven-day weeks. We're on VHR; this morning I woke up early hoping to be busy and, so far, it's looking good: only two hours in and we're sitting on the ground at one of the forward operating bases near Musa Qal'eh, a place called FOB Edinburgh. It's a small, well-kept base in the middle of the desert where we can get fuel and then wait to launch in support of patrols in the local area. We flew here at dark o'clock, fuelled up and took up our current positions on the dust-suppressed patch to the north of the FOB: me in the front, Stu in the back and all the time in the world.

'Got it,' laughs Stu into the intercom.

I wheeze something in reply and return the Fruit Shoot to its position on the dashboard. I'm saving it for later.

My tummy throbs from laughing, and while Stu fiddles with the borrowed camera I reflect on how glad I am that we're paired up.

One week in, and we're already working together like a well-oiled machine; I feel as if I'm half of a synchronized pairs diving team, which is always how it feels when you fly with someone who has enough capacity to do their own job and to pay attention to yours. Even if we're both on separate radios dealing with different dramas, I'm trying hard to get the TADS slaved on to something that matches my map, Stu is flying the aircraft

224

through a complicated manoeuvre and I decide we need to start our run-in to the target, all I have to do is waggle my finger above my head through the blast screen, and the aircraft will suddenly be heading the right way. He doesn't even have to stop talking on the radio, and neither do I.

But that's not why I'm so glad; it's because we have so much fun. Whenever a dull moment presents itself, with it arrives a golden opportunity for comedy. We giggle our way through long transits, banter our way through take-offs and landings and tease viciously through TICs. I love it, and it's certainly making the last five months of my army career go faster than they otherwise would.

Camera away, I see Stu look up in the rear-view mirror. 'Where's that bacon sarnie? Honestly, he's SO SLOW,' he mutters.

We have started a running joke in our flight about the speed of the other crew's front-seater. On our very first shout, he took almost an hour to get to the aircraft while we all waited on dispersal with engines running. He faffs and dithers at every pass in an attempt to get everything perfect, and we are remorseless with our banter. He also had a horrible stomach upset in the first week here, so we regularly add his 'leaky bum' to our list of insults. He's done a load of jobs in the army and is senior to me but, as an Apache pilot, he's a newbie and it's his first tour. As a dad of one with another one on the way, he's also a devoted family man; he spends hours Skyping his wife and mentions her at every available opportunity.

As I look up, I see his pink cheeks making their slow way past the front of our aircraft, heading for the tiny gap in Edinburgh's HESCO fortifications that forms the entrance. He's concentrating hard on finding his footing as his slight frame crosses the rough ground. I'm guessing he's gone to check up on the bacon sandwiches he ordered for us an hour ago from the cook tent.

I quickly type a message into the IDM, our form of text messaging between aircraft: 'WHAT'S TORTY UP TO NOW?'

We call him Torty, for Tortoise. I look over at JB sitting alone in his aircraft and see him pressing the 'receive' button then laughing. He starts typing, and as Torty passes our cab and moves slowly towards the HESCO wall we receive a response: 'GONE FOR OUR BREAKFAST. BACK IN TIME FOR LUNCH.'

The four of us make up Two Flight – and the three men have all taken well to having me in charge. It's a big compliment.

Fifteen minutes after Torty set off for the food, I am covered in bacon grease from my sarnie and hydraulic fluid from my gloves. I stuff the last of my sandwich into my mouth with my filthy fingers, cracking the cockpit door to chuck the crusts out on to the dirt.

'Good breakfast, huh? Eventually.' I look up at Stu in the mirror, but he's obscured by bread.

'Mmmphs vrygd. Youwnt nthr wn?' is the reply I receive.

God forbid he gets a radio call in the next two minutes; he can't even speak to me through the volume of bacon in there. Torty had eventually waltzed out with two bulging packets of sarnies – the chef was pretty excited about having visitors – and Stu took six. Not having much facility for leftovers in the tiny cockpit, and never one to waste food, he is now committed to eating them all.

'No thanks, I reckon we're about to go. Sun's fully up,' I say, pointing at JB, who is sunning himself by his cab. 'Terry will be wide awake and ready to fight by now. Just hopping out for a wee.'

I unplug my comms lead and jump out, then decide I'll just check what's happening before I go. I stroll into the ops room inside camp to phone back to HQ.

As I walk in, I see the internet chat window shared by the whole of theatre suddenly flare into life. One of the patrols we're supporting this morning has come under heavy contact.

I start running and have a moment outside the tent, turning left for the loos, then right for the cab, then left for the loos again, torn between supporting the TIC and relieving myself before the three-hour flight. I decide I'd better get airborne fast, turn right and start a familiar adrenaline-fuelled sprint to the cab. As soon as I'm in eye-shot, I signal to Stu to start up and, by the time I'm plugging in, the rotors are whirling.

Overhead Musa Qal'eh, I get radio comms with Widow Seven Nine, who is out on the ground with an Afghan National Army patrol. They have been coming under contact from multiple firing points for twenty minutes and are trying to return to base.

'Ugly, can you just have a look into compound 71? We think that's where it's all coming from.' I can hear gunfire in the background, and my breathing speeds up.

I dig out the right mapping – there are over twenty maps for a town the size of Musa Qal'eh. The cockpit is already starting to fill with grids, maps and paperwork as I plug the coordinates into the TADS. The sights slave on to an area where three men are standing around, with another two in bulky clothes making their way up the road from where the last contact was. On the corner of the track is a rectangular compound with speakers on the roof.

'Widow Seven Nine, this is Ugly. That building is a mosque . . .' I see something else '. . . and to add to that, there are children playing in the field next door.'

Below us, five youngsters of varying heights are kicking a football through the dust, harbouring desires to make it to the country's national team and become their equivalent of Wayne Rooney.

'Bloody hell,' I gasp to Stu over the intercom, 'I can't fire there! There're kids, it's a mosque, and I haven't seen any weapons.'

Widow sounds like he's in trouble, so I decide to put a warning burst down to try and defuse the situation. I slave the sights on to the dirt patch next to the mosque and pull the trigger. Twenty rounds spatter neatly down into the dirt.

'That's the compound, Ugly! Engage!' Widow is understandably keen to get his patrol to safety.

Suddenly I see one of the guys with the bulky clothes adjusting his robes. He has gone to the far side of the mosque to do it, so I can't see him, but zoomed right in as I am, I make out his shadow, and in it the shape of a weapon. He darts out from behind the mosque, dives into a ditch and heads west. A couple of his mates follow.

I report back: 'Widow, Ugly. I think I've got weapons.'

'You're not the only one, Ugly. Greeneyes has PID'd weapons at that exact grid too!' Greeneyes is the UAV operating in this area.

'That's a bit better,' says Stu. Now we're in a situation we both recognize – good guys under contact, enemy forces a nice safe distance away and obviously carrying weapons.

'Ugly, I need you to engage!' I can hear Widow panting as he tries to continue his patrol. We wheel immediately around and track the bulkily dressed weapon-carrier along a treeline. He's not stupid, and has chosen the perfect place to hide. The early-morning shadows obscure the Day TV and the water at the bottom of the treeline muddies the FLIR picture.

As Stu turns the aircraft north to set up for a strafe along the treeline, I unexpectedly catch sight of another enemy head bobbing along the path.

Stu hasn't seen and is asking, 'Do you want me to tip in west or east?'

There's no time. 'Never mind that, we're engaging now!' I cut in, pulling the trigger with my left finger, the laser with my right, and trying to hold the whole thing steady. It's a poor shot; we're facing away, we're in the middle of a tight turn and

I'm rushing. The rounds land all over the treeline, but it's not a very tight group.

'Mong,' Stu teases.

'Thanks, just try and fly straight, loser. Bring me on to west.'

Then the radio pipes up: 'Ugly, this is Widow Seven Nine, we've just heard from the Taliban that you've killed one and injured another. Apparently the third is now on the run. Good shootin'!'

He's still on the move, but it sounds like we've taken the pressure off.

Stu is in fits in the back and has all sorts of useful comments.

'Twenty of the worst rounds I've seen today, and you hit two of them – hardly! He probably died laughing at your shooting!'

'Yeah, well, the other one probably injured himself falling over his mate while he was laughing at your flying.' My attention to the banter is only partial; I'm still frowning into the sights trying to find the third guy, but he's sensibly gone to ground. Torty has been shadowing us through the entire engagement but he has no luck identifying number three either.

A twenty-minute search finds nothing, despite Greeneyes' assistance, and soon we need to go home for fuel. We watch Widow's patrol until it's back to safety, have one last scan for the missing enemy fighter, and head for Bastion as a pair.

'I've just found a bit of bacon on my lap,' smiles Stu, sounding pleased with the find.

'In that case, enjoy your second breakfast and I think it's my turn to fly,' I say, shoving fistfuls of maps into the dashboard and taking the controls. We weakly josh about whose turn it is to make the brew when we get back, and who makes the worst tea, but mostly I'm thinking it'll be nice to have that long-awaited pee.

A week later, and I'm back in Musa Qal'eh. We've been here the past two days and, unbelievably, the enemy forces keep

229

using the same firing points each day. I run the TADS over the familiar face of compound 23. It has four smooth, stone, arch-shaped doorways facing south. It looks like an old colonial building, which once saw plummy-voiced Brits sipping tea from china cups inside its walls after the first Anglo-Afghan war of the 1800s.

Stu flies towards the arches so the TADS can be directed into them and, although I can't make anything out in the shadows, I know that the enemy is in there.

'We're still taking fire from 23, Ugly,' Widow Five One shouts into his radio.

His twenty-man patrol is on the northern side of the compound, so he can't see the doors. What he can see are small 'murder holes' the enemy has made in the wall facing him, and guns poking through the holes like accusatory fingers through a blanket, with angry muzzle flashes and rounds coming towards him. It's a pretty well-known tactic, and we can use simple rules of engagement to deal with it; the only problem is that you never know who else is in the compound. Sometimes the enemy fighter will just barge in on a family, use their house for a few hours then leave. It would make the British forces look pretty bad if we blew up every single one of these temporary sniper positions.

Compound 23 is easy, though; no locals have been near it for months.

I know that, at some point, the enemy will come out of the buildings, and I am waiting to catch them. Ideally, I would put a Hellfire into the compound from the south and blow the whole thing up, but the patrol is too close to where the blast from the missile would be. I'm going to have to pick off the individual snipers with my gun.

We circle and wait. Widow Five One takes more rounds. It's a dangerous gamble to let this continue, and soon Widow's patrol suffers a minor casualty. I hatch a new plan to force the enemy out.

'Fly straight towards those arches for a second,' I tell Stu.

'I'm going to stick some rounds inside the building to make them relocate.'

He wheels the aircraft round and I tell Widow about our plan. He's happy.

'Just get them, Ugly. I don't care what you do as long as you're planning to stop these guys. And soon.'

We run towards the compound and I line the crosshairs up with the first doorway and squeeze the trigger. Rounds spray around the doorframe, but some find their way indoors.

As Stu pulls the aircraft right to avoid over flying the compound and losing sight of the enemy, I see one of the fighters dart out of the door we just shot and run into the building next door. The aircraft, banked steeply over, is in no position to fire, and we miss.

'Bugger,' I sigh.

We reposition the cab and I ready myself, fingers hovering over the triggers.

Another man runs out of the right-hand door, which I wasn't expecting. I move my line of sight and fire but, by the time the rounds land, the man is safely inside.

For a few comedy moments this continues: the enemy run in and out of the four doors, trying to find safety, and each time I miss them by a split second. It's frustrating, and I tell Stu it reminds me of the arcade game Whack 'Em, where the targets pop in and out of little holes and you bash them with a foam hammer.

'Think there's something wrong with your hammer then,' he laughs, 'or your aim.'

Finally, one of the enemy leaves the compound altogether and makes a break for it down the road. He doesn't get far before my rounds hit him. He's motionless and lying just metres from the building.

'That should discourage the other little bastards.'

'Maybe it would be better if they all came out; we could pick them off one by one,' Stu wonders.

I have a better idea. 'No. I want to keep them there. I'm going to get Widow Five One to withdraw so we can Hellfire it.'

The patrol moves north a few hundred metres, and I put down a few bursts of 30mm while the patrol is vulnerable, then I make my move.

We wheel around to the north and I action a Hellfire. We have to act quickly before the enemy cotton on to the fact that we can't see the arches any more. I have to fire the missile in this direction to keep the blast safely away from the patrol.

'That's missile away,' I tell Widow as the Hellfire skims off the rails.

We all wait for impact, and Stu and I breathe simultaneous sighs of relief as the compound vaporizes in a huge cloud of dust and smoke.

'Direct hit,' announces Widow Five One, 'and firing has stopped.'

'And I didn't see any leakers,' says Stu, who has been watching for anyone escaping.

Good. I feel satisfied that we've stopped these guys now.

'Looks like they won't be using old number 23 again,' says Stu as we turn towards home.

A day later, and twelve pilots file into the debriefing room and sit down on the filthy canvas chairs; the other four are flying. The room stinks of old sweat and adrenaline. I choose to sit right at the back so no one can see my grimaces and promise myself I won't get angry.

We're here for a 'weapons debrief'. The idea is that the weapons officer chooses clips of gun tape to illustrate 'good' and 'could have done better' shooting, and then we have an open forum where we swap tips and advice. We also discuss rules of engagement if there have been any tricky situations recently. I think it's a great idea in principle, but often these sessions have a 'name, shame, and explain yourself' air to them.

Also, during the good clips, there's always a nauseating display of willy-waving. I hate it.

The first few clips are from the pilots who are flying, so we draw our conclusions and move on without any of the normal protests. One guy in the front adds his own personal sound-track. He starts up as we are shown a Hellfire hammering towards a compound: 'Whoooosh!' He then peppers the sporadic gunfire with a chorus of 'Pow! Pow!' Idiot.

Then up pops my gun tape from Musa Qal'eh the day before. As the tape is played, paused, rewound and replayed, I can hear the usual sucking of teeth and see heads shaking.

'Right,' the weapons officer starts, 'can anyone tell me what could have been better?'

I decide to bite the bullet and go first. 'Yep. Those were all snap-shots, taken on an opportunity basis. If I'd had more time, I could have set each one up, aligned the gun with the nose of the aircraft and stored each target.' There. That should head off all the 'helpful' remarks, I think.

But no. Soon there is a veritable chorus of: 'Didn't you think to use an automatic range?', 'Why were you so close?', 'Why didn't you come in from the north?' and I feel like shouting back, 'YES, I DID THINK OF THAT BUT I DIDN'T HAVE TIME,' but stop myself because I know everyone is just throwing out ideas. I feel paranoid, as if they're all picking on me specifically, but I know that isn't the case. It's my tiredness starting to show, and I take deep breaths and explain again that the shoot was fast; it was over before it began.

The next clip is to illustrate some rules of engagement issues. As the tape starts to play, the mission leader for that patrol talks us through the shot. Two ramshackle compounds sit in the middle of the desert, nothing around them. A track joins the two; chickens roam around one of the compound's yards. The friendly patrol is off-screen to the north.

'The friendlies were taking fire from their south' – he points to the TV screen – 'and we saw this guy here' – his pencil tracks across the screen as an enemy fighter enters the area and moves towards the compound without chickens – 'going into this southern compound. We watched the compound for another fifteen minutes, and no one went in or out, but the friendlies continued to take fire from it. They'd already sustained serious casualties, so when they asked us to destroy the compound we were happy to oblige.'

We all continue to watch as his Hellfire missile blasts into the compound on the TV, then the Boss pauses the tape. Everyone is nodding their agreement and murmuring that they would have done the same.

'Good shot,' one of the pilots says.

The Boss clears his throat and speaks: 'Now watch what happens.'

He fast-forwards the tape and then presses 'play'. We watch as some Afghan men and women appear from the southern compound and approach the smouldering compound. They look tormented – one woman has her hands on her head, another is gesturing wildly. Both have their mouths open, and it seems strange that the tape has no sound; they look as if they're screaming the house down. Two of the men climb through a smoking hole in the wall. Moments later, they emerge carrying the body of a small child. It isn't moving. The women crowd around the body as the men go back in, and soon they bring out another small body. After this come two teenager-sized men, staggering and limping. One of the women falls to her knees and puts her head on the ground over the first body. The tape cuts out.

The room is silent, and the mission leader looks ashen-faced. He's not quite looking anyone in the eye; his emotions are unreadable.

The Boss is the first to speak again, and when he does he asks the audience, 'Does that change anything? Was it still a valid target?'

The mission leader shakes his head slightly and quietly says, 'Yes. It doesn't change a thing.'

234

Someone else joins in: 'I agree. It's terrible, but the enemy were obviously using that compound too. You saw them go in and had no way of knowing the children were there.'

I feel confident when I add, 'Anyone would have taken that shot.'

There is general assent, but the mood is sombre. We all think about the difficult choices we've had to make in similar stressful situations, and we're relieved that, this time, it's not us who will battle our conscience tonight when the lights go out.

As I walk back towards the accommodation, my mind drifts away from the dead children, not because I am a heartless bitch but because I try never to dwell on the consequences of a decision. I still can't quite reconcile it in my mind and would drive myself mad thinking about it, so I comfort myself with the knowledge that, logically, it was the right decision. We didn't know about the children; the Taliban did. While the babies and children sat on the dirty floor playing, men around them fired shots from grubby weapons with the intention to kill.

I return to brooding on the honesty debrief and what people said about everyone else's engagements. I can feel my anger returning and, when I get to my room, I tuck into two mini Bramley apple pies and sulk, before strolling in a more reflective mood to email Jake. As I type in my password, a flurry of new messages appear. There're loads from Jake and Mia, and one from Louise. She's deployed in Iraq at the moment doing a similar job to the one she was doing for us on my first tour. I love reading her descriptions of camp life in Iraq – so similar in many respects to here: dirt and sand everywhere, men talking about work and a lack of clean clothes.

We've been swapping honeymoon stories to keep up our morale – I tell her about the pure blue water in the Maldives and, in her latest email, she gushes about the stunning hotels and white beaches in South Africa. It's good to be able to talk to her about being apart from her husband – hearing her pining for Tom makes me feel less lonely, somehow. Tom is back in

Afghanistan, although I only learned this from Louise; his being stationed at a remote base near Sangin means we never come face to face. Louise is dealing with the combined concerns for her own safety and the much greater worry over Tom's – and with her intelligence job, she is only too aware of the dangers he faces. I don't envy her one bit.

I reply back to her:

Hi hon, I can't believe how good South Africa sounds – I'm salivating just thinking about it. Do you really get mortared every few days? We are really lucky at Bastion and have only ever had a couple of scares; it's Kandahar where we have to be careful. I tried to look into Tom's base the other day as I flew past, but I couldn't see much activity – guess maybe they were out on patrol? Jake sent me a parcel this morning with some random photos to keep me entertained – he stuck in one of your hen party with all of us in Jane Austen outfits – remember? Keep safe, hon, speak soon, Charlie x

I step away from the computer, and my head is filled with the azure sea and milky-white sand of the Maldives. But, for me, I can't wait to go home.

My first big test comes four weeks into my five-month tour, in the shape of Operation Shahi Tandar. I will be mission lead – in charge of not only the Apaches but also the other helicopters involved. While I know my every move is being watched and monitored, I can't help feeling as if a simple insertion, our involvement in the bigger plan, has been turned into a complex and public planning process just because it's at Kandahar. The CO's boss is here, and high-ranking officers from Canada, America and other countries are also based here, so I feel under pressure to look good, as if I'm 'representing' the JHF.

The aim of this mission is to bust a series of factories which intelligence officers know are filled with bomb-making equipment and weapons, and to disrupt a group of terrorists in the western Panjwayi and Zhari districts. The mission is part of a bigger operation in the area.

I spend the day with the intelligence officers and the CO confirming the safest landing sites, liaising with the ground troops to find out where they intend to patrol while on the ground and when they need resupplies of food and ammunition, and making sure that all the maps, timetables and other products have been completed and printed. Stu is with me all day, helping out and loading up the data cartridges we'll need for the mission.

Orders kick off. I stand up and start the introduction. There are over sixty people gathered in the too-small, too-humid room for the presentation. As my momentum builds, I gain confidence. Everything goes smoothly, and it's over within an hour.

Afterwards, the pilots chat through the finer details of the take-off and transit; details that are only pilot-relevant. I end up standing at the bird table next to a Chinook pilot who has been rude to me all day for no reason. I vaguely remember his face from a course I'd been on back home.

'Hiya,' I say to him casually, taking my place and setting down my maps.

The back of his bald head shines in the fluorescent lights, gleaming at me. I try to ignore the fact that he silently keeps his back to me. His thick shoulder blades are level with my eyes.

Five minutes pass as we wait for all the pilots involved in the mission to arrive, then the rude man abruptly turns to face me. He's actually quite good-looking, with well-defined features and bright blue eyes, but the effect is utterly ruined by the way he's sneering.

'Are you the mission commander for this?' he asks, putting the emphasis on 'you'.

'Yes,' I answer, hoping I say it with at least some confidence.

'The whole thing?' he asks.

'Yes.'

'Hmm.' He doesn't sound impressed. I feel like I'm the scissor monitor in junior school and someone just asked me why I think I can run for prime minister.

'Don't you think we need a Chinook lead too?' he asks.

'Not really,' I answer. 'I think we just need someone in overall charge, that's all.'

'And you think that should be you?'

'Well, I don't really give a shit. The CO nominated me, so here I am. And I didn't notice you caring earlier, when I spent three days running around planning and preparing the orders.'

He sniffs, and his back appears in front of my face again. Fucking hell, this is all I need.

The last two pilots arrive. I start running through the JMB (Joint Mission Brief) format and find myself getting into the swing again. As I outline who is going to line up in what order on the runway, I feel the rude man's eyes on me once more. I falter, but manage to finish when, out of the corner of my eye, I see his shiny head shaking in disapproval.

I look over and raise my eyebrows in a question.

'No, no, no,' is all he says. Again I am transported back to my school years and feel as if I'm being told off in the play-ground by the cool gang but, in reality, I'm being reprimanded in front of a group of more experienced, older pilots who are all watching me for my reaction.

My first reaction is to feel my cheeks glow and my breathing become shallow. 'What?'

'That's not how we're doing it. Plan's changed.' He sounds smug. Obviously, he has changed his mind about the plan in the five minutes since my orders.

'Would you care to brief it, then?' I say, overly sweetly.

He briefs his practically-the-same-as-the-original plan, taking care to say things like 'unlike what Charlie just briefed' several times. I wisely bite my tongue, and soon the painful JMB is over.

No one else seems to pay the slightest bit of attention to what I feel is an obvious display of discord, but it's been a long day for everyone, and each pilot is concentrating on his role in tomorrow morning's flight.

Nine hours later, we're back around the same bird table having a confirmatory brief. It's 5 a.m. and we're due to launch in forty-five minutes; this is a standard check for weather and any other problems. The rude bald man is nowhere to be seen.

As Stu and I walk slowly to our cab, I rehearse the mission in my head. Two Apaches, three Chinooks and two Sea Kings will lift at the same time, in the dark and carrying hundreds of soldiers. We'll fly low level over the desert to a small village and drop the soldiers off in four different landing sites, from which they'll spread out and surround the factories.

We climb into the aircraft and start the APU, but the first thing I test – the radio – is broken. We have no crypto, meaning we can't talk to anyone securely. This is a no-go, and we spend the next thirty minutes trying to sort it out. I start to panic that we'll delay the whole operation. Eventually, we get one of the four radios working securely and start the engines in good time – only for one of the Chinooks to go unserviceable moments before take-off.

'Ha. Hope that's Baldy,' I say out loud.

'Who?' Stu asks.

'Never mind,' I answer quickly. No time for that now. 'It does bloody mean that we're lifting late.' Strike one against the mission lead – a late take-off. Plus our other three radios are insecure, which means I'll barely be able to pass any information over them. Bugger.

The transit goes according to plan, and the Chinooks are preparing to land when Stu spots that one of them is heading for the wrong HLS.

'Check nav!' he says urgently down the radio, but it's too late and the Chinook lands in an updraught of dust. The pilots have an extremely high workload in the final stages of a dusty approach, so it's no wonder they didn't hear. Wrong HLS – strike two.

The soldiers stream off the various helicopters in Etch-a-Sketch lines and head towards the nearest buildings. The men that climbed off the errant Chinook go towards the wrong buildings, understandably thinking they're at a different HLS.

I try and radio-check the JTAC, but when he gets his radio set up five minutes into the mission, he's nowhere near the lost patrol and has no comms to them. Wrong buildings, and nothing I can do to correct it – strike three.

A few tense minutes pass, and someone on the ground eventually realizes the error. As they start to set off towards the right building, I feel reassured. I adjust my arse across the lumpy seat and settle down for the long haul as Stu and I scan the perimeter of the area to look for any threat.

When we reach bingo fuel – the point where there's just enough fuel left to be relieved by another flight and get back – two hours later, we check out with the JTAC and return to Kandahar to await the request for a resupply.

That afternoon, as we prepare to fly out again, I learn that the REME and signallers have not, in fact, sorted the crypto out, as they had assured me they would. We are going flying again with no secure radios, and I'm incandescent with rage that this hasn't been fixed. I want to do my job to the best of my ability, and this will screw me over.

'There's no time to deal with it now, for fuck's sake,' I say testily to Stu. 'We'll just have to roll with it and kill the signallers later.'

'I'll do that for you,' he says with an evil smile. He has a running feud going with one of the signallers over a petty disagreement, and is always planning ways to harm him. It's a form of self-therapy for him when we come back from stressful flights.

The resupply goes without too many hiccups, considering I

have no working radio and am supposed to be running the mission. I'm very careful what I say, as anyone with a simple radio scanner will be able to listen in. I become more and more furious at the situation as the sortie drags on.

Back at Kandahar, I storm into the ops room to find the captain in charge of signals. I have tunnel vision and stare around the room in a rage looking for him, so when the rude bald man steps into my line of vision I'm startled.

'How was that?' he sneers.

I have absolutely no morale left, and no inclination to be polite. He clearly knows it wasn't a huge success and has come to bask in the fact that as I was mission lead, it will reflect badly on me.

'Great,' I snap. 'Apart from the fact that *someone* landed in the wrong place, I think everyone managed to play their parts well.'

He looks taken aback and I'm glad.

He says, 'Well, I just heard that the Marine commander radioed through to say that this morning was the smoothest insert he's ever been involved in.'

I don't know whether he's genuinely trying to compliment me or whether he thinks that, despite me, the Chinooks did their job well.

I plump for the latter, exhausted. 'Well done,' I say.

He walks off, and I find the signallers and let rip, before Stu cleverly extracts me with promises of a strong tea and a double-choc-chip cookie at Tim Hortons.

The following morning, first thing, we have a post-op wash-up, and it's clear that, since the Marine commander is happy, everyone is happy. The sun is shining from my arse but it was a lucky break – it could so easily have gone the other way.

An hour later, it's time to go back to Bastion, and as we fly towards home, leaving Kandahar province behind us, I feel the weight lifting from my shoulders. The op is over.

I take the controls from Stu and see him in the mirror

enjoying a huge stretch, making the most of the rare opportunity to take his hands off the cyclic.

'Home sweet Helmand,' I say as I catch my first glimpse of the Green Zone. It glows in the early-morning light, with fog sitting by the river and all the familiar FOBs dotted along it.

Moments later, my happy feelings are smashed as we fly straight into a flock of small birds and I feel a vibration through the pedals.

'You feel that?' I ask.

'Nope,' Stu answers. 'Probably your shit flying.'

'No, seriously, I think we've just hit a bird,' I tell him.

'Oh, man,' he sighs. 'Just what we need after yesterday's fiasco.'

The aircraft seems to be flying fine, so we just let our wingman know and keep trucking towards Bastion.

When we do our post-flight walk-round, I find a bloody mass of feathers and bones attached to the front of the aircraft but no other damage.

'I'll just go tell the REME about this so they can check it,' I tell Stu.

The crew chief responds with good humour: 'So, ma'am, you are telling me that you got through the whole day-long, seven-aircraft mission in an unknown area without a scratch . . . and then went U/S because of a sparrow?'

I really like the chief – he's intelligent and interesting and a huge asset to the REME out here. He has a totally bald head which looks as soft as a baby's bum but enough hair on his muscly arms to make up for it. With huge puppy-dog brown eyes and a smooth, deep voice, he exudes manliness.

I see his point and nod my head, laughing. 'Pretty much,' I say.

There's a voice behind me. It's Stu. 'Girl pilots, huh? Shouldn't be allowed.'

Escorting Chinooks to pick up casualties is one of the worst jobs we do; it seems to be almost every day when we're on

VHR, sometimes more than once. For every fatality, there are countless injured and maimed soldiers.

One evening, we're called out around 10 p.m. on an escort job to pick up casualties from Gibraltar, an FOB between Sangin and Gereshk, where one of the commando regiments is based. It's also where Tom has been working for the past two months training Afghan National Army soldiers.

As we fly north-east, we learn on the radio that there are four serious British casualties, and I feel a familiar burst of sorrow and anger. That's a lot of casualties from one incident. I have a terrible gnawing feeling of fear in the depths of my tummy: how will Tom be coping with this? He has enough to deal with already, living in such a dangerous location.

An unfamiliar voice comes up on the radio, and I'm momentarily confused, before the explanation arrives: 'Ugly callsign, this is Untrained Observer. My company commander and JTAC are both injured. I will guide you in.'

I acknowledge, then exhale, 'Shit,' into the intercom.

We know it's been a full-on fight tonight, because we've followed it all in the ops room, but we didn't know until now who it was who'd been injured. This is really bad, and it sounds like the fight is still going on. Poor Tom; God knows what he and his colleagues must be thinking – with no company commander, they have lost their leader.

There's a delay while the casualties are prepared. Untrained Observer, who I assume to be one of the Marine platoon commanders, tells me they are moving the casualties towards the landing site for pick-up. It sounds like hell down there.

The untrained observer warns us that the casualties are ready but the emergency landing site is still hot. The Chinook pilot bravely decides to go ahead regardless; it's my job to make sure I protect him as best I can. I peer down towards the landing site and flip down my NVGs. Normally, I'd be able to make out a small line of men snaking towards the Chinook carrying stretchers. Tonight, though, there's too much tracer in the air for me to see – the friendlies are firing everything they have at the enemy to keep them at bay while the helicopter is on the ground. I can't think about Tom. I concentrate hard on my job of keeping the Chinook safe, knowing that, later, there will be time for me to think about what our soldiers are going through on the ground.

With the casualties on board and the Chinook safely airborne, we start back towards Bastion at top speed. Untrained Observer keeps asking after his guys, and the JTAC in particular.

Stu radios the Chinook; we are able to speak directly to the loadie, who is sitting in the main body of the helicopter assisting the casualties.

'You got any news on the state of the four casualties?' he asks.

'Affirm,' the loadie replies. 'Two dead, two critical.'

It's like a punch in the stomach. More losses.

The loadie is unable to tell us which ones have died – the medical team has its hands full dealing with the life-threatening injuries on board.

'Untrained Observer, this is Ugly,' I transmit. 'MERT call-sign has two dead and two critical, but they can't tell us who's survived at this time.'

'Roger.' His voice is cracking. 'Can you let me know as soon as you hear?'

'I'll try,' I respond.

A few minutes later he asks, 'Do you have any further update on the two surviving guys?' He sounds distraught, as if he's desperately trying not to cry.

'Sorry, no. I'll try and get one for you,' I answer, without much hope. I'll be out of the loop as soon as we land; these guys will be under the hospital's care then. We radio the loadie again, but with the same result. And I don't want to keep bothering him – he needs to focus his attention on the patients.

244

It's horrible – it's only too clear how close these guys are to each other.

I check out with Untrained Observer as we leave radio range.

'Roger, Ugly. Thanks for your help tonight, and any updates would be appreciated.' I'm overwhelmed by how professional he is; he's speaking to the aircraft as if he's been doing it all his life. They have no commanding officer, no JTAC, and have lost four of their thirty men, yet they carry on. They don't have a choice.

'I don't know how they do it.' Clearly Stu is thinking the same things I am.

We fly on in silence, and I notice that the weather is turning. There are huge clouds building in the distance, and the wind is picking up. At Bastion, we close down as quickly as possible and scamper back to our accommodation. We know to take any sleep we can get.

At 3 a.m., after just forty-five minutes in bed, I'm woken up, and immediately feel guilty about being asleep. I gather myself and sprint towards the flightline in pouring rain, still half asleep but knowing that whatever mission we've been woken for will be vitally important.

Over the radio Zero briefs me: 'You're escorting the commandos' 2I/C to Gibraltar.' The remaining group of Marines will need some strong leadership and their morale boosting. It's a good decision.

As I climb into the cab, the weather's almost scary it's so bad. The rain beats down against the cockpit glass, and in the scattered lights of the airfield it looks as if the clouds are only a few feet above us. Lightning streaks across the camp.

'I'm not sure about this weather,' I say to Stu. I'm not looking forward to flying in this.

'We've got to try it whatever,' he points out. He's right, the Marines at Gibraltar need help.

As soon as we lift, we're practically blinded by cloud. The Chinook carrying the 2I/C is in the lead. The FLIR can't see through the low stratus, and everything outside the window is obscured by heavy rain. My heart starts beating faster as I realize I can't see the ground or the sky.

'I've just lost the Chinook through the rain,' Stu tells me, as we climb through a hundred feet. This is bad, and we both search frantically for the enormous helicopter that would mean instant death if we crashed into it. A heart-stopping few moments pass and we both silently scan the sky. The rain beats against the cab like a drum and I'm scared to blink in case I miss something.

A radio call from the Chinook makes me jump: 'Ugly, this is Tricky. The weather is too bad; we're turning back. Currently at fifty feet, five miles east of the airfield.'

I let out a huge sigh of relief and acknowledge. 'They're below us,' I confirm to Stu. 'We're safe.'

The return to Bastion is hairy, and I'm so glad to be back on the ground my whole body feels floppy. There's no way both helicopters would have made it the eighty kilometres to Gibraltar tonight, no matter what the mission was. I'm gutted that we couldn't deliver the 2I/C though.

'Thank God that weather wasn't here earlier,' I say to Stu as it occurs to me. 'We wouldn't have been able to pick up those guys. The surviving two probably wouldn't have made it either.'

Stu nods tiredly as we trudge back through the downpour towards the VHR tent.

Back in bed, I toss and turn – I can't get thoughts of the Widow and OC, the two men who died, and the people they'll leave behind out of my mind. I know in these very moments when I'm trying to slip into oblivion, the mothers and wives of the guys that didn't make it will be getting the heartbreaking, life-changing news. And these are Tom's friends – the men he spent twenty-four hours a day with. God, he must feel awful. I seriously doubt he's managing to sleep. The rain thrums gently against the roof and I can smell wet earth.

246

After a while, I give up trying to sleep and, as soon as I think I can get away with it, I throw the covers off, pull on my trainers and a pair of shorts and head to the nearest gym through the muddy puddles; we're off VHR this morning, so I can finally do some exercise. As I enter the gym, ten local Afghans look up; they're using dirty grey rags to wipe the machines. I can't help but think that all they're doing is evenly distributing the germs. I start to stretch, and ten pairs of eyes gaze at me, up and down, their lips curled and beards twitching. It feels as if they are taking in every single bit of bare flesh. I feel pretty disgusting – like a piece of rancid meat in the butcher's window.

Back in JHF later that morning, one of the other pilots tells me that Widow Six Five came this morning from the hospital looking for the crews that were flying last night. He's injured but alive. He's recovering with the OC, both of them having taken blast injuries from an explosion.

'It was the two others who didn't make it,' he says.

What two others? Who? What about Tom?

'Do you know their names?' I ask, my heart in my mouth.

'Tom and Danny – a captain and a corporal. Brilliant blokes, by all accounts.'

I'm practically winded. 'Tom?'

Please no.

'Tom, you say. Are you sure? It's just – my friend Louise – her husband is called Tom. He's in that company.'

Fuck, no, please, no.

'Is your friend in the RAF? That's him – he was twenty-six, I think they got married last year, or the year before? She will've been told by now. But that's the one.'

Oh God, I can't take this in.

I think back to their wedding day. I threw pink confetti over them as they left the old country church where they'd just said their vows. They laughed, overwhelmed with happiness, as the photographer snapped away. I automatically think of Jake. My whole world would collapse if I lost him; every tiny thing I do reminds me of him, from the toothpaste we both use to arranging my pillows in a certain way at night.

What will I say to Louise?

It seems impossible to take in – the kind of news that makes you feel outside your body, like it can't possibly be happening. I try to deal with it practically; I don't even want to start thinking about the emotions of it all. I can't. At the first possible opportunity, I go to visit the two surviving men in hospital. The Marine OC is fine – he had his ankle broken by the blast and has shrapnel injuries – but Widow is really shaken – he keeps saying that Tom saved his life by taking the blast. Widow's injuries are worse than the OC's – he has serious shrapnel wounds to both legs. Tears roll down his cheeks as he keeps repeating the same thing: 'He saved my life, he saved my life.' Both his legs are swathed in bandages.

'The missile went straight into Danny,' he says, wiping his nose with his hand. 'He died instantly, but Tom took the lion's share of the blast through his head.' He pauses. 'He died as the helicopter was speeding towards the hospital here.'

The Widow and OC go back to UK hospitals tonight.

What the hell are we doing out here?

I start planning the letter I'll write to Louise tomorrow. I'll tell her everything I know – she'll want that; anything that might make it even a tiny bit easier to live with. At least, being in the military herself, she'll understand what he was doing.

I send an email to her and get no response, so I email her sister and find out that she's been at home on R&R for a week. At least she's not in Iraq. Her sister tells me that Louise and Tom were due to be on R&R together, and that he had been about to come home in a few days. I read her email through my tears, and reply saying that I'll phone as soon as she thinks Louise is ready.

When I hear that a soldier has died out here, it makes me feel sick and anxious and terrible yet, unlike our friends on the ground, I don't usually have to put a face, a personality or a life outside the military to that name. Yet now I do, and it haunts me. I see Tom's face on every Marine – and understand the risks they are all taking by doing their job; that every one of them may have a girlfriend, a wife, children, friends, colleagues, parents; how a single death may change a hundred lives for ever.

Two days later, my flight moves on to air-testing duty. The other three go to Kandahar, but the Boss asks me to stay at Bastion to work on some operations. I have loads of work on, but the time drags. I can't believe Tom is dead. During the day I can't stop thinking about him, and at night I dream about Tom and Louise together; it goes round and round my head like a 100 degree wash. It physically hurts. I can't imagine how she's coping; Tom died in such extreme, tragic and brave circumstances and, since I've known her, she's only ever been with him. I want to call her, but I'm not sure if she'll be ready to talk. I email her sister again to ask how she is and await a response. I wonder whether I should take photographs at the vigil but then think it may be inappropriate. I feels as if I have a hundred questions I want answered but I'm not sure what they are.

Three days later, I walk towards the main square at Bastion; it's not my first vigil, but I know it will be the most poignant so far. The sun is slowly lowering in the sky across the golden, scorched earth. Everyone stands in formation, on three sides of a square. I slot in with the others on one side near the back. It's silent.

I look around; there must be over a thousand people here. It's a sea of eyes and mouths. We are commemorating three soldiers; Tom and his colleague, and another who lost his life the day after they lost theirs. Vigils for soldiers have to be bundled together to save time.

It's not safe for the Hercules to land at this time of day, so there are no coffins; they'll be dispatched home at three o'clock the following morning under the cover of darkness. It doesn't make it any less real.

'The Last Post' rings out on the trumpet. A minute's silence follows. I try not to think about anything too hard and stare at the back of the head in front of me. As a cannon mortar goes off, the senior staff at the front salute. There's a stream of readings, peppered with the words 'loyal', 'hero', 'inspiration', 'passionate', 'devoted'.

'You OK, Charlie?' Bertie asks me in a whisper as we stand at the back.

'Of course I am. What right do I have to be upset?' I feel angry at everything. 'It's just that this has made me realize how many people are affected by every one of the deaths . . . and there are so many.'

Bertie nods and squeezes my arm.

Afterwards, I follow some young Marines out of the main square. One turns to his mate and says: 'I don't know what we're achieving here.'

My head feels bruised inside, like a pear at the bottom of a rucksack.

I ease into an existence in which we are totally detached from the real world. We don't know what day of the week it is – day and night blur into one and there is no concept of there being twenty-four hours. There's a never-ending list of tasks and we snatch sleep where and when we can, trying to reset our confused body clocks. My ops-officer role is another 100 per cent more work than just flying – when the others go to bed after a mission, I trudge towards the JHF. But, generally, I don't miss my time off; the job's keeping me occupied, and I'm grateful for that.

I'm finding myself becoming slightly obsessed with the men we are losing. One afternoon, I hear that one of the Widows we worked with up in Musa Qal'eh was killed by a stray RPG. The sound of the JTACs' deep voices as they run for cover has become familiar, comforting. I try to think of them as just voices; but now I know that they are real men and I struggle to deal with it.

But there are also some unexpected positive developments to drag me out of my morose frame of mind and, being married now, I feel slightly invincible on camp; as if no one can touch me.

I phone the groundies one day to find out if an air-test I've been waiting to do is ready. The head groundie answers the phone.

'Hi, it's Captain Madison.'

'Did you phone to tell me you love me?' he asks, a cheeky smile in his voice.

I smile and tell him no. I'm also feeling less like an army officer and more like a person now that I'm almost finished.

'Is my air-test ready yet?'

'Nope, but the REME have got something up here I think you should see,' he answers, but won't be drawn on what.

When I finally go to sign for my air-test, I see what the groundie meant. The crew chief sits smiling, as usual, behind his desk, but looks as though he's just bought a new car and can't wait to show someone. God knows how he can always be so cheerful, but I'm glad he is. It's always great so see such a happy face after a mission.

'All right, Chief?' I say, fishing my pen out of the pocket on my arm.

'Fine, thanks. You seen our new addition?' He grins like a hyena.

He steps aside and proudly introduces me to my porn-alike, which is Blu-Tacked to the wall behind him. It's a very large-breasted, tiny-waisted lady from *Hustler*, with my face glued on. Far from making me paranoid and disgusted, I'm quietly rather flattered. They obviously think I've still got it, which can only be a good thing. Then I wonder whether, if

I'm pleased by a porn-alike, it means I'm truly past my prime.

'Erm, very nice,' I say, then smile politely and stroll away, not sure how I'm supposed to react. 'Gym sessions have obviously paid off.'

In mid-February a new op, Operation Diesel, kicks off in earnest. Every operation takes weeks of planning, but it's only once it's started properly that the buzz starts. More than five hundred soldiers on the ground are involved, most of them Royal Marines from 3 Commando Brigade, in a complex operation centred on Sapwan Qualeh in the Sangin Valley. Again, we know there are drug- and bomb-making factories there, and we need to destroy them.

The heroin problem out here is still very real; the strife-ridden area still produces over 90 per cent of the world's heroin, and Helmand alone is responsible for two-thirds of that. While there are indications that poppy production is on the verge of decreasing, it's still one of the major issues that has to be faced and the problem is compounded by the fact that the refined drugs are everywhere and corruption abounds.

Airborne for the first mission of Diesel, we spend an uneventful hour on station but, in terms of the ground picture, that's good. The Marines send decoy units out into the desert while quietly moving large columns of troops into hidden positions surrounding the sprawling network of compounds close to the Helmand river. The Marines encounter hardly any enemy resistance, which lets them get on with their main job: finding the narcotics and getting rid of them.

It's the middle of the night, so the only scenery we see is through our NVGs or the FLIR, but I can just make out the tiny figures of the Marines as they move from compound to compound. All the guys on the ground carry a radio of some description, and I visualize the web of communication this creates; in the relative silence of my cockpit, I wonder what they are all saying to each other.

'God, this is dull,' Stu remarks. 'I just want to blow something up or go home.'

'I know. At least usually you can have a laugh and a joke with the JTAC, but this one has no sense of humour at all.'

I have only intermittent chats with the JTAC, callsign Nowhere Two Six, as he has nothing for us to do except keep a wide look-out. He's probably preoccupied with his job on the ground anyway, but it means that, tonight at least, he's no good for banter. We check out a couple of suspicious-looking guys for him, and search a few compounds, but other than that Stu and I are just chewing the fat and providing a deterrent. The only possible job Nowhere has for us is the destruction of an enemy truck they've found.

'We might need to deny that, Ugly, but I'll get back to you,' Nowhere tells me about an hour into the sortie.

'Roger,' I reply. I always try hard to sound efficient and professional on the radios – female voices so easily sound whiny.

Immediately after this short conversation with Nowhere, a funny noise comes through my headset – a sort of muffled buzzing, like radio interference. I wonder if our aircraft is causing it. If so, everyone on the radio net will be able to hear it: all the ground commanders, all the JTACs and all the aircraft – there are tens of helicopters and several fast jets and UAVs all listening in.

'What's that weird noise?' I ask Stu. As I speak, the noise temporarily stops.

'God knows. All I can hear is a really high-pitched voice . . . might be coming from the front cockpit, but I'm not sure,' he replies. 'Anyway, I mainly tune out women's voices.'

I ignore him. 'It stops when I speak though . . .' I pause. 'Yep, it stopped then too.'

'Whatever,' Stu sighs. 'I can't hear anything.'

'I'll just have to keep yabbering away then,' I say merrily. 'What shall I talk about . . . let me see. This is a pretty boring sortie, huh? I'm quite excited about denying that truck though. A Hellfire before breakfast would be good, don'tcha think? Stu?'

'Oh, would you just shut up, you're ruining my nap,' he chuckles back.

I continue with a diatribe of similarly useless babble in order to keep the weird buzzing at bay, until the noise vanishes on its own after a couple of minutes.

The first thing that happens after the noise vanishes is that Nowhere speaks to me, slowly and deliberately, as if trying not to laugh.

'Um, Ugly, you might want to check your pressel there. You've been on constant transmit for the last two minutes.'

Oh. my. God. 'Roger. Out,' I manage to squeak into my radio.

'Ooooooh myyyyyy Gooooood!' I hope Stu will tell me that it doesn't matter, I didn't say anything bad. I didn't even have my pressel down – there must be a problem with the radio.

There's no response at first, and for some reason I can't see him in the mirror – maybe it's too dark.

'I don't think I said anything too bad, did I?'

There's a huge gulping sound over the intercom as Stu takes a wheezing breath and finally sits up straight, recovering from the head-on-lap, convulsive-laughter position he had assumed.

'I'm actually . . . crying . . . with laughter,' he announces between roaring giggles. He wipes his streaming eyes. 'You're such a knob!'

He convulses away from the mirror again, in uncontrollable hysterics.

'And now . . . everyone in Helmand knows what I have to put up with!'

I'm silent, trying to replay everything I said in that two minutes, and trying to imagine how many professional soldiers have just heard my vomit of conversation. I cringe at the thought of facing any of them again.

The next ninety minutes drag, and when we finally get back to Bastion I can't wait to escape to my bed. I sign in the cab while Stu pretends to slip the crew chief a fiver for 'fixing' the switch before our sortie. I can see he'll get a lot more mileage out of this one.

However, while it's not my finest moment, the operation is deemed a huge success; not only is £50 million's worth of heroin found but there is not a single casualty. Apart from my dignity, of course.

I sometimes find it hard to take the meetings around the bird table seriously – they always make me feel as if I'm on the set of a Second World War film, the bit where they gather around the dog-eared map with little models of tanks and soldiers and move them around with a billiard stick.

In fact, not much has changed as far as our planning table goes: we still have a massive square table in the middle of the room with a map of the area on it. All the planning for major and minor operations, short-notice tasking and routine escorts happens using this antiquated set-up. We cram around the edges, stretch across to point out high ground or vulnerable areas, and the intelligence officer uses a long pointer to tell us, 'The enemy are here, here and here,' and we act out our flights using marker pens, hands or sweets – whatever is to hand.

Today we're clustered around the bird table for the second of the twice-daily briefs. I always stand towards the back but angle myself so I can see the map properly. The intelligence officer is giving his brief and everyone is standing around fanning themselves against the heat created by the crush of thirty sweaty bodies.

'There has been a real surge of activity in Sangin over the last twelve hours,' he informs us in his monotone voice.

I crane my neck to look at Bertie, who raises her eyebrows.

'I assess that EF [enemy forces] will almost certainly attempt to fire at the Chinook tomorrow from this area,' the officer drones on, pointing out the offending area with his stick.

I make eye contact with Bertie and rub my hands together gleefully – I could do with some action. She forms her fingers into devil-horns, knowing that we're both hoping to do some shooting.

'Edinburgh and the Musa Qal'eh areas are both nothing to report,' the officer sums up.

The brief wraps up with the medical officer telling us that the hospital at Bastion has reached capacity and some casualties will have to be moved to the hospital in Lashkagar. It's a sobering way to finish.

It's March, over two months into my tour and we're staying at FOB Dwyer. The camp is about 200 metres square, and it feels as if we're living in a miniature town from an old Western movie, or on the set of *M*A*S*H*. Everything is built from sweat and wood, apart from the tiny runway outside the wire. It's very much a building site at the moment, and everywhere you go you bump into pallets of wood, HESCO, barbed wire, food and water. The going is very rough wherever you are – a headtorch is an absolute necessity to avoid banged shins and broken ankles.

Everything is tented; there are no proper buildings. The camp is surrounded by a HESCO wall and there are 'HESCO houses' everywhere, which are just three-metre-high cells with eight camp cots in them and holes for doors. The lucky pilots are staying in an American tent – the camp is half American – and the girls have poncho-walled off our end for some privacy, so it's very comfortable. I'm glad Bertie is here too.

The showers are in an iso-container, like the metal containers on huge freight ships. They are switched on for a couple of hours a day and solar-heated, so you take your luck. The loos are unisex wooden stalls where, firstly, everyone can see your feet and, secondly, *everything* goes in a plastic bag each time –

there is no drainage or plumbing. The boys wee into little tubes that poke out of the ground all over camp (they call them 'desert roses'), but we girls go through the bag rigmarole each time; the boys only have to bag poo.

'It took the boys at least two days to work out that I wasn't going for eight poos a day,' Bertie tells me. 'I mean, what the fuck do they think I'm eating?! Morons.'

The food is ration packs cooked up centrally by a chef, apart from Sundays, when you pick up your own twenty-four-hour ration pack and do it yourself – it's the chef's day off. Lucky him.

Running water is rare, and it's all saltwater. Doing your laundry is a bit of a nightmare, because dust storms are common and your stuff ends up in a worse state than it was before.

We work sixteen hours on, eight off here, which feels amazing, as I have dedicated 'time off' for the first time. It's wonderfully relaxing to know that, for eight hours, I am not liable to be called in for anything at all. As well as sleeping, I can sit and read my book or type letters home.

I'm also over the moon to discover the all-important HESCO-gym, which has a corrugated-iron semi-roof, complete with two dusty, sickly crosstrainers and a nearly dead running machine, along with some bikes and a rower. Unsurprisingly, the meat-head section of the gym is well stocked and permanently filled with beefy Americans in their combats pumping iron. The only downside is that, since the ceiling doesn't meet the wall in many places, the dust and wind attack you while you run, making you feel like you're in some sort of dirty wind tunnel training for the Navy Seals. I just try to think of the extra calories I'll burn.

Everyone wanders around camp wearing whatever they want, but the Americans have the craziest outfits: combats and T-shirts are the norm, but some add trainers, flip-flops or baseball caps too. Some people dress totally in civvies and everyone is free to carry whatever weapon they feel like carrying. Sometimes it feels as if we're on the set of an R&B music video.

The local celebrity is the sniffer dog, a brown and white spaniel called Travis. His British owner walks him around the tiny perimeter several times a day and answers the same questions over and over again: how long have you had him, what happens to him after this tour, what kind of work does he do . . . ? Travis is very good-natured and really cute, but so attached to his owner that he whines the whole camp down if he even nips off to make tea.

A few nights into our stay, there's an awful storm, and I'm sure it'll take our tent down any second. I can see flashes of lightning reflected in the spooky-white walls of the tent liner, mixing like a kaleidoscope with the flashes of the boys' torches as one by one they wake and check the structure of our shelter, weighing up whether it's going to survive the long night.

It's a bizarre place to live, this tent. It could comfortably fit twelve people, their camp cots and all their stuff, so with only six of us it's a little large. I sometimes wake up feeling like I'm in the bit of *The Nutcracker* where the room becomes massively oversized and I'm lying, tiny, in a corner in my squeaky camp cot. Other times I feel like I'm in a lovely clean hospital ward; the rest of camp is so brown and dirty that this white haven feels very out of place.

Tonight, though, it's like living in a child's nightmare. The tent walls thrash and smack against our beds, the tunnel-shaped structure warps noisily, creaking and bending with the gale-force wind. Sheets of rain and other debris slam up against the thin plastic material next to my head, and through my issue ear-defenders I can still hear everything as clearly as I can hear my heart thumping.

At around 6.30 a.m. I can finally see morning starting to break through the cracks in the Velcroed-down window flaps in our tent. I immediately use the excuse to climb out of bed, grab my wash kit and head out. The wind is still strong, kicking up puffs of grit, but the worst is over. I'm exhausted after a sleepless night. I zip the tent door up behind me and wander towards the American shower tent. I know there will be no water, but at least they have lights in there.

I survey the devastation. The tin roofs have been ripped off the HESCO houses, and all the sunshades and windbreaks that people have put up have been torn apart. The aircraft look pretty sorry for themselves too, and I see the engineers checking them out. All the pallets of food, loo roll, water and building supplies are strewn everywhere and there are inches of dust on everything. As I reach the wooden toilet block, I find that this includes the loo paper, wipes, seat and everything I touch. I'm filthy by the time I reach the shower tent and cursing the fact that the showers won't be switched on for another twelve hours. The usual military duties start and, like worker ants, everyone is out pitching in to get things back in shape. I squeeze through the tent flap and dump my stuff at a sink. I wearily brush my teeth and have a wash by pouring bottles of water into the sink. I fantasize about the running fresh water at Bastion.

In the cloudy, windy afternoon, Stu and I are lazily reading our books in the tent when the Motorola crackles, 'Hangover'.

'We have a shout!' Stu shouts.

'OK.' I grab my dog tags and dive out of the tent.

We find out that there's a casualty about 60 kilometres to the south. We're to launch immediately and escort a Sea King down there to pick him up and, within fifteen minutes, we're airborne, following the Sea King across the expanse of deserty nothing. The only snag is the weather – it seems that the worst isn't over and, as we fly south, the visibility level is dropping to dangerous levels. Soon it is dipping in and out of our legal limits.

'I can't see much any more . . . you? I'm putting the NVS on,' Stu says. The night vision system will 'see' through the dust storm slightly better than the naked eye. When we reach the HLS, still at 200 feet to stay visual with the ground, the wind has picked up to 60 knots and we're struggling to stay in the air with the downdraughts. It's tough work, and neither Stu nor I have space in our brains for anything else but flying safely.

The Sea King quickly has the casualty on board and we turn north for Dwyer. Suddenly all we can see is dust: no Sea King, no ground, no sky, no way of telling which way is up. I can feel the slow trickle of sweat as it runs down my back. My eyes are gritty.

'I'm going up,' is all Stu needs to tell me. He starts climbing. This is the tried and tested procedure; otherwise, there's nothing to stop us crashing into the ground.

'Roger,' I reply. I get on the radio and tell the Sea King we've lost all references. We trade height and heading information to make sure we're not going to crash into each other. I double-check that the radar is on and that the settings are correct; it's saved my arse before.

We climb to 6,500 feet before we can start picking out the way ahead of us, and fly on in silence. I look down intermittently to see if there's a way through the shallow dust storm yet and, after about five minutes, I see a thinning of the dust that will allow us down.

'Look low, eleven o'clock,' I say to Stu. 'Let's go through there.'

'Okey-dokey,' he says, and lowers the collective.

Arrival back at camp is hairy but workable. It takes us two attempts to get in, because we can't even see the runway properly, but we land in one piece, shaken but relieved. The groundcrew and REME walk to our cab for shutdown, but as the rotors are about to stop, I realize I can't even see the furthest groundcrew any more. I look up and see that the aircraft parked fifteen metres in front of us is no longer there; there's just a wall of dust. Talk about lucky timing.

Suffice to say, the weather is so bad that, for the first time, I actually don my hideous, uncool goggles to get back to the tent. I look like a knob, but at least I can vaguely see as I gingerly pick my way across camp. My eyeballs ache.

We weather out the rest of the storm hiding in the tent watching *Prince Caspian* on DVD on a borrowed projector.

The next day is Sunday, and US-style rations arrive. We sit outside the back of our tent on camp cots and greedily tuck into the big cardboard box. Food is scattered all over camp on big pallets – there's no chance of anyone stealing anything out here. We've selected a random menu from the pallet outside the back of our tent and are eagerly unpacking the unfamiliar contents.

The eighteen-man ration pack contains everything you need. In it are four twelve-by-nine-inch plastic trays of ready-cooked food: spaghetti, meatballs, green beans and a cake. Each plastic tray has a water-activated heating system which starts when you pull the rip cord. The trays then stack up inside a separate cardboard oven and cook for forty-five minutes – the smell is tantalizing.

While we wait we dissect the entire contents of the box: there are eighteen sets of food, eighteen plates, eighteen pairs of plastic gloves in case there is no way to clean your hands, three plastic serving spoons and a cake slice, three different pots of seasoning and a packet of ready-made icing for the cake, napkins and binbags and even a tiny pot of picante sauce. They've really thought of everything, and the UK ration packs pale in comparison.

'Whoever invented this is a fucking genius. They deserve a medal,' announces JB.

We eat hungrily, the eight of us making more than our fair dent on the eighteen-man pack.

Stu says that he has put on five stone during the meal; he is the master of overstatement. We play a card game in the cookhouse and, when he loses, he describes himself as 'utterly heartbroken'. Later, we watch a film and, when a bungee falls from the ceiling on to his leg, he is 'absolutely petrified'. In the morning we walk to an air-test and, when his bootlace comes undone, he calls for a 'total mission abort'.

I start to think I'm enjoying my time down here; as if it's total R&R – albeit with a difference.

On day six at Dwyer, another shout comes in the afternoon when we're sleeping, having been up all night. We dive out of our beds and out of the door, sprint like idiots across camp to find out what's going on, realize that someone else has the Land Rover, so continue our run all the way, almost a mile, to the flightline.

It's another job intercepting an important Taliban type; we may know he's a high-level commander, or similar, but that's it. They are by far the most exciting, but only about one in ten actually goes ahead and they usually involve hours of waiting on the ground or circling in the air.

I have two main issues with these jobs, despite the fact that they're always highly enjoyable. When they do go ahead, pretty much the whole world watches the gun tape afterwards and your shooting takes on a political importance as part of the bigger picture: Is Apache a good strike asset? Should we use the armed Predator instead?

The other problem is that we inevitably circle for hours, then get 'GO GO GO!!' on the radios without ever having seen what it is we're then expected to fire at. It's all about the element of surprise, so we're normally a few miles out from where the strike will happen.

It's always easier if I'm flying with my whole flight together, because our drills are pretty slick by now, and less chatter on the radios equals quicker results.

Today, my wingman is from another flight, as it was already in the area. We brief on the radio before we meet in the holding area.

'OK, Ugly Five One,' I tell them, 'I'll take tactical lead for this. Do you have the target grid?'

Ugly Five One answers straight away: 'Happy with that. Yes, we do.'

'Roger. When we get the call to run in, I'll go first and fire rockets or missiles, depending on the size of target. You follow me in and clean up with rockets.'

Five minutes later, we circle together in the hold, separated by 500 feet.

We circle out of earshot for a long time, with me squinting down the Day TV as it fades as we start to lose the light. All I can see are loads of people in several fields, farming. We have no comms with the JTAC, who goes under the call-sign of Mayhem, so we're doing everything through a UAV, Arnold, a slow-speaking American who sounds as if he hates the world.

'Ugly Five Four, Bravooooooo is oneeeeee of the paxxxxx in the field at grid 628714. He is currently stationary but we are waiting for the go-ahead from Mayhemmmmmmm,' Arnold tells me. It takes him twice as long to say this as it would a normal person, and I pray we don't have to make any snap decisions based on information from him.

'That field seems pretty full of people,' I say to Stu.

He looks at the TADS video picture on his screens. 'Yep, I count at least thirteen people in there. And was that kids just walking away to the north?'

'Yeah, it was. This isn't making me feel comfortable. I hope Mayhem takes his time and tells us who we're killing,' I say.

I speak to Arnold: 'I can see about thirteen adults in that field, with two children departing north. Can you give me an exact location for the Bravo?'

He gives me a ten-figure grid, his voice like one of those awful recordings at call centres. The kit on the Apache only takes eight figures, so I'm no better off. He tries to give me a laser spot, but his spot is so big it just drags the TADS to the field of thirteen pax again. He refuses to give a description of the actual Bravo and says he'll pass it on later. There is also the world's most obvious bright white car near one end of the group of pax, but Arnold claims not to be able to see any cars. I'm getting nervous.

I ask wing: 'You happy with the Bravo?'

'Nope. Just a huge bunch of people there. Could be anyone.'

I speak to Stu. 'So, for all we know, there's a teddy bears' picnic going on next to someone's Skoda.'

I'm starting to get twitchy. Just as I'm considering telling Arnold that under no circumstances can I engage with so little information, he starts drawling: 'Ugly, you are cleared in on those pax. This is time-sensitive. How long to engage?'

Stu turns in towards them without a word – we've practised this a thousand times – while I start shouting at Arnold: 'Which ONES? Are they near the CAR??' No answer.

We speed towards the pax, and I'm starting to feel maxed out; like I can't handle it. It's a nasty sensation and one I can't remember feeling before. I action the weapons and wonder what I'm going to do. Can I really engage all thirteen pax just because a UAV controlled by someone in Las Vegas says to?

Then: 'Ugly, abort plan, I repeat, abort.' It's Arnold; he adds that we need to stay out of earshot to avoid alerting the Bravo to our plans.

Stu does a screeching-halt-and-handbrake-turn-style man-oeuvre, suddenly lowering the collective and pushing the cyclic hard over to the right. Our wingman sees us and does the same, breaking the other way. We go back to circling at an acceptable distance. Now it's too dark for the Day TV to work so, to add insult to injury, I can only see hot things in a field next to a cold car. I go back to breathing normally but it takes a good three minutes.

'That was close,' I say to Stu. 'I wasn't happy with that at all. Not sure I would have engaged on that scanty amount of information.'

'It would definitely be helpful to know who we're going for,' he agrees.

After another five minutes, I tell Arnold that our fuel

endurance is coming to an end, and he disappears off radio frequency to chat to Mayhem. Moments later, he's back.

'Ugly, I need you to run in and destroy all of those pax. Mayhem has confirmation that they are all involved closely with the Bravo and are all valid targets. Bravo is to the south of the group. You happy with that?'

That's more like it, I think. That tiny bit of information has made everything click into place – I know Mayhem has positively identified our targets as the bad guys and now we're back doing the job we are here to do. I'm relieved – he will have all the information that we don't have up here and if they are enemy, I'm happy.

'Roger. Happy with that. It'll take us three minutes to have weapons on target.'

His slow voice responds immediately, 'Cleared to run in. All pax are targets.'

I know both aircraft have practised this before on the ranges, so all it takes is a quick confirmatory call to wing.

'Shooter-shooter, my lead. I'll fire a kilo Hellfire, you follow up with flechettes. Happy?'

The plan goes exactly as we wanted, and moments later a Hellfire and sixteen flechettes fly into the field. It's too dark to see any battle damage, but Arnold is suddenly taking more of an interest, interjecting with 'Keep firing, Ugly', and 'Any hot spots within fifty metres are valid targets'.

Buoyed up by this top cover and wanting to make certain we get the Bravo, both Apaches fire hundreds of rounds into the area. I do a flechette run just for good measure. Soon nothing is moving on the ground, and our fuel has also run out. We're forced to leave station before Arnold even has a chance to find out who is left. He asks us to come straight back.

We speed back to Dwyer, land and are immediately flocked by groundies – I feel like I'm at Silverstone, but in the dark. We refuel, and are simultaneously reloaded with weapons. The groundies are really professional, as always; they don't ask what we've been shooting at or why we need to go again in a hurry, but just give us what we ask for. I feel really proud of everyone.

Just as we finish our über-fast re-arm and are preparing to take off, we're told to stand down. We're given no reason. It's really disappointing.

We hear over the radios from the unit's commander that the Bravo in question got away. I know that there's nothing more we could have done without Arnold telling us who the prime target was. It's a shame, but we also have confirmed kills on a number of enemy fighters, so it wasn't a wasted mission.

All the further tasking gets cancelled, so we eventually finish and trudge off, in desperate need of a shower.

We get our kit together in the dark as everyone else is peacefully asleep, grab our torches and make our way to the American showers, which are clean, bright and lit 24/7. The dust is ankle-deep here, so as I close the curtain behind me and look down, my flip-flops have vanished and it looks like I've got little dirty brown boots on, like Uggs.

I push the metal button and nothing happens. There's no water. I get dressed, now a little peeved, and walk over to the Brit showers in the iso-container, which are dark and fed by cold saltwater. I repeat the process, but there's still no water.

I shuffle next door to the dark, dank, smelly, saltwater sinks where at least there should be water. There's no light, though, and, without my torch, it's pitch-black, desert-dark. I put my stuff down and go to use the loo: balance plastic bag over hole, wee in bag, throw bag away. It's not ideal at night. I've got too much stuff in my hands, so decide to balance the torch on the heavy wooden door to grab a wee-bag. In slow motion, the torch topples from the door, bangs on the rim of the loo and disappears inside like it's going through a basketball net. Bollocks.

I peer inside, expecting and hoping to see a net and, below it, dust and dirt. Instead, I'm witness to someone's messy diarrhoea attack. Clearly they didn't have time for the bag. My torch lies like a beacon, illuminating the whole stinky mess. I take a deep breath and almost pass out. I don't have a choice, as life with no torch is the worst situation imaginable. It's almost as bad as the hideous, hideous stench coming from my torch as I pick it out with two fingers in a sort of minimal-damage pincer movement.

In the sinks, I leave water running over the torch, soap it, cover it with alcohol gel and wash it again. I can't see a thing and do everything by touch. After a thousand washes I take a sniff; it still reeks. I'm forced to wash my face and hands in the dark, and brush my teeth with bottled water, and I leave the torch in the sinks, marinating in alcohol gel. As I drop off to sleep, I begin to suspect that I have (someone else's) shit on my nose. It feels like it's embedded in my nostril.

In the morning, my mood has improved and I make my way to the mini-control room we have set up. Two signallers sit with JB in the roasting-hot tent sharing an ancient newspaper.

'How was the mission?' JB asks.

'Fine, although I lost my bloody torch last night.' I tell him the whole story in detail and, as I do, I notice that the two signallers are enjoying it a whole lot more than I expected. By the time I finish, they are in stitches. JB, on the other hand, looks less than amused.

'Ha, ha,' one of the signallers finally gasps. 'JB "found" a torch in the sinks this morning and has been boasting about it all morning! In fact,' he says, turning to look at a red-faced JB, 'didn't you have it in your *mouth* while you were rummaging in that tool kit earlier?'

JB fishes in his pocket, slams my torch down on the desk and walks away. I then realize that the one thing he's not wonderful at is taking the piss out of himself.

Back at Bastion, it feels great to have a long, hot shower. I do miss the remoteness of Dwyer and the lack of pressure, and stepping back into the JHF is like coming home from a holiday with that plummeting feeling of just knowing there is heaps of paperwork to catch up on.

It's not long before another big op is in the offing. Planning for Operation Aabi Toorah, Pashtu for 'Blue Sword', has been going on while we were away, and I immediately pick up where I left off, reading the documentation and making sure I am 100 per cent sure of everything.

Over five hundred Marines of 42 Commando Group and Afghan National Army soldiers will be patrolling the region 100 kilometres south of Garmsir in the southern Helmand valley, in an area known as the 'Fish Hook' because of the prominent bend in the river there. The aim is to gather intelligence and gain an understanding of the district. It's the first time such a sizeable reconnaissance force has been into the region, which is notorious as an ungoverned space that allows freedom of movement for insurgent fighters, equipment and narcotics.

The Marines have already spent nearly a month in the field, laying up in the desert preparing for the long haul. Over three hundred more men will then join the mission and move rapidly eastwards to clear compounds, talk to the village elders and gain as much knowledge as possible to feed back for future operations. It's 42 Commando Group's final operation before they can go home after six long months on the ground.

It's taken weeks of orders, rehearsals and plans but, when the time finally comes, I'm desperate to get started. After returning from Dwyer, I've been swotting up and I feel I have a thorough knowledge of the plan. All the pilots are still convinced that nothing is going to kick off – every major op we've done recently has been so quiet.

As the Boss, Bertie and the rest of Two Flight have a last discussion over their maps on the morning of the op, I catch Torty's eye and we sneak away from the bird table.

'Shall we?' I ask.

'Definitely. We don't want to get embroiled in *that* briefing. We'll be here for hours.' Torty pulls a meaningful face and starts gathering his maps. One Flight are known for their ultra-long briefs, whereas we specialize in a brief-with-a-tea-on-the-way-to-the-flightline.

I've been up for two hours and it's only 4.30 a.m., so I grab a cup of tea from the table by the back door of the tent before we step out of the JHF into the warm, starry night. I can hear some of the US Cobras running up at the northern end of the airfield, their rotors making the air thrum gently, and wonder what they're up to. The air smells sweet – a strange yet familiar mixture of shit and aviation fuel.

Torty and I have agreed to 'fluff' some cabs, leaving JB and Stu in bed. It takes about twenty minutes to get one of the aircraft properly warmed up: APU on, TADS cooled down, weapon inventory correct, and so on, and although we can do it quicker, it means missing out checks. So Torty and I head to the flightline to start up the cabs we'll be flying later today, while the Boss's flight starts its own. If one of theirs goes unserviceable, they'll be able to jump quickly into mine or Torty's with everything already up and running. It's a well-practised procedure and it saves a heck of a lot of time.

'I can't believe we're even up . . .' Torty tries to check his watch. He's right; this is our umpteenth early start, and we're not in a position to just go back to bed mid-afternoon to make up for it. I feel like I'm dragging my heavy legs through honey; my tired eyes struggle to focus.

'Tell me about it.'

I'm concentrating more on my feet than on the conversation. I only ever seem to lay eyes on my headtorch during the daytime; as soon as the sun sets it seems to disappear, so I've become expert at avoiding the multiple holes, tent pegs and wires scattered on the wasteland between the JHF and the hangar. I've still not managed to replace the shitty handtorch either.

I go to chat with the REME and sign out my cab, and the crew chief is already up. I give him a grin and a chirpy, caffeine-fuelled 'Morning!'

'Morning, ma'am. What's the plan today?' he asks. His boss is a bit of a scatterbrain when it comes to passing on information from orders groups, so I was expecting this. I tell the chief the outline plan:

'Right. All the Marines are here at Bastion already – about 450 of them. The Boss's flight and the Chinooks and Sea Kings are going to insert them into Marjeh in four waves starting at 0500; that'll take a few hours. The Cobras are relieving the Boss's flight around 0730, then I'm relieving them around 0830. This gives the Marines constant overhead protection while they move to their new bases. Then the Cobras take over from me again, and finally the Boss takes over from them. That should cover the Marines moving through the most dangerous areas of Marjeh and take us up to 1500.'

'Right. So two Apaches, three times,' the chief summarizes. I nod, signing out my cab.

As I walk across the dispersal with my stuff, I see Bertie and her front-seater walking to their spots. I wave, and she waves back. I know we both want this to kick off; it's been ages since we had any really good action. Despite my mixed feelings whenever we're involved in heavy fighting, it's our job out here, and there's nothing worse than feeling like our time is being wasted.

Everything in Torty's cab and mine sparks up fine, and even our radios seem to be working. Exactly on time, the Chinooks, Sea Kings and two Apaches take off in radio silence in a cloud of grit and dust. They look like a pack of flying hunters, disappearing into the pale dawn sky.

As they leave the airfield heading south, Torty and I simultaneously shut down our APUs and climb out of the cabs. We're lifting at 0835 exactly, so everything between now and then is, in my case, valuable bed time, and in his, Skype time, and we power-walk towards the accommodation. We take the illegal route through the nest of antennae on the side of the JHF to avoid becoming embroiled in anything inside, and head straight for our beds. I check my alarm clock; it's 5.25 a.m. I let a tidal wave of sleep crash over me.

'Captain Madison! Captain Madison!'

I'm jolted awake by loud banging at my door and a signaller calling my name. I turn to my alarm clock. The faint yellow LCD winks back at me. It's five to six.

'What?' I demand angrily. I'm sick of getting woken up so early, and I know I'm not on until later. I start pulling my boots on automatically.

'I have a message for you, ma'am,' the signaller says. I can only just see his outline in my doorway against the weak light outside, but I can see that it's Airtrooper Turner standing at my door. He looks even younger than his eighteen years with his wide eyes and a mottled spotty forehead.

'Come in then, you're waking everyone up,' I answer stroppily, then quickly tell myself off – this isn't his fault.

He walks in, his boots clumping noisily on the cheap laminate floor. I'm glad Bertie is already up and flying. He does a double-take when he sees me sitting up in bed, hair all over the place, fully clothed with the duvet still strewn half across me and one boot on. Now he probably thinks I always sleep in my flying clothes, but I'm too tired to care.

'Major James's aircraft is U/S and you are to relieve him,' he reads slowly.

The Boss. The Cobras are meant to be relieving him, I think. What the hell's going on?

I'm dressed in two minutes and following Turner to the signallers' Land Rover; they have an allocated vehicle for collecting meals and mail and for picking angry pilots up in the dead of night. Stu is nowhere to be seen, so I get the signaller to drop me at the JHF and go back for him. As I pull open the door and enter, I know instantly that it's all kicking off – the place is buzzing, and the CO and another fistful of officers are all clustered around the ops desk staring intently at the computers and the UAV feed and muttering. There is the constant, urgent swell of radio traffic in the background, and I can make out both Bertie and the Boss's voices.

'Charlie. You're finally here,' the CO greets me, looking pointedly at his watch. Cheeky fucker, I think, I was only woken up eight minutes ago. Officers of lieutenant-colonel rank from all three services – the Army, Navy and RAF – rotate in this job, and it's the turn of my regiment's commanding officer. As well as being highly intelligent, he's witty and likeable; he instantly gained the respect of everyone in our regiment when he took over and the response has been the same out here – everyone is glad he's in charge. Bertie and I have an additional reason to be glad – the CO is extremely good eye-candy. His floppy blond hair and overly pronounced jawline are reminiscent of those of a Disney hunk, and he looks unusually young to be doing his job. He loves his phys, and his toned torso shows nicely when he strips down to his T-shirt in the sweltering ops room, but the most noticeable thing about him are his incredibly blue eyes. When he speaks to you, he barely blinks and never breaks eye contact, to the point where I sometimes feel quite dizzy. Bertie and I also spend a fair amount of time contemplating his backside as we stand around the bird table, but this pales in comparison to the amount of time the boys spend in front of the porn display in the brew tent.

I notice that he looks fit even at this time in the morning. I mumble something incoherent and stare at his arse for inspiration. Reaching into my pocket for my map and some chewing gum, I lean over the bird table for the brief, hoping that my Airwaves gum is overriding my morning dog-breath.

'Right,' the CO starts. 'The Boss's gun is U/S, and I don't want to bring the Cobras forward. You're going up to replace him as a singleton. Bertie has taken tac lead from the Boss. You need to lift asap.' He turns back to the screens.

I ask for the current friendly positions and intelligence circles some grids on my map just as Stu emerges through the JOC's front tent flap.

'Come on,' I say, and lead out the back way.

We jog towards the cab, and I fill him in on what's happening. He grunts sleepily without a word of complaint. We're on APU within fifteen minutes of him being fast asleep in bed, and airborne within twenty. I glance in the mirror as we lift off from Bastion, and he looks half asleep still.

I check in with the Boss as soon as we are at 1,500 feet, and he tells me that a helicopter was shot at two miles from Bastion this morning, so to avoid the southern sector.

'Oops,' says Stu, as we both look at our location on the tactical situation display and see we're smack in the middle of the bad area. I shrug; not much to be done now.

The Boss continues, 'The primary HLS for the operation was unsuitable for the insert due to the number of enemy forces on it; I made the choice to use the secondary one.'

I start scribbling.

'At the secondary HLS, the Chinooks were shot at with RPG during their departure. Also, the latest grid for the AAA [anti-aircraft artillery] from the IntO this morning is 41PR56323361.'

More powerful weapons which can take out aircraft have been slowly on the rise since my first tour and the development seems to have culminated in this large weapon at Marjeh. It's been having a pop at everyone who has gone past in the last few weeks. We don't know what sort of weapon it is – only that it's huge and that, despite a few exploratory patrols to try to find it and nail it, no one has managed to get a whiff.

Stu starts plugging the grid in while the Boss reels off about six different 'current locations' for the enemy forces, and I struggle to keep up. He then tells me the Marines have been on the ground for just over an hour and already they've engaged in multiple locations with grenades, small arms and Javelin anti-tank missiles. The Boss gives me a laser spot for a burning enemy car and a pile of dead enemy.

When we get on station, Stu and I work furiously to plug the grids in and identify all the areas on the ground, slaving the TADS to them one by one. I take over where the Boss left off with his British JTAC, Nowhere Six Three, while Bertie carries on with Nowhere Six Four. I scan the areas he is passing me, but I can't see any enemy; I've obviously arrived during a tiny lull. We listen to Bertie's radio chat up north and realize she's pretty busy.

I glance in the mirror again and see Stu staring back at me, wiping sleep from his eyes.

'You woke me up for *this*?'

He's joking, but I know he has the same sixth-sense feeling that I do; despite the eerie quiet, we both know this could be big. I feel my skin start to prickle.

Bertie is preparing to Hellfire into a compound and, since it's quiet, I decide to check out that area too. I stick my laser spot tracker on when I think she'll be lasing the compound, and get a good spot straight away. I peer through my sights.

Bingo!

I immediately see some enemy leaking from the compound. The front one has a weapon, and the second guy is carrying a bulky backpack. They are hurrying away, glancing stealthily behind them. I'm only about two kilometres away when the TADS picks them up, so their outlines are pretty clear – they look about the size of a thumbnail in my sights. I make out their man-jammies billowing behind them as they run, and the shape of the weapon underneath the front man's dark, heavy cloak.

I get straight on the radio to Nowhere Six Four, while Bertie's Hellfire blows the compound to pieces. A plume of thick smoke fills my sights.

'Anything leaking from that compound is a good target, Ugly.'

274

Stu is already on the radio to Bertie getting deconfliction; they agree to stay north of the compound. I store the guys as a target and pull the trigger: my first twenty-round burst of the morning.

It hits one of the guys straight in the head. I see the explosion of the rounds above his shoulders – and it also gets the second man, who immediately bursts into flames. He goes from walking along the road to rolling on the ground in a ball of flames – a secondary explosion, no doubt from an RPG warhead in his backpack. I curl my finger a few more times to cover the areas in rounds and make sure neither man escapes, then pause to zoom in.

I can see that, for now, neither man is moving, and I feel satisfied. I like clear-cut engagements like this: there was no question that those two were enemy and they will not escape to fight another day. I feel like I'm making a small but real contribution to the fight. I don't ponder on anything else; now isn't the time.

'Good shooting,' Stu comments. 'Glad we got that in before handover time – the Cobras should be due in any second.'

As he speaks, I hear Livewire callsign checking in; they are on time. There's a girl in charge of the pair – I met her for the first time yesterday in the orders group – and she asks Bertie for a brief.

'Whoa, there,' Stu shouts as soon as he hears her voice. 'Three girl pilots at once – that's too many empty kitchens!' He laughs at his own joke, while I ignore him, peering at the TADS and trying not to smile.

Bertie is still firing at something she's found to the north, so her handover is punctuated by the sound of a missile coming off her rail. The JTACs are silent, giving us time to do our own handover and, no doubt about it, the three of us girls in the air will not have gone unnoticed. I feel quite smug. Talk about baptism by fire.

Looking back down into the TADS, I see that the enemy

who's been shot in the head is lying on the road motionless, so I leave him alone, but backpack man is trying to crawl back towards the compound. The fire seems to have burnt itself out, but I can't imagine he looks pretty down there.

I'm half-listening to Bertie's handover when I hear her address the Cobras:

'Livewire, this is Ugly Five Four. That's all I have for you; call Ugly Five Four for further,' and Livewire radios me.

I squeeze the trigger, aiming at backpack man; the rounds splatter towards the ground but he keeps crawling slowly away. I transmit to Livewire in between: 'I have two EF east of compound 8 – look out for my splash.' She'll be watching for the impact of the rounds now. The guy eventually stops moving.

Bertie is low on fuel but our cab has more, so after Livewire tells me she's happy, we decide to check out the AAA grid from the Boss. We fly south and scan the area.

Even since my last tour out here, I can see a noticeable improvement in the Taliban's weaponry and tactics. On my first tour, there was just one Heavy Machine Gun (HMG), in Now Zad, and it was a big deal – all assets were bent on destroying it, and when one of the Apache crews finally laid eyes on it, they hit it with Hellfire, rockets and 30mm. Now they pepper the whole Green Zone; every village has some sort of anti-aircraft gun.

And as far as tactics go, the Taliban are quick to learn and practise top-level sneaky warfare. Gone are the days when they would just mill around with their rifles or try and fight the troops in groups; now they almost exclusively use hit-and-run tactics. The Marines will be patrolling from their bases when they come under sudden ambush, and while they deal with the initial casualties, the Taliban will scoot. Sometimes Taliban fighters will press their momentary advantage with a follow-up attack but, either way, when the dust has settled, they will have melted back into the population, indiscernible from the farmers and market traders. And by the time the Apaches turn up, nine times out of ten, we're searching for a needle in a haystack. Or, more aptly, one black turban in a sea of black turbans and man-jammies.

'Ugly, Ugly' – Nowhere Five Three breaks into the silence – 'you are being engaged by AAA.'

In the silence that follows, we hear the *tick tick tick* noise of rounds shooting through the air beside us. I feel that rush of adrenaline again and squeeze myself as far back as I can into my seat, trying to fit my whole body behind the skimpy three-inch-wide bullet catcher, and peer down my sights, desperate to see anything.

Nothing.

Still nothing.

Nope. The fucker is still hiding.

We give up after a few minutes; it would be an impossibly lucky break to actually see the AAA – to be the ones to have an opportunity to kill it.

'It's like trying to find a fart in a sandstorm,' Stu comments cheerfully.

We route home and he starts up again about who let so many females get through pilot training.

'Let's hope you all manage to park up properly when you get back to dispersal, eh?'

'Don't max yourself out multi-tasking, peabrain. I know how hard you find it doing more than one thing at once, so just concentrate on flying in a straight line.'

Stu moves on: 'Oh well, at least we've killed two EF before breakfast. Now *that's* worth getting up for.' I briefly consider the fact that I think nothing of killing a handful of people before I even have my cereal, it's as if it's just like taking the rubbish out, but reason that I'm only doing my job and I'll have time to make sense of it later.

Back at Bastion, we stay on APU, as we only have half an hour until our planned take-off time.

277

'I'm starving,' Stu moans.

'Me too,' I agree, the thought of it making my tummy rumble. 'I'll go get a drink for us, at least. Don't get your hopes up though, there's never any milk.'

I leave him in the aircraft and go to find food, but the only thing in the groundie shack is cereal, and all the milk shipments have gone to the FOBs. I make tea and stir in some milk powder, which sits in lumps on the top. I gingerly sip it as I head back to the cab. It tastes like heaven. I pass Stu's through his door and contort myself back into my cramped cockpit, settling in for another three and a half hours.

Torty and JB check in with us over the radio as soon as they're on APU, and we send them the data files for the last targets we engaged. We've been following the fight over the radios, and it sounds pretty quiet – the Cobras haven't shot anything.

'I'm surprised they haven't been engaging – they usually find a fight,' I comment.

'Mmmm. They were certainly talking the talk at the brief earlier. There really must have been no targets,' Stu agrees.

We lift on time, and I take the northern sector where we were earlier; Torty takes down south with Nowhere Six Three. My JTAC tells me that, although the Cobras couldn't positively identify anything, the Marines have been in constant contact since 6 a.m. – the enemy is hiding in compounds and tunnels and moving frequently, like rats through the sewers.

We have Kisling, an armed Predator UAV, working in our area as well, and Stu and I are tasked to scan a line of buildings for enemy fire. After about forty-five minutes we see some dickers (enemy using radios or phones to cue fire on to friendly troops using a Motorola-style radio), but there are trees everywhere and we can't see anything properly. It's a blur of treetops and muzzle flashes.

Slightly alarmingly, the JTAC reports fire towards our aircraft, but we can't hear it or see anything.

'Where are these bastards? I'm sure Widow's right about them and, if it's our aircraft they're going for, I definitely want them dead,' I seethe.

They must be crazy to take on an Apache, or maybe that's the thrill. Just you wait, little fuckers, I think.

'My line of sight – muzzle flashes,' Stu suddenly indicates. I slave the TADS to his head and see flashes coming through murder holes in the wall of a compound surrounded by trees.

Stu sets up to run in along the line of the wall, and we attack along the buildings. I see some movement from behind the wall of the same compounds and fire another few bursts; the movement stops.

'No more fire coming from that location, Ugly, but there is still sporadic fire coming up towards your cab. Move your sights east and prepare to watch for leakers from Kisling's engagement,' instructs Nowhere.

'This is pretty full-on. I don't envy the Marines one tiny bit,' I say to Stu.

'Me neither,' he replies, 'but I'm not too keen on whoever's shooting at us either.' He has a nervous edge to his voice.

Kisling Hellfires a compound, but the missile only takes out half of it, and there is movement from the part of the building that survives the blast.

We mop up – and take a few runs to finish off whoever it is inside. I hope these were the idiots that were having a go at us. The cab is buzzing; I can hear Nowhere Six Five to the north asking us for help, having been pinned down and surrounded, so I shower the area with bullets.

We barely have time to inhale before I turn my attention to Nowhere Six Five. Torty is still involved in a heavy contact down south and can't come to their assistance, so we break off our engagement as soon as movement stops. Stu swings the cab round to the north.

We have fifteen minutes of fuel left by the time we reach

the overhead of Six Five's position, and we spend it searching every building around him. Every time we think we see a muzzle flash or a streak of colour moving through the maze of buildings, it's gone before we can be sure. We can't just fire indiscriminately, so it's a sweaty-palmed game of cat and mouse. Nowhere Six Five is still reporting constant fire; the whole thing is very annoying.

'Ugly, check out building 15,' Nowhere pants down his radio. He's on the move.

There's a tiny movement as I slave the TADS to the compound, but then it's gone. I report back.

'Ugly, there are EF everywhere. We're taking incoming from at least three directions. Try the compounds to our south.' I imagine I hear frustration in the JTAC's voice.

I'm glad when Livewire checks in with us at 1115 – I'm tired, hungry and frustrated. I can't even imagine being a Marine down on the ground, with no option to escape this fighting. I'm so relieved to be able to get the hell out of here and back to relative safety.

'Shall we give the AAA a miss this time?' Stu asks as we leave station.

'I reckon so. Shame to get shot to bits before we've even had breakfast.'

That afternoon, there's a vigil for three of the soldiers killed last week; I find it more emotional every time one of these takes place. From the speeches, I find out that one of the dead boys had only been in theatre a week.

Having a vigil in the middle of an operation like the one we're in only brings everything that much more sharply into focus; we've got to do a good job, the best job.

In one of the back rows I spot Widow Six Five, the guy who was lying next to Tom when he was killed two months ago, and I track him down after the vigil. I thought he was still at Selly Oak Hospital in Birmingham (one of the major destinations for servicemen and women who suffer trauma injuries, with one of the best burns units in the country) recovering from his injuries, which were major. He had horrendous shrapnel injuries in his legs from the blast.

'I decided I had to come back out here . . .' he says. 'I just felt like I had to finish my tour, you know . . . finish what I started.'

He looks visibly shaken by the vigil – his eyes are rimmed deep purple and his face looks drawn. We walk towards the JHF, where he has a desk job; he limps heavily now. I want to help him along but I resist.

It's odd speaking to him; I've tried not to think about Tom too much, as I find it really difficult, but seeing Widow has made it all seem real again. I head back to the accommodation, shattered, and email Louise to see how she's coping. The sleep can wait.

I set my alarm in preparation for the second phase of Op Aabi Toorah tomorrow and drift off into an uncomfortable sleep filled with dreams about the shooting I've done today. My ears are throbbing with the sound of rounds and shouting. Everything I look at has crosshairs hatched across it.

I wake to a loud knocking on my door and have a moment of dislocation in which I wonder briefly if yesterday was a dream. My alarm clock says 3.30 a.m., and when I look across the room, I see that Bertie is stirring in her bed. It must be a new day, but it hasn't started well. I had my alarm set for five.

'What?' I say to the closed door.

'Captain Madison? You have to brief at 0400,' the signaller says through the door.

Surely not . . . I'm so tired.

'Is that it? What for?' I ask.

'Don't know. Sorry, ma'am, that's the whole message.' He sounds apologetic.

'OK, thanks. Can you make sure you wake Stu?' I ask.

'Already did.' I hear his heavy boots walking away as I sit up and start scraping my hair into a ponytail. It looks as if today is going to be another long one.

It turns out we're doing a round-the-houses escort with the Chinook before we take up our planned tasking overhead the operation, continuing with yesterday's efforts. Stu walks into the JHF five minutes after me.

'What do you *do* in the morning?' I tease. 'You always get woken first and I still beat you here.'

We fly an uneventful circuit around the FOBs before taking up our scheduled tasking. As we depart the JHF I hear over the radios that the Marines are now in contact – sounds as if the enemy is awake and angry. We're told we'll be lifting in thirty minutes.

My flight rushes to the cabs and manages to taxi on time. We're constantly listening to the operation frequency, and it's getting really busy – there seem to be several contacts going on at once, and the gunshots on the radios sound like popcorn in a microwave oven.

Tower holds us on the runway for what seems like an age, and my patience runs out.

'Tower, this is Ugly, say reason for hold.'

Tower sounds pissed off; we're not the only ones being held. 'Ugly, the airspace around Bastion is hot for rockets firing. We do not control the airspace, we are trying to get you clearance from controller.'

'Can't they stop the rockets? This is mission critical!' Stu is as annoyed as I am.

While we are waiting helplessly on the runway, Three Flight declare that they are fuel critical and have to depart; this leaves the Marines with no overhead protection but with several enemy positions identified. I'm breathless with anticipation and my heart thuds against my harness.

'Jesus, it sounds horrendous already,' I say to Stu. I feel adrenaline pumping as the frustration builds.

'Tower, my playmate is now off station, request expedite my departure clearance.'

Tower is really testy with me now and assures me, 'Ugly, we are doing everything we can. Stand by.'

Finally we are cleared to take off, but as soon as we're airborne Crowbar tell us we are in hot airspace with no clear route out. There are still rounds in the air from the rocket test and there's no way of telling where they are. There's nothing to do but carry on. At least if we get hit we won't know about it – we'll be blown straight to pieces.

'Fabulous! We're going to get shot down by our own GMLRS,' Stu says.

We reach the operation area unscathed, passing Three Flight on the way. They give us the lowdown, telling us where all the suspected enemy are, but telling us they couldn't positively ID anyone with weapons so haven't engaged. We spend a frustrating two hours searching endlessly for enemy fire, with the JTACs reporting that they're taking small-arms fire from multiple areas. The enemy have obviously talked to each other overnight and agreed that it is better to lie low when we're overhead.

Towards the end of our fuel endurance, I decide to leave Torty searching a few final areas for the JTAC and head down to the AAA area. We think the weapon is mounted on a vehicle, which makes it easy for the enemy to drive it somewhere, shoot at the helicopters, then drive it away and stow it. It's going to be almost impossible to find due to its relatively tiny size (it will be the size of a pinhead on the screen in my eye) and mobility, but we can only try.

I slave to the latest suspected position, which intelligence gave me this morning. British forces haven't been this far south in Marjeh for months, so the area is pretty unfamiliar territory for Apaches; this hopefully means that the enemy won't be as helicopter-aware as they are further north.

'Come on out, you bastards,' Stu whispers, looking out of the window for anything suspicious.

Almost as soon as we're in the overhead, we start hearing the distant metal-on-metal *tick-tick* noise of something firing at us; we redouble our efforts to find it but can't see a thing. I widen my search pattern with the TADS, and then almost jump out of my skin when the video picture scans past the jackpot. It's not the vehicle-mounted AAA, but there is a guy in man-jammies strolling slowly across the road carrying in his hands the biggest gun I've ever seen. It's over a metre in length – like the daddy of all tripod-mounted weapons. It's not the thing that intelligence has been on about – but it's big. He carries it as if it were a briefcase, so I can see the whole outline of it against the dirt road behind. He's walking towards a lean-to and is being followed by a handful of others.

I get straight on the radio to Nowhere, trying to keep my voice from sounding squeaky with excitement – finally we're going to get to kill some baddies.

'I've got PID EF with long-barrelled weapon, Nowhere.'

I watch the guy through the TADS. He's pretty fat, wearing billowing pale robes and flip-flops. He meets up with some mates, other fighting-age males, greeting them with embraces. They're in animated conversation about something as they walk towards the lean-to, which is attached to a small building. They're probably discussing how to kill more British troops, I think.

'There are about seven fighting-age males and they are gathering in a small building at grid 41PR458788. There are more weapons inside.'

Nowhere acknowledges just as I spot a sentry sitting on the roof of the building. He's using a radio or mobile phone, which is further evidence that he is enemy – regular Afghans can't afford them.

'If only he'd get that weapon out and have a pop at us,' I say. Under the rules of engagement, my hands are tied until he takes a hit at us. It's like waiting for the trailers at the cinema to be over before the main film starts. You have no control over the delay, but you know when it starts it'll be good.

The radio crackles. It's Nowhere Five Two.

'There are friendly troops in that area, Ugly, abort, I repeat, abort.'

What?!

I acknowledge, and we both peer more closely at the TADS picture. They don't look like friendlies, even if the friendlies are dressed in man-jammies. They're not moving like friendlies either. I've spent a long time watching these guys, and they're moving like Afghans.

'That's weird,' Stu says.

'Yeah. Maybe the friendlies are just close by. They must be a bit close for comfort though.'

We continue to circle, wondering what the hell to do.

'Five minutes of gas left,' Stu tells me. God, this is disheartening.

Just as he finishes, an enemy guy emerges from the lean-to, picks up the PKM machinegun from the ground and props it on the roof, aiming at us.

'Whoa there,' Stu shouts, and I feel the cyclic twitch as he tightens his grip on the controls, ready to manoeuvre away.

'Self-defence – let's go,' I say, looking into the mirror. We grin at each other – at last!

We wheel around until the TADS is facing the open side of the lean-to. I action a Hellfire while Stu positions us. As we turn to run in, I pull the trigger, and we watch as the Hellfire slams straight into the centre of the group. It's a bull's-eye. We turn to take a look: there are no leakers; we can see bodies in the rubble and they are perfectly still. I can't make out anyone particular in there, but I am confident that we've just taken out a whole nest of Taliban.

We turn towards Bastion to refuel and I rewind the video-tape, preparing to watch the shot back as soon as we are on the ground. It's almost 11 a.m.; we've been flying for five hours today, and I'm looking forward to a cup of tea.

The radio crackles, but instead of a JTAC or a signaller, we hear the CO. This must be important if he has moved from his desk.

'Ugly Five Four, confirm you did NOT engage the grid you passed for PKM.' His voice is gruff and monotone; he sounds really serious.

Stu and I exchange a glance in the mirror, and I suddenly feel horribly anxious, my heart starts beating hard and my mouth goes dry.

'Wrong. We *did* engage at that grid. Why?'

'Confirmed friendlies at that location, we just had a call with their location. Out.' The CO's voice is clipped.

I think we're going to crash; we're both stunned into silence. We say nothing as we complete our approach and land, then I break the silence.

'But they didn't look like friendlies . . .' I start.

'No,' Stu replies. 'And I think by now we'd both know . . . you get a feel for it.'

'Anyway, whoever it was pointed a weapon at us. No way would one of our troops do that, even if they were trying to look like enemy.' We are trying to reassure ourselves, but I feel sick to my stomach. The colour drains away from my vision and I feel paralyzed. A list of questions starts to spin through my head: How could what I have just seen possibly be friendly troops? What will people think of me? How will I ever forgive myself? Will I be able to trust my judgement ever again?

We reach the refuel point and the groundies pass us sausage rolls and cheese and onion crisps; not the best combination any time, but today neither of us can stomach anything. I snatch it from their hands without saying a word. As we take on fuel, we watch the tape back and can't see it any other way. We convince ourselves we've done the right thing.

But I'm still visibly shaking with shock; my hands are clumsy on the controls as I consider the possibility that we have shot and killed British troops. I can't take it in. Our boys. My fault.

'Either way, we need to go and watch this tape back and find out what really happened before we fly again. I'm in no state to go back down there not knowing what we might have done.'

'OK,' Stu agrees immediately. 'We shut down and go straight in.'

As we taxi to our parking bay, Zero is on the radio again.

'Ugly Five Four, you are to return immediately to Op Aabi Toorah – the Cobras have cancelled their second slot.'

I look at Stu in the mirror and know he will agree with me: 'Negative. Find another callsign; we need to come in and assess our gun tape.'

'No need, there were no friendlies there. We made a mistake. Out.'

'Thanks for telling us!' Stu explodes. I am too relieved, and too angry with Zero to respond. The relief is overwhelming, like it's a drug pumping through my veins. I feel I can breathe again. Colour starts to filter back into my vision.

'Guess we'd better head for Marjeh then.' Stu sounds calmer.

I sigh with relief and tuck into my cheese and onion crisps as Stu steers us into the air again. My hunger is back with a vengeance.

Back at Marjeh, it's spookily quiet. The locals have cleared out and enemy are nowhere to be seen. They may be regrouping. Looking down, the only movement is that of a handful of stray dogs rampaging the streets for scraps of food.

'Hopefully they've all had the good news about their buddies down south and are licking their wounds,' comments Stu, refer-ring to our Hellfire this morning. I hope so, too.

We head towards the heart of the action in Garmsir, and it is immediately obvious that we're going to have to split up; I leave Torty at the northern end of the area with Nowhere Six

Five, who is under heavy fire, and head down to the desert on the south-western side of the area to help Norseman Two One, the Danish JTAC.

'I see them,' Stu says almost as soon as we're overhead. We're trying to locate Norseman's patrol so we can follow his instructions about where he's taking fire from. I slave the TADS to his line of sight and see a line of tanks in the desert, facing the Green Zone. From the sky, they look like toys someone has laid out on their bedroom floor, in preparation for battle.

'There it is again, Ugly,' Norseman is shouting over the radio. I wonder if it's an inappropriate time to think how sexy his accent is. 'I think maybe now it's shooting at you. It's coming from exactly east of me.'

I scoot the TADS over to the Green Zone. I can hear the huge, scary gun firing every time Norseman presses his radio pressel. And, as an added bonus, it's firing at us.

'I hope this is "the big one",' I say. In most villages there is a 'big one', operated by the man at the top of the pecking order. I know this morning we knocked off something good in Marjeh, but it would be quite another thing to locate *the* Big One, the one that's been terrorizing aviation for weeks. Every time intelligence intercepts any Taliban radio calls, they're talking about wheeling it out.

'Me, too, we can kill that one too,' Stu agrees. We both want it to come out – two in one day would really be something to boast about.

We try circling in the area Norseman indicated in an attempt to draw the fire towards us so that he can identify exactly where the weapon is. We keep circling and, although the gunman keeps up his sporadic engagements, we have no luck. Norseman is getting increasingly jumpy about the fact that we're being shot at and keeps trying to make us scarper, but we decide to ignore that and get on with hunting this thing down. And, I'm enjoying listening to his voice.

Bizarrely, neither of us is nervous about being shot; any of those feelings have been overtaken by a desire to find this weapon. Adrenaline makes me feel slightly, if not totally, invincible. It's as if the Grim Reaper is standing across a crowded room staring me out. He's eyeing me up – and I'm ignoring it.

'Ummm, I reckon our luck might run out soon,' Stu says. We've been circling around the same area dodging bullets for the best part of half an hour. Stu has been trying to fly as erratically as possible to avoid us being hit, but it's inevitable that, sooner or later, the *tick-tick* noise will become more serious.

Torty radios us saying he could do with another set of eyes up north. Nowhere Five Five is still taking heavy fire and the enemy are everywhere – it's like the run-up to Christmas on Oxford Street down there. Norseman sounds disappointed that his overhead cover and bait are going, and I hear the gunman having one last go at us over Norseman's radio. Arsehole.

Up in Nowhere Six Five's area, things are really hotting up. He has several patrols out, all pinned down by enemy gunfire, and he is singlehandedly trying to control all the contacts. When I arrive, the Marine's patrols are in various locations along a north–south running strip of compounds; they think they are taking fire from the east. To complicate matters, there is some sort of anti-aircraft gun in the area, which has been firing intermittently at Torty's helicopter.

Torty's back-seater fills us in. 'We've been taking airburst and God knows what else, but we can't ID anything. Stand by for laser spot on to latest suspected enemy locations.'

Two Apaches obviously present a once-in-a-lifetime target, and I follow Torty's laser spot around the area.

This time, though, it sounds as if we've got them on the run. As long as one pair of British eyes is watching the fighters, they can't blend back in.

Nowhere Six Five reports that both cabs are now taking fire from an unidentified gun.

'Not our day . . .' Stu comments.

'Nope,' I reply, squinting into the TADS. 'Just imagine how

much they want to shoot us . . .' I start to get a slightly sick feeling in my stomach when I contemplate how hard those bastards on the ground will be working to take us out.

'I've been checking out the compounds in the east for the last thirty minutes, but I can't PID any EF,' Torty says. 'And I have no idea where this gunner is hiding.' He tells me he's seen a couple of possible firing points and the murder holes the enemy are using. Nowhere Six Five has intermittent sightings of the enemy, but from rapidly changing locations.

Stu and I put down some warning shots on a compound where we can see muzzle flashes. We hear the *pop-pop* noise of incoming fire start up in earnest.

'Ugly callsign!' Nowhere Six Five cuts in. 'Your northern aircraft is taking some sort of airburst fire – confirm you can see it?' That's Torty's cab.

'Negative,' I reply, knowing both aircraft are more interested in finding the men who are firing at the troops on the ground.

'I just wish the little bastards would come outside,' I say angrily.

'No chance – they know they'd die instantly.' Stu stares intently out of his left-hand window at the fight on the ground as he manoeuvres us around for another warning shot.

Torty's Hellfire goes off, and as I watch the explosion on the TADS, his back-seater radios us to tell us an RPG has just gone off behind our cab. This is a larger burst than the gunfire – visible from the ground and in the air; gunfire is mostly just noise and a streak in the air.

'Great,' I say sarcastically. I try to think of this as one less RPG on the ground waiting to be fired at me but, in reality, this is really bad. An RPG would rip right through our armoured flying tank and take out anything in its path. Worst-case scenario: it goes through one of the cockpits; the occupant wouldn't survive it. Anywhere else, it would certainly damage a hydraulic line, crucial electrics system or one of the rotor drive shafts, and that could be fatal.

'Those RPGs are straight from hell. That would definitely finish us off,' Stu says, echoing my thoughts.

I know there's nothing I can do about the RPGs apart from hope that his aim doesn't improve. I use every last speck of energy to concentrate on the TADS – I don't think too hard about the fact that I'm being shot at. I also trust Stu to manoeuvre the aircraft skilfully; for now, while I'm busy scanning the area, I'm trusting him with my life. Another round of popping fills the cockpit.

'Leave us alone or come out and play, you fuckers!' Stu shouts, frustrated.

I'm scanning the southernmost compounds in the line-up when Nowhere radios again to let us know we're now being engaged by AAA, airburst and RPG – the deadly three.

As I acknowledge him, on automatic, my mind is suddenly filled with a picture of what the air around us must look like in freeze frame: countless dotted lines of bullets snaking their way up to the cabs like airborne acid drops, waiting to eat their way through the first bit of metal or flesh they touch. The fireworks display of airburst rounds is suspended all around us like clusters made of dynamite, and each cluster has the destructive power of a hundred normal bullets. And the RPGs – huge, powerful rockets each coming towards us like a lorryful of explosives, desperately seeking, wanting to just glance off one of our surfaces . . . When you look at the whole picture, it's mind-numbing.

'Better off not knowing, I reckon,' I say into the intercom.

'Yep. Ignorance, please,' Stu agrees, as another round of popping is heard in the cockpit.

I start searching the treelines leading out of the compounds and ignore the fact that the sky has become a mass of killer metal.

Torty's Hellfire hasn't stopped the firing in the compound he was targeting, so now he's attacking the murder holes with 30mm. I want to save our ammunition for when we see the enemy, so we don't join in. All of a sudden JB's Scottish voice comes over the radio. It's urgent.

'We've got PID EF, southern side of the compound we just engaged,' he tells us. I look at the smoke plume from Torty's Hellfire and slave the TADS to it. Sure enough, I see three fighting-age males with weapons leaving the building and running towards the road.

'Oh, yeah,' I whoop. 'The targets have entered the room!'

One of them is trying to stash his weapon under his man-jammies as he runs, but it's too late: I've seen him and we have it all on videotape. As soon as the guys get to the road, though, I stop feeling so smug.

There are thick trees lining both sides of the road, and keeping track of the men on the ground from up here is a nightmare. I see them join another couple of men, and they run south as a pack. Stu is already positioning us perfectly; we'll run up the line of trees so we can fire at a moment's notice.

Torty lets off a burst of rounds as the group becomes briefly visible between the trees. In the thick line of leafy green I see a brief flash of white robe and immediately squeeze the trigger. The rounds take a few seconds to reach the ground and the men have vanished. I aim for the next gap and fire early, trying to ambush them. The rounds scatter in the gap, but the men don't appear.

I'm too early.

'That's the only way we're going to get these guys,' I say to Stu, who is trying to keep us in a racetrack – a flying pattern that sees us following an elliptical route round a fixed point – so we're vertically above the road. 'We'll take opportunity shots at them in the gaps—' I break off, seeing a flash of black robes whizzing past.

As I squeeze the trigger again I see Torty's rounds landing long of the fleeing men. Mine land short, and then they're gone again, hidden between the trees. Adrenaline is coursing through me with the thrill of the chase.

Nowhere Five Five chooses this moment to tell us we're still being shot at – as if we don't know that already: 'Ugly, you're taking consistent and sustained fire from AAA and RPG – it's going off all around both callsigns.'

I feel as if the aircraft is flying through more metal than air; I start to wonder how we can possibly both be unscathed – or at least not hit anywhere we've noticed. It's like trying to run down the street in heavy rain and avoid every drop.

But when I look out the window, I see only beautiful blue skies around me; the kind you'd kill for on holiday. The inside of my cab smells of the apricots I was munching on the way here, and other than the sounds of gunfire, which I have tuned out, this could be a summer's day in England.

I look at Stu in the mirror. He makes his special 'We're going to die, but what the hell' face, screwing his eyes up and rolling them towards the ceiling while grinning maniacally, then goes back to scanning the trees. I try to ignore the clicking and popping noises all around us. I glance at Torty's cab just in time to see a white puff to the right of him. Stu has seen it too and radios them immediately.

'Ugly Five Four, you are taking RPG fire on the right-hand side.'

'Roger,' comes JB's smooth voice. 'Jealous?'

We continue hunting.

We give chase for another twenty minutes, before a simultaneous burst from me and Torty explodes all around the group. I see two of them go down.

'Finally!' I breathe, and redouble my efforts.

'You start from the back, I'll go from the front,' I quickly tell Torty.

Burst by burst, we start picking them off one by one. As each one goes down, I mentally cross them off my to-do list. Two of them break off and Torty pursues them; I hear him flechette them in an open field.

The gunfire around us doesn't let up, and every now and then another innocent white cloud rears up ahead of us.

I spy two more fighters running south along a road with deep ditches either side. I glance at the clock and do some mental maths. We're only allowed to fly for eight hours a day; it's a safety measure for when it's as stressful and full-on as this – it would be so easy to injure our own troops accidentally in a moment of misjudgement. So far, we've flown seven and a half hours, and it's a fifteen-minute flight home. If we want to finish these guys off for sure, we're going to need an extension.

'Can you get Zero to extend our flying hours?' I ask Stu.

He nods and starts transmitting. The pair of men dive into a ditch and I immediately pull the trigger. Then Stu sees what I don't: a further enemy crawling along the bottom of the TADS picture. He is still trying to ask for our extension.

'Hello Zero, this is Ugly Five Four, we require . . . *No, look, there they are!* . . . an extension to our flying hours . . . *Down and right, Charlie. Move bloody down!. . .* [rounds going off] . . . to eight and a half. Over.' He's kept the pressel down for the whole thing, and I smile in spite of my stress as I prepare to fire again, imagining the poor signallers trying to write that message down verbatim.

I follow his instructions and we pin them down and finish them off with 30mm. I see my rounds flying into one of the enemy's faces and feel a flame of satisfaction. All movement on the ground stops as we circle.

By this time, Norseman has joined Nowhere Six Five in telling us how many people are shooting at us. They can hear it clearly from the ground, and can now see the multiple lines of gunfire arcing towards the cabs, mixing with the puffs of RPG fire. It's nothing short of a miracle that neither of us has been hit yet. I'm so amazed by this realization that I have a brief *Sixth Sense* moment during which I wonder whether I'm already dead and this is what comes after. I bloody hope this isn't all I have to look forward to when the Grim Reaper does strike.

All I have time for is to acknowledge the transmissions – Stu is on the other radio and I'm poised to shoot any leakers. There is nothing to do but keep flying and hope for the best. I'll think about it all later. Right after our engagement is complete, we get an IDM from Torty: '*NICE RADIO CALL, MORONS.*'

'Ha, ha, he's just jealous,' I say. It's well known how cheesy it is to pull the trigger while you're transmitting. I realize that the stress we've been going through in this cab will be exactly the same in Torty's. I feel a familiar sense of 'togetherness' from knowing that I am in a pair. How different this mission would be if we were alone trying to find these enemy forces, knowing that we were the only target, that if we were shot down there would be no one to see. The IDM has relieved the tension a bit, and I return my attention to the TADS, craning my sore neck down once more.

'At least if all these guys are risking getting their big weapons out we must have upset them,' I speculate, watching the treeline with the FLIR for any moving hot spots.

'Yeah, we must've killed enough to piss them off,' Stu replies, sounding smug.

We circle in the overhead after finishing off the last of the group, checking that there are no further EF. Widow confirms that for now he is no longer taking incoming.

He adds: 'You are though, Ugly. It hasn't let up.'

I can hear that, but we've come this far; we're certainly not going home until the job is done. We wait ten minutes until I'm happy we've finished our job. Both cabs are out of fuel. We check out with Widow and head back.

We've been fighting for almost eight and a half hours, and my whole body and brain feel limp. I marvel at how ridiculous that is, when all I've physically done is sit on my cushioned seat and press buttons. I think about the Marines on the ground, who have another three solid days of this. The Cobras are back overhead now, and I know we won't be flying again today.

I climb wearily on to the EFAB when we've shut down and pull my helmet off my sweaty hair. The sun is high in the blue sky and the hot, shitty air feels nice on my wet face. I stretch gently on the side of the aircraft, trying to ease the cramps in my legs. As I start pulling my maps and kit out of the cockpit, one of the other boys taxis past on his way to an air-test and gives me a fake salute from the front seat. I laugh and wave back. Stu and I do an exaggerated high five.

As I walk towards the office, a good-looking young officer is showing some nurses around one of the aircraft. He nods over to me and smiles a white-toothed, tanned-face smile; I see the nurses swooning at his chiselled face as he points out the 30mm gun. On the far side of dispersal, the 'Diet Coke ad pilot', as Bertie and I call him, is loading rounds into his pistol, wearing a tight-fitting T-shirt and mirrored Raybans. I look for a moment too long and nearly walk into a group of groundcrew moving missiles into the ammo bunkers. They laugh and joke with each other, looking so young in their tank suits and dogtags. I have a sudden vision that I'm on the set of a movie – some sort of helicopter *Top Gun*, with bronzed and rippling-torsoed men strolling around, hips slung with pistols while aircraft taxi in from hairy missions. I must be tired.

The gun-tape debrief takes nearly two hours, and I chew on a just about defrosted sausage roll in the breaks while Sergeant Tucson rewinds and asks questions: 'When did you first see these guys? What colours were these robes here?'

And then, 'And I have another little treat for you,' he says, putting a different tape into the player.

It turns out the Marines have footage on their cameras of us being shot at this morning. One of the company commanders has already handed it over. On the tape, it looks as if there are little balls of smoke appearing from thin air around and behind the cabs. I think it kind of looks like Apache-farts but, for once, the boys don't find a fart joke funny.

'Lucky to be alive, I'd say,' the Boss concludes. He watches as many gun-tape debriefs as he has time for, and has been watching from the back of the TPF.

'Thank goodness we are, or I wouldn't be here enjoying this lovely sausage roll,' I whisper to Stu, biting into another piece of frozen, meat-flavoured gunge.

'You've got filo pastry on your chin, minger,' Stu whispers back, pointing.

I escape as soon as possible, and find Bertie in our room. She looks at my tired face and hands me a chocolate HobNob; her fiancé sent them to her, and we've been rationing them – special occasions and emergencies only.

'Long day?' she asks, rhetorically. I guess my eye-bags say it all.

'Ugh,' I answer. 'Give me *Grazia*.'

I flop down on my plastic mattress as she throws me an old, grubby copy of *Grazia*.

'Want to discuss it?' she asks. We sometimes talk over difficult missions or hard, split-second decisions we want to rehash or be reassured about. I know we worry about little details so much more than the boys, and I like reminding myself she's the same.

'Nope,' I manage around a mouthful of biscuit. She nods, throws me another HobNob and turns back to her studying – we're both trying to study for our civilian-pilot licences, which we start from scratch when we leave the army, so we try to fit revision sessions in where we can.

I pull my boots off, revealing dripping-wet socks, and immerse myself in Kate Moss's latest antics. Heaven.

In the evening, I phone Jake, but the days have all washed into one. I can't think of anything specific apart from shooting that man in the face; obviously, I can't tell him about that, so I just mumble responses to his questions about how I am and excuse myself after five minutes. I can't wait to get home.

*   *   *

Six weeks exactly before I'm due to go home, Jo arrives, and I'm unaccountably excited. Having Bertie out here has been an incredible bonus, a lifesaver. We've had so many conversations that really put my mind at rest, or made me forget that I'm in Afghanistan, that I really can't imagine how I coped on my first tour.

I know that Jo will be girly and will make me feel instantly as if I'm back at home, and when she arrives and I pop over to see if she's moved in, I'm not disappointed. Her room looks great – she's got a duvet from home, a little rug beside her bed and a photo of her boyfriend already installed on the wonky table. An upturned box serves as her cosmetics cache, and I scan the Clinique and Clarins tubs.

'Hi!' she greets me, her permanent smile beaming. She exudes a happy, settled feeling, and I grin back and waggle two hot-chocolate sachets in the air.

'You don't even need to ask,' she says, filling the kettle with a bottle of water. 'I've even got biscuits.'

As she rummages in her luggage for biscuits and a mug, I wonder aloud how she can be the kind of girl who packs biscuits for an op tour but keeps such a great figure – her legs are amazing.

'Gym, run, gym,' she replies, pointing at a tall stack of gym clothes. Brilliant – we've got that in common too . . . now if only I could get that body.

Over the next week or so, I spend a lot of time with Jo. She asks millions of questions about everything, from rules of engagement to hot-water availability. She's especially curious to hear about all the different scenarios I've been faced with out on the ground; she's more conscientious than anyone I've handed over to before. We also discuss careers, babies and clothes. When I'm busy doing something else, I even catch myself planning when we can next have a good gossip – she's such a breath of fresh air I feel as if I have a girl crush.

*　　*　　*

In the first two weeks of April, I start to pass over my operations officer tag to Torty so that we have a decent handover before I come home. He needs to get up to speed before I leave and he's champing at the bit to take the reins. We finally find the time during a mid-week lull in the fighting – it's the middle of the poppy harvest, and the lower-ranking Taliban fighters make more money from working the land than from fighting, so there have been fewer IEDs and hit-and-run attacks recently.

We sit out at the back of the JHF at the wobbly, home-made wooden table, and I take my notebook out. My handover follows the same format as the one I received from Wiggy almost five months before.

'There are quite a few people you need to make contact with,' I start, and reel off a list of the names, ranks and locations of all the JTACs running FOBs.

I summarize what operations the Boss and I are currently planning, who will be involved and the timings, and then we walk inside to the ops officer's planning board. The planning board is the main tool of every ops officer. It shows timings and crews for everything. With everyone on different sleep patterns, crews being swapped to suit the different operations and requirements changing at the last minute, it can get pretty complicated, but all the crews refer to it daily for their tasking. I've got my board down to a fine art, and it works like clockwork, but I know Torty wants to do things his way.

We then run through the computer systems, talking until Torty looks like he'll explode, or I think I will, then we stop for a drink and a break before carrying on.

I'm so tired at the moment I feel I could die of exhaustion and, typically, I pick up a hideous bug from Bertie. It's a weird flu thing and knocks me sideways. I'm reluctantly grounded until I'm well enough to fly again. The doctor says it should be a week – I know this will never happen, but I agree to lie low for a day and a half. One morning, with Bertie out flying,

I sweat into my sheets, my temperature sky-high and my throat like razor blades. My head feels as if it's being split open by one of those pneumatic drills used to break up tarmac. I sob quietly into my pillow, as the normal noises of camp whirr around me: armoured vehicles clatter past, a Big Brother voice comes across the Tannoy, making announcements, and the girls who have been on night shift cackle as they clean their rifles in the corridor. At that moment, I physically hate my job so much it hurts. I'm too tired to move and just toss and turn until I eventually fall into a deep, troubled sleep.

When Bertie comes back, she fetches me some food and tries to make things as comfortable as possible for me, but I long to be at home, where Jake would bring me fresh orange juice and dish out endless sympathy.

Restored to health, I start to tune out. The weeks are beginning to linger in a way I never thought possible; each minute is painful. I look at my watch, expecting half an hour to have passed, and it laughs back at me: five minutes since I last looked. I'm going around constantly muttering, 'I'llgetthroughI'llgetthrough.' And matters are certainly not helped by the fact it's so quiet, and half my job – as ops officer – is now redundant. However, I embrace my position as line pilot purely in charge of my flight and actually even surprise myself by having no proper idea what's going on. I don't listen in briefs, don't look at the board and don't care. The only negative is that now, when new people arrive in theatre, I'm not 'Ops O', I'm not anything. It's a hit worth taking. My mind is on the new life I'm about to start when I get home: being a wife, thinking about our future family, holidays, anything that isn't Afghanistan.

Conversations home are becoming more difficult – I try to call Jake every day, but it's hard to know what to talk about. There's a two-second delay on the line and it's starting to infuriate me; and I can't talk about what I'm doing so we rely on his news, but there is very little of it, as he's just working hard and waiting for me to come back.

He always sounds distracted – and I guess I do too. I'm worried that all my memories of him and us seem 'worn out' and tired, as if I've thought about him too much. I just can't wait to get home.

In an attempt to stay focused, I up my quest to go out with the Medical Emergency Response Team (MERT). I'm keen to see what actually goes on in the Chinook when we escort them to pick up casualties. In each team of four, there's a paramedic, a trauma nurse and two doctors, one of whom is also an anaesthetist. Their skills and equipment make the MERT the most advanced first-response airborne combat medical team in the world. We regularly show doctors and nurses the Apaches and explain what we do and, after one visit, I'd emailed one of the friendly nurses, who put me in touch with the head of the MERT.

Two weeks before home time, it's cleared by both their top man and the Boss, and I can't wait. On the pre-selected morning, I go to wait in the VHR tent so I'm near the flightline. The shout comes, very sociably, at about 10.30 a.m. I'm just finishing my third tea when the phone starts ringing, and I can tell it's a MERT call. I run out to catch a lift with them, but as soon as I rush up the Chinook ramp into the cab, I realize I'm well outside my comfort zone. I don't know where to sit and, when I get on, feel I'm constantly in the loadies' or medics' way.

I finally plump for a spare seat near the pilot, next to piles of important-looking equipment. I gingerly move what looks like a heart lead from beneath my thigh.

The rules on who we can treat have changed: we now pick up and try to help anyone in need of treatment as part of the hearts and minds effort – from Afghan policemen who have shot themselves because they're high on drugs to innocent children or guilty Taliban with life-threatening shrapnel wounds.

As we get ready to take off, one guy with the radio receives information from Zero; we're heading to Sangin to pick up an ISAF casualty who has a gunshot wound to the chest. A note is passed round, so that all the medics understand what they will be dealing with.

One of the guys next to me points out the relevant details. He's a heavy-set man with an almost ghostly pallor, but he seems to be full of energy.

'It's the full monty,' he mouths over the sound of the rotors as the Chinook lifts off the ground. It's one of our men. I stay silent and nod; I'm not entirely sure what to expect. Suddenly I think I might feel really sick when the casualty comes on board and sneak a sick bag into my pocket.

When the Chinook touches down on the sandy ground there's a hive of activity. I'm the only one who doesn't move. I feel quite in awe of the medics and slightly guilty for doing nothing. The casualty is brought on – it's a Gurkha. His face is contorted with pain, and beads of sweat rest on his forehead. He's covered in blood and field dressings. I'm surprised how much has been done already on the ground. Every patrol that goes out has a medic with them – and they are as good as any paramedic.

As the stretcher is put down on the ground, the MERT team clusters around like worker bees, hooking him up to machines and doing vital checks in a clearly well-practised manoeuvre. I watch as blood drips through the exit wound in his back and through the stretcher, making a small pool below. The medics communicate in some sort of sign language over the deafening noise. They signal for chest drains and dressings and God knows what. The whole operation is seamless.

The doctors had already asked whether I would like to see the whole process, from pick-up on the ground to being put on the wards, and I decide to go the whole hog, getting off with the casualty at the hospital HLS and hopping in the ambulance.

As it pulls up outside the hospital, about twenty people, all in scrubs, are waiting. They shout urgent questions at each other – it's all numbers and abbreviations.

A scary-looking colonel, who looks as if he's seven foot tall, asks who I am as soon as I step inside the hospital door. I tell him and say that I want to see the most useful job in theatre. He smiles back, explains that he is the consultant anaesthetist and instructs me to follow him. I rush to keep up with his long strides. He barks orders at everybody.

The casualty is whisked through reception, where he is X-rayed. I'm pulled behind a filing cabinet, and the images flash up on to a screen. The image of a chest glows against the black. It means nothing to me, but he is taken straight into the operating theatre. He looks as if he's sleeping.

'Shut up! Move away from the table if you're not required,' the colonel shouts. 'I only want to hear two voices, and one of them is mine.'

The surgeons stand with their hands against their chests in order to keep them clean: they look like meerkats sniffing the air. The Gurkha is hooked up to some breathing machines, cleaned, catheterized and given blood before the surgeons step up.

I watch, amazed, as they slice his chest open with a knife. Everything is covered in blood. At one point I hear someone asking for 'a mallet', and sure enough it's a hammer-and-chisel affair to get through the breastbone, then I see sawing and rib-spreaders are put in before he's pulled open like a book.

It's not quite the sedate affair I imagine when I curl up in front of *Casualty* and *ER*. I stand back, shocked and overwhelmed. The surgeon pulls out the liver, lungs, stomach and spleen one by one, checking them. A friendly trauma nursing instructor explains everything. He wears normal combats and has a medical badge sewn on to his arm to identify him. He is short and has a soft Welsh accent; his short dark hair is speckled with sweat.

'They're checking the heart now, see?' he says to me, then reels off which organs are being waved in the air as if he were reading out a Tesco shopping list.

While I stand open-mouthed, one doctor strolls in with a

steaming cup of tea, a pair of Crocs poking out from his scrubs, and takes a seat in the corner, as if he were in a café.

'I'm sweating,' one of the surgeons announces, and one of the bystanders rushes forward to mop his brow with what looks like a hankie on a stick. It feels like it's 10,000 degrees in here, with all the fluorescent lights and people. I ask the nurse why it has to be so hot.

'Because the casualty is undressed and cut wide open, and he'll get really cold if it's not,' he explains.

'But it's about a million degrees in here.'

'Yeah, we have heating on, even when it's in the forties outside,' he tells me, as I stare around, agog, at the surgeons and assistants, who are wearing lead aprons over two layers of combats. No wonder everyone's so thin.

I wipe the sweat out of my eyes.

Later the casualty is wheeled out; the operation was a success, and I'm told by the nurse that he'll make a full recovery. It's a life saved and, to me, that matters more than anything else.

A week before the first pilots are due to fly home, we're scheduled to have a session with a psychiatric nurse specializing in Post-Traumatic Stress Disorder (PTSD).

I walk over to the briefing room with Jo. It's a perfect day: topaz sky with no clouds and no wind to stir up dust. The sun beats down on us, and by the time we join the other fifteen pilots in the rows of filthy canvas chairs, I can feel sweat starting to run down my back.

'Is this the first time all the Apache pilots have been together in one place?' Jo whispers to me.

I shrug and nod. 'Suppose it must be.'

The nurse turns out to be a portly, silver-haired man in his mid-forties, and the start of the lecture is really disappointing.

'I'm afraid no one really knows what to expect with Apache pilots in terms of stress. The job you do is so specialized, so different, from that of the typical PTSD sufferer. We won't really know how you'll fare for a while.'

He points at a Powerpoint slide on his laptop. It shows an irrelevant graph of time since being deployed in an operations theatre against number of PTSD patients to admit they need help. Most cases appear in soldiers who have been out of theatre for a few years at least.

'Our job is halfway between that of the soldiers on the ground and the fast-jet community's – surely you have data from both of those?' the Boss asks.

'We do,' says the lecturer. 'One issue for soldiers who are out on the ground is adjusting back to the safety of home. They are no longer fighting for their lives every moment, and it is no longer acceptable to lash out at anything that seems threatening. Life back home can also seem frivolous and without meaning when compared to the stark survival lifestyle in theatre. This is coupled with the problems of integrating back into home life that apply to any soldier who has been deployed: young children may not recognize their returning parent, wives will have learned how to cope without husbands, and friends may find it hard to accept the ways in which the soldier has changed.

'Fast-jet pilots tend to be less affected, but that doesn't mean they don't have problems. The destruction and loss of life caused by each bomb dropped in anger is hard to comprehend, and the speed with which the pilots have to switch between flying over a hostile battlefield and being back in the relative safety of an airbase is mentally tough.

'The problem we have with you guys is that you spend a lot of time deeply involved with the battles on the ground, and your sights allow you to see things up close; often closer than the troops on the ground. But within minutes of firing rounds into the enemy, of taking someone's life, you are back in camp planning another mission and making sure your shirt is tucked in and your beret's on straight.'

At this, we all pass knowing smirks to each other. He must have heard about the new rule in Bastion that all soldiers must wear headdress at all times, wear shirts instead of T-shirts and keep their hands out of their pockets.

'That's such a ridiculous rule in the middle of a war zone,' Stu comments from behind me.

The lecturer continues: 'The constant flipping between one set of rules – shoot anything that shoots at you – and another – look smart, check your emails – is emotionally draining and can be very confusing.'

He's right, of course – I guess I'd never really looked at it that way. He makes a few more less relevant points and dismisses us. Jo and I leave the lecture together and head briskly towards the accommodation.

'That was a bit rubbish,' I say. '"You might all be really screwed up in a few years, but we're not sure. Good luck," seemed to be what he was saying.'

'Yeah, not helpful.'

It does get me thinking, though – I consider the problems Jake's two friends have had readjusting, and the issues I've had pretending to be normal when I'm with my friends. I can't help but worry about settling back into life at home and then, when I leave, how everything will work out.

When I get back to my room later that night I try to sleep, but I can't. I'm thinking of all the injured guys lying in the hospital right now, a huge number of them amputees. I just don't understand it. How can these guys cope with going from being the fittest, most motivated men on the planet to having no legs and no longer doing the job they loved? It seems so unfair, and I wonder briefly what I'm doing to the families of the Afghans I kill.

I push the last thought out of my head and swing my feet off the bed. I need company, or I'm going to drive myself crazy, so I go to find Jo, who's in the room next to ours.

I really hope she's there.

I knock on the door and a happy 'Come in' makes me feel better straight away; it doesn't pay to be alone with your thoughts sometimes, and I'm fast learning that female company is the best antidote to war.

She automatically reaches over and puts the kettle on while I slouch in, wearing my PJs. The room is warm and smells of hot chocolate and clean clothes. I slump to the floor, cross-legged.

'What's up?'

'Oh, you know . . . can't sleep I guess,' I mumble, accepting an instant hot chocolate in a mug on which is written, 'It's hard to be perfect all the time.' 'I don't think anyone at home knows what I do. None of my friends appreciates the mental toll this takes on you.' I tell her about Margery denouncing me and that she thinks I have a desk job.

She tells me about the similar troubles she and her other half go through. He's in the army too, and they share all the problems Jake and I have.

'When we go out, everyone always asks about his job,' she tells me. 'They assume I'm just a housewife or something. Then when John says I'm an Apache pilot, they're totally shocked. But then they start asking me why we're out in Afghanistan, what I think we're achieving and stuff. As if I chose to come here!'

I agree. 'I know – it's pretty rare to get support from anyone. It really gets me down. Everyone but Jake – he behaves so perfectly when I get home; he knows exactly what I've been through and wants to know but isn't at all voyeuristic about it – he lets me tell him what I want when I'm ready. But I don't think my friends have any idea. They just assume I'll be fine to step back into the partying and gossiping, like I was never away.'

'Why don't you just tell them, then?' she asks, stating the obvious. 'I haven't been here before, but I always try and tell my mates as much as possible about other tours I've done. Having lots of military mates helps too, I guess.'

'It's too hard. You can't talk just a little bit about Afghanistan – you can't answer "So how was it?" with "Oh, you know, killed a few people, the usual" to someone who hasn't a clue. You either say nothing or go all-in.'

'So tell them everything, go all-in.'

'I tried that once,' I start. 'And I'll never do it again. One of my friend's friends has always been interested in my job. Last time I went home we were at a wedding and he asked how my tour had been and I started to tell him. I tried to make it funny, so I told him about the man I shot who was carrying explosives in his backpack – when they exploded he was thrown through the air like Buzz Lightyear. But instead of laughing, he looked a little horrified and excused himself.'

I feel slightly embarrassed at the memory; at the time, his response made me feel as if my job were something to be ashamed of.

'I guess you lose sight of where the social boundaries are – I don't know what makes a normal topic of conversation any more,' I say, shifting my butt position on the floor.

Jo is sitting cross-legged on her bed with a pillow in her lap, and I almost feel like I'm at home, sleeping over at a friend's house or something. Jo always looks so great, even when we've been flying all night, and now her eyes are shining and wide awake as she smooths down her stripy pink PJ bottoms.

'I can see what you mean. I was sitting at breakfast and some other pilots were absolutely pissing themselves that they had blown someone's leg off that morning. They were laughing that there was blood everywhere and all sorts . . .' She tails off, then says, 'It's a bit messed up, really. It's not right.'

Something else has been playing on my mind, too. Some of the boys keep a 'kill count' in their logbooks. I don't, but I have some idea of the scale of what I've done.

'You know,' I say slowly, wanting to gauge her reaction, 'I've killed more people than Harold Shipman, Myra Hindley, Jack the Ripper and any other serial killer you can name all put together. If that's not fucked up, I don't know what is.'

I've been calculating this tonight, lying in my bed. I want to see if she looks horrified and thinks I'm a bad person.

She looks me straight in the eye. 'You know, I kind of think of our job as being like an airborne hit-man. You run into the JOC, get a scrap of paper with a grid on it and get told to kill whoever's there. It's kind of cool. And we're on the side of good, don't you think?' She leans back on her elbows looking at me.

Now this is the difference, I think to myself: this is her first time out here and my last.

'I used to think it was cool. I was always so satisfied with myself when a mission went well, when I could see the gun tape of me shooting the bad guys. But now I'm not so sure. I don't feel satisfied, I almost feel soiled. And I feel more soiled every time. I know we're supposed to be on the right side, but that's what those guys think too. And they have mothers, and kids . . .' I stop, not wanting to go down that road.

'I guess we just have to do what we're trained to do, and do it as well as we can,' Jo says reassuringly.

'Well, regardless, I do know that we're doing what we're told. If the prime minister isn't enough top-cover for your conscience, I don't know who is,' I say lightly.

I feel as if I've sorted out the mess in my brain a little. If Jo doesn't think I'm nuts, or a bad person, then there's a good chance that, tomorrow, I won't either.

'Night,' I say, unfolding myself from the floor, and head back to bed.

The time comes to pack my things and leave Bastion, and it's not a moment too soon. I feel overwhelming relief when I hand in my ammunition, knowing that this is the last time I'll be here, or ever have to carry a rifle. I can't get my stuff packed up fast enough – I fling everything into my Bergen, grinning. Not only is this my last tour, but it also marks the end of my time with the military. Other than a couple of days back at the squadron base, I've racked up so much holiday that I'm on leave until my official end date late in the summer.

I don't even make a big deal of saying goodbye, mostly because I don't want to prolong my stay, but also because I know how annoying it can be to hear people saying their joyous farewells when you've just shown up.

I get lucky with the flight manifest and fly out before the Boss and everyone else. I tell them I'll see them in the UK.

As I board the Hercules to head home I expect to feel tidal waves of relief crash over me, just like I've imagined so many times over the last few months. Instead, as I settle into my seat and don my helmet and body armour for departure, I feel a creeping feeling of nostalgia. All the fun times I've had out here, the laughing until I think I'll suffocate, the euphoric feeling after a successful mission, the hours spent playing Cluedo and Nerf come flooding back to me. And then the sensation I knew I'd feel but hoped to suppress – an almost crushing grief for the people I'll never see again, or at least not for long. I've been closer than family to my squadron for years, and now I'm heading off into an unknown future without them there to laugh at me, stick Post-It notes on my back and support me. I'm a little bit frightened. I console myself with thoughts of all the time I'll be able to spend with Jake, Mia and my family, and remind myself that I'm doing the right thing for me. I fall asleep, exhausted, even before the plane takes off, and dream of landing back in Bastion and finding it filled with my friends from home.

Back home, it feels like the other times I've returned from Bastion: very green, very alien and very emotionally uncomfortable. I know it will take me weeks, even months, to get used to being here, so this time I try and go with the flow. We have a long trip to America to see my dad and brother planned for the summer, and I hope that six weeks of total relaxation will help me feel better.

A week after my return, Jake holds a 'welcome home' dinner party. Mia and her fiancé and one of Jake's military friends and his wife sit around the table. Glasses clink, conversation flows, everyone is in good spirits. Dishes cleared, Jake sits at the piano and plays a mixture of songs – all our favourites, from Elton John's 'Your Song' through to Beethoven's 'Moonlight Sonata'. As I lean back into my chair, I realize it's been months since I've heard music. As the notes rise and fall, I'm transfixed; it sounds incredible. Such a simple pleasure, yet so beautiful. From then on in, I know I'll never take anything for granted ever again.

Epilogue

As we drive to the Remembrance Day service, I stare out of the windows at the fields and trees flying past; there was a frost last night and everything looks incredibly beautiful, as if handfuls of diamonds have been scattered from the sky. The trees' golden leaves are ringed with white, and the horses and cows we pass are surrounded by a fog of frozen breath that is suspended in the air.

We arrive at the country church and step out of the car on to the frozen gravel, Jake in his uniform and me in my thick civilian coat. It's six months since I've returned from Afghanistan and, two months ago, I finally waved goodbye to the army. Jake looks handsome in his shiny ceremonial gear, but it's always been a double-edged sword for me. I know that, for him, it stands for bravery, integrity and doing something meaningful with his life. Yet, in just a few months, he's due to go on operational tour and I'll be the one left at home worrying that he could be taken away from me. Being on the front line is what he enjoys most; it's where he's at his best and feels fulfilled – I know this, but it makes me uneasy.

The church is cold, and I wrap my arms around myself as Jake walks to the podium to give his reading. His voice booms out and I feel pride almost bursting out of me watching him.

Before the minute's silence, the vicar encourages everyone to remember not only the lives lost in the World Wars but in the current conflicts around the globe. I'm surprised to hear a murmur of agreement from the pews around us; heads nod emphatically. I think about how aware everyone now seems to be about what is going on overseas – the forces are getting more press; people are becoming more aware of the sacrifices.

During the silence I think about the man who died behind the dusty outhouse, Mathew Ford, Louise and Tom, and about all the other brave young soldiers killed every week in Afghanistan – and the people they leave behind. I ponder on how transient life can be and find my mind running through a roll call of the people who are most dear to me – my parents and family, Mia and my friends, my old colleagues with whom I shared my time in Afghanistan and, most importantly, Jake. I think about our life together and hope that we will be given enough years to make the most of it.

The last few weeks have been the first time we've properly lived with each other in the same house, and they have been blissful. Jake comes home every evening and always seems more pleased than the previous night that I'm there. We've talked about things we've been putting off, like starting a family and moving to a bigger house. Now I am out of the army, he's been able to take a new job, the one that is going to take him away from me in a few months, but he's so excited about it, it's given him a new lease of life. And I have the exciting decision of what to do next; I feel that the world is opening up before me.

As the service ends, Jake and I step back outside into the cold air and go home.